VIOLENCE AGAINST WOMEN

SERIES IN HEALTH CARE FOR WOMEN
Series Editor: **Phyllis Noerager Stern**, DNS, RN, FAAN

Helpers in Childbirth: Midwifery Today   Oakley and Houd

Menstruation, Health, and Illness   Taylor and Woods

Silent Sisters: An Ethnography of Homeless Women   Russell

Violence Against Women: Nursing Research, Education, and Practice Issues
   Sampselle

VIOLENCE AGAINST WOMEN: NURSING RESEARCH, EDUCATION, AND PRACTICE ISSUES

Edited by

Carolyn M. Sampselle, PhD, RNC
University of Michigan
Ann Arbor, Michigan

●HEMISPHERE PUBLISHING CORPORATION
A member of the Taylor & Francis Group
New York   Washington   Philadelphia   London

VIOLENCE AGAINST WOMEN: Nursing Research, Education, and Practice Issues

Copyright © 1992 by Hemisphere Publishing Corporation. All rights reserved. Printed in the United States of America. Except as permitted under the United States Copyright Act of 1976, no part of this publication may be reproduced or distributed in any form or by any means, or stored in a data base or retrieval system, without the prior written permission of the publisher.

Chapter 12 is reproduced from Ladwig, G., & Anderson, M. (1989). Substance abuse in women: Relationship between chemical dependency of women and past reports of physical and/or sexual abuse. *The International Journal of Addictions, 24*(8). Reprinted by permission of Marcel Dekker, Inc.

1 2 3 4 5 6 7 8 9   B R B R   9 8 7 6 5 4 3 2 1

This book was set in Times Roman by Hemisphere Publishing Corporation. The editors were Deena Williams Newman and Nancy Niemann; the production supervisor was Peggy M. Rote; and the typesetters were Rosemary Chandler, Lori Knoernschild, Darrell D. Larsen, Jr., and Laurie Strickland. Cover design by Debra Eubanks Riffe.
Printing and binding by Braun-Brumfield, Inc.

A CIP catalog record for this book is available from the British Library.

Library of Congress Cataloging in Publication Data

Violence against women : nursing research, education, and practice
   issues / [edited by] Carolyn M. Sampselle.
       p. cm.—(A Health care for women international publication)
     Based in part on a conference held in Indianapolis on April 21, 1990.
     Includes bibliographical references and index.
     1. Family violence. 2. Abused women. 3. Nursing. I. Sampselle, Carolyn M.
   II. Series.
     [DNLM: 1. Nursing Research—congresses. 2. Violence—congresses.
   3. Women—congresses. 4. Women's Health—congresses. WY 20.5 V795 1990
   RC569.82'92—dc20
   DNLM/DLC
     For Library of Congress   91-7082
   ISBN 1-56032-217-9   CIP

Contents

Contributors

Marcia D. Andersen, PhD, RN, FAAN, CS
President
Personalized Nursing Corporation, PC
100 Tower
Renaissance Center
Suite 1585
Detroit, MI 48243

Karen S. Babich, PhD, RN
Senior Research Staff Fellow
Violence and Traumatic Stress Research
    Branch
National Institute of Mental Health
Rockville, MD 20857

Evelyn L. Barbee, PhD, RN
University of Wisconsin, Madison
School of Nursing
Health Sciences Center K6/246
600 Highland Avenue
Madison, WI 53792

Linda Bernhard, PhD, RNC
Ohio State University
Department of Women's Studies
Columbus, OH 43210

Jacquelyn C. Campbell, PhD, RN, FAAN
3777 Greenook
Ann Arbor, MI 48103

Susan M. Cohen, PhD, RN
Women's Health Care
University of Texas Health Science
    Center at Houston
School of Nursing
1100 Holcombe
Houston, TX 77030

Janice M. Dyehouse, PhD, RN
University of Cincinnati
3110 Vine Street
Cincinnati, OH 45219

Lee Ann Hoff, PhD, RN
Northeastern College of Nursing
102 Robinson Hall
300 Huntington Avenue
Boston, MA 02115

Rita B. Kerr, PhC, RN
Capitol University
School of Nursing
Columbus, OH 43209

Diane K. Kjervik, JD, RN, FAAN
University of Texas at Austin
School of Nursing
1700 Red River
Austin, TX 78701-1499

Gail B. Ladwig, MSN, RN
Jackson Community College
Jackson, MI 49201

Theresa F. Mackey, PhD, RN, CS
University of Michigan
School of Nursing
400 N. Ingalls
Ann Arbor, MI 48109

Angela Barron McBride, PhD, RN,
    FAAN
Indiana University
School of Nursing
610 Barnhill Road
Indianapolis, IN 46223

Judith McFarlane, PhD, RN
Texas Women's University
College of Nursing
1130 M.D. Anderson Blvd.
Houston, TX 77030

Nancy Opie, DNS, RN
University of Cincinnati
College of Nursing
Cincinnati, OH 45221

Mary Jo Perley, PhD, RN
Senior Associate Executive Director
Chief Nursing Officer
Presbyterian Hospital of Dallas
13003 Fall Manor
Dallas, TX 75243

Martha Pitzer, PhD, RN
Ohio State University
College of Nursing
1585 Neil Avenue
Columbus, OH 43130

Carolyn M. Sampselle, PhD, RNC
University of Michigan
School of Nursing
400 N. Ingalls
Ann Arbor, MI 48109

Phyllis Noerager Stern, DNS, RN,
    FAAN
School of Nursing
Dalhousie University
Halifax, Nova Scotia
CANADA B3H 3J5

Ecford S. Voit, Jr., PhD
Assistant Branch Chief
Violence and Traumatic Stress Research
  Branch
National Institute of Mental Health
Rockville, MD 20857

Diane Wind Wardell, PhD, RN
University of Texas Health Science
  Center at Houston
School of Nursing
1100 Holcombe
Houston, TX 77030

Preface

The genesis of this book occurred within the membership of the Women's Health Research Section of the Midwest Nursing Research Society. A planning committee which was composed of the authors of the first chapter in this volume recognized the significance of woman abuse as a health problem. The planning committee further recognized that the burgeoning literature dealing with violence against women required synthesis in order for recommendations to be made about the research agenda and nursing practice.

The Midwest Nursing Research Society affirmed the importance of nursing's role in addressing woman abuse through the funding of a synthesis conference. The goals of that conference were to review current research and theory about violence against women and to generate research priorities and clinical applications.

The conference entitled "Violence against Women: Implications for the Mental Health Research Agenda and Clinical Practice" took place in Indianapolis on April 21, 1990. Nurse researchers with combined expertise in woman abuse and the respective disciplines of Anthropology (Dr. Lee Ann Hoff), Law

(Dr. Diane Kjervik), Psychology (Dr. Theresa Foley Mackey), and Nursing (Dr. Jacquelyn Campbell) presented state of the science literature reviews. Dr. Angela McBride identified the common base among the various literatures and made specific recommendations for nursing's continuing research agenda on violence against women. Dr. Karen Babich, who represented the National Institute of Mental Health, provided an important link with a major federal funding agency. Dr. Phyllis Stern, the editor of *Health Care for Women International*, alerted those at the conference to extend their view beyond North America and to consider the charge to nursing that is sounded from the world community. The papers presented at that conference formed the initial nucleus of this volume.

Both the presenters and the audience were energized by the conference proceedings. It was very clear that a strong feminist framework linked the different perspectives. In addition to the outcomes that were specific to the research agenda, there were also important implications for education and research. It was evident that the research focus should be expanded beyond the target and perpetrator to include the context of violence. Conference participants were convinced that nursing could make a substantive contribution to decreasing woman abuse.

A similar conviction is apparent in the various chapters of this volume. Each author has elected to take no honorarium; rather, all book royalties will be donated to support research that addresses violence against women or agencies whose purpose is to assist abused women. Moreover, many of the chapters have been dedicated to particular women or groups that the respective authors wished to acknowledge.

Part One

Implications for the Nursing Research Agenda

Chapter 1

Violence Against Women: The Scope and Significance of the Problem

Carolyn M. Sampselle, Linda Bernhard, Rita B. Kerr,
Nancy Opie, Mary Jo Perley, and Martha Pitzer

INTRODUCTION

There is an epidemic of woman abuse in the United States. Consider some recent examples: In March 1990 a Detroit woman who was leaving her lover after a 12-year relationship was pursued by him in a high speed automobile chase that ended with her being thrown from her car and seriously injured. Her former partner's comment was "I told you I'd kill the bitch." Though because of his suicide he will never be tried, officials believe that Charles Stuart of Boston killed his pregnant wife, Carol, in order to collect on her life insurance. In a New York City social club 87 people died in a fire reportedly set by a man angry with his former girlfriend, who happened to be a club employee.

In 1989 at a college in Michigan a 21-year-old man was convicted of walking a girl home from a campus party, forcing her to have oral sex, and raping her. She bled later that night and was admitted to the hospital in shock; she subsequently transferred from that campus to a school in another state. The judge sentenced the rapist to three years probation and ordered him to pay his victim $200. The reasons that he gave for this leniency were, in the judge's

This chapter is dedicated to women of all cultures who have gone before; we share the conviction that our work for change will build upon and affirm their lives.

words, "There wasn't any slugging, there wasn't any threat" and his concern that the prison record could interfere with the rapist's goals of finishing college and becoming a police officer!

Violence against women is a significant problem for women at every age across the life span. Whatever the developmental point, women are consistently more likely than men to be the targets of physical, sexual, and emotional abuse. This disparity holds whether the crime is incest, rape, or battering. Women are the recipients of physical and sexual abuse at least 10 times more frequently than are men (United States Department of Commerce Statistics, 1989).

Awareness and dismay about the extent of violence against women is growing in the United States and internationally. The Alcohol, Drug Abuse, and Mental Health Administration (ADAMHA) was charged by the Congress of the United States in 1984 to study and consider the needs of women as a special and priority population. The expert panel convened by ADAMHA highlighted the causes and mental health effects of violence against women as one of five priority avenues of inquiry (Public Health Service, 1985). The urgency for addressing the antecedents and consequences of woman abuse was further underlined by the 1987 National Institute of Mental Health and National Coalition for Women's Mental Health conference on implementing a women's mental health research agenda (Eichler & Parron, 1987) and the National Black Women's Health Project, which identified violence as the number one health issue (Avery, 1990).

Because of nursing's commitment to the promotion of optimum health, the problem of woman abuse is salient to both nurse researchers and clinicians. Additionally, in light of nursing's tradition of preventive intervention, we are mandated to look beyond the pathology of an isolated family unit to examine underlying societal attitudes and the changes that must occur in order for the problem to be addressed effectively.

Substantive research about violence against women has evolved in several social sciences, but this knowledge has not been synthesized for application to nursing practice. Nor has the current body of research literature been reviewed with consideration of how nursing's unique research perspective might advance this knowledge base. Thus, the general aim of this book is to examine the current level of understanding about violence against women, to use that base as a springboard for new directions in nursing research, and to recommend applications for education and clinical practice.

THE PREVALENCE OF VIOLENCE AGAINST WOMEN

Estimates of physical abuse of women in the United States range from 1.8–4 million yearly incidents (Hotaling, Finkelhor, Kirkpatrick, & Straus, 1988; Straus, Gelles, & Steinmetz, 1980). This means that 1 in 10 American women is abused by the man with whom she lives. Moreover, experts in family violence agree that reported figures based on police and family court records, seriously underestimate the actual incidence (Appleton, 1980; Walker & Browne, 1985). Portents of assault to come after marriage can be found in the prevalence of courtship violence reported; this is abuse occurring during a time when individuals are typically on their best behavior (Billingham & Henningson, 1988). It is also disturbing that women who are the targets of courtship violence are as unlikely to report the assault as are their married counterparts. There has also been a marked increase in the United States in forcible rape, which is up 35% from 1978 to 1987; the total number of rapes and attempted rapes reported in 1987 was over 91,000 (U.S. Department of Commerce, 1989). It is estimated that the actual incidence of rape far exceeds the numbers that are reported.

In general, women are reluctant to report being battered and raped. For example Koss (1985) found that only 5–8% of women who had been sexually assaulted actually filed a report of the crime. There are many reasons for this reluctance including self-blame, fear of reprisal, and lack of confidence that justice will be done.

There are also flaws in the survey instruments used to collect statistics on woman abuse. In a recent review Koss (1990) points out that the National Crime Survey, a key index of various criminal acts perpetrated each year, is flawed in its ability to elicit accurate data about sexual abuse. The survey questions that tap aggravated assault include "Did anyone beat you up, attack you, or hit you with something, such as a rock or bottle? Were you knifed, shot at, or attacked by some other weapon by anyone at all in the last six months?" The next question that is the screen for sexual assault is "Were you assaulted in some other way?" Note that there is no cue to elicit data about a sexual attack, nor is there any attempt to determine if the individual experienced some assault that may not be immediately conceptualized as a crime (e.g., date rape). Also childhood sexual abuse is not considered by this survey. Thus, there is good reason to believe that the problem of woman abuse is of greater magnitude than is documented in official statistics.

Indeed, the body of victimization studies reflects substantially higher levels of violence against women than do official statistics. Specifically, of adults reporting retrospectively, 15–38% experienced sexual abuse in childhood (Finkelhor, 1984; Russell, 1983). Among adult women 23–39% reported at least one attempted or completed rape (Kilpatrick et al., 1983; Koss, Gidycz, & Wisniewski, 1987). The incidence of wife beating ranges from 28–31% (Strauss, Gelles, & Steinmetz, 1980; Hanneke, Shields, & McCall, 1986). The consistency of the estimates across various categories of woman abuse adds to the confidence that can be placed in the statistics. The bulk of the evidence supports the conclusion that approximately one third of the women in this country experience life- and spirit-threatening violence at some time.

The bulk of research that examines the extent of violence against women has been done in the United States. There are clear signs, however, that this is a global problem affecting women in many different cultures. For example, *The Proceedings of the International Tribunal of Crimes Against Women* (Russell & Van de Ven, 1976) indicted such culturally sanctioned violence as: Dowry murder, where women are killed for their dowry portions; genital mutilation, particularly clitoridectomy, which is done to ensure that women will be faithful wives; and violation of the right of due process, where a mere accusation of adultery is grounds for immediate imprisonment.

Continuing concern at the global level about violence against women was an important theme at the Third and Fourth International Congresses on Women's Health Issues (1988, 1990). International speakers reported such practices as: Execution of Egyptian women who are carrying an illegitimate pregnancy; the high incidence of female infanticide in countries where government policy is to limit fertility to one child; and the statutory limitations in many societies that equate women's legal status to that of a minor, with power residing in the woman's father, husband, or eldest son.

The prevalence of violence in women's lives in the United States and abroad is shocking. Equally troubling is the disproportionate level of violence that is perpetrated on women by acquaintances or significant others, that is intimate violence. It is more likely that a woman will be raped by someone she knows than by a stranger (Koss, 1985), and wife battering, by definition, is carried out by one with whom the woman has had an intimate relationship. Women are, by all accounts, the primary targets of this category of abuse.

Intimate violence arises from a sector that societal norms define as safe. The expectation is that family and friends will protect and nurture, not do harm. To be the target of abuse at the hand of someone who is known imposes a burden that compounds the physical trauma. When the abuse arises from someone familiar, a sense of betrayal and exploitation is added. Intimate violence can shake a woman's confidence in her ability to judge another individual and can rob her of critically needed sanctuary. That the crime was perpetrated by one who knows her, can seriously compromise her sense of self-worth. This may provide a partial explanation for the long-lasting physiological and psychological dysfunction that many abused women experience (Becker, Skinner, & Chichon, 1986; Burgess, 1983).

MYTHS THAT SUPPORT WOMAN ABUSE

Historically, the problem of violence has been attributed to the individual characteristics of the perpetrator and his target. That is, some character defect or developmental deficit is believed to account for the violent behavior of the inflictor as well as the "invitation" extended by the recipient.

This premise is reflected in a number of myths about violence against women (Brownmiller, 1975; Boston Women's Health Book Collective, 1984).

One such myth is "Deep down, all women want to be raped." This myth operates in advertising images of women who are wide eyed and vulnerable, while their body language openly invites sexual attention. Frequent examples are found in romance novels where women are routinely overpowered by men and, as a result, transported to greater sexual fulfillment. This misguided belief is woven into the fabric of our society. For instance, Texas gubernatorial candidate Clayton Williams compared Texas weather to rape, saying, "If it's inevitable, just relax and enjoy it" (Ann Arbor News, 1990). Thus, it should not be surprising to note that a sense of entitlement is demonstrated in research about masculine attitudes. A survey of college age men found that 51% reported they would rape a woman if they knew they would not be punished; they further thought the victim would enjoy it (Malamuth, 1981).

A variation of this myth is that women invite assault by their dress or behavior; that is, they seduce the rapist or incite the batterer. In advertising, women are frequently seen in varying levels of undress or disarray, regardless of the product message. This myth of seduction effectively excuses the perpetrator and blames the victim. Rapists have avoided punishment by arguing that the dress of their victim enticed the attack.

From a slightly different perspective, the notion that women issue an invitation for assault allows society to look the other way in cases of wife battering. "She must have done something to make him so angry," and "Why would she stay if she didn't think it was partly her fault?" are examples of this attitude. These attitudes also explain the guilt and shame that research tells us is the overwhelming initial response of abused women.

The myth that men have uncontrollable animal urges operates to excuse the perpetrator. This belief suggests that a "real man" may be forced to make unwanted sexual advances due to his higher level of need. It can also minimize uninvited propositions as nothing more than a healthy, red-blooded response to a woman's attractiveness. The woman is pressured to view such an advance as a complement rather than the sexual harassment it actually is. At a darker level, this attitude can set the stage for rationalization of incest as an understandable outcome when male sexuality is frustrated (e.g., young girls are told "Your mother isn't being a woman for me"). Yet another variation of this theme is that physical violence is manly and attractive (e.g., "You have to show her who's boss").

Society also holds fast to the myth that abuse is not that common or widespread. It is widely believed that rapes are committed by perverts, not ordinary people and that battering and incest are primarily problems of poverty.

A compelling body of research exists to challenge the myths about woman abuse. With regard to the invitation to rape attributed to women, it is noteworthy that most rapes occur indoors, usually in the woman's home. Also, rape occurs with frequency among the elderly and physically handicapped (Boston Women's Health Book Collective, 1984; U.S. Department of Justice, 1982).

The contention that spouse abuse is a two-way street is unfounded as well. Invariably the pattern of family violence that is documented is one of men attacking women, with women's violent acts almost exclusively precipitated by the preceding abuse (Dobash & Dobash, 1978; Walker & Browne, 1985). Finally, violence against women is not restricted by socioeconomic or other demographic factors. Abusers and perpetrators represent all races, ages, socioeconomic classes, and occupations (Gayford, 1975; Horning, McCullough, & Sugimoto, 1981; Straus, Gelles, & Steinmetz, 1980).

The inconsistency between myth and reality has led to the recognition of a system-based cause of woman abuse rather than one of individual deficits. From this perspective violence against women is viewed as the natural result of a sexist social order (Chapman & Gates, 1978). Collectively men are seen to use violence against women as a means to maintain power over them. This can be a troubling concept for women who have relationships with men whom they are certain would never behave this way. However, the question is not so much whether a *particular* man uses violence, but rather that *so many* feel entitled to express anger or frustration in this manner.

SOCIETAL CHARACTERISTICS THAT SUPPORT VIOLENCE AGAINST WOMEN

In her classic anthropological review of 186 societies, Sanday (1981) demonstrated that men were not genetically programmed to rape and commit other woman abuse. In fact, cultures could be differentiated by their levels of violence; distinct characteristics distinguished rape-prone as opposed to rape-free societies. Where violence against women was integral to the fabric of the culture, roles for men and women were gender-based with little value placed on women's roles, power was held by men, and women were viewed as property.

Given the high incidence of woman abuse in our contemporary society, it should not be surprising to note that the cultural traits identified by Sanday are also present. Case examples of the societal characteristics that support violence are readily found in the news and advertising media (Table 1-1).

Devaluation of Women

Feminist philosophers point out that traditional Western society has been shaped by the male-dominated majority culture (Belenky, Clinchy, Goldberger, & Tarule, 1986). Traditional values, often deeply entrenched and rarely questioned, support negative attitudes about women. The patriarchal view is that of women as a subspecies whose behavior and characteristics are deviant from and less capable than those of men (Bardwick, 1980). This is readily seen in the negative connotation reserved for words that depict feminine images (e.g., buddy vs. sissy or master vs. mistress). It is also reflected in the attitude that a

Table 1-1   Case Illustrations of Societal Characteristics that Support Violence

Devaluation of Women

1   "Hey, horny, over here," some fraternity boys yell at us as we walk across the street. . . . All the rushees make a supreme effort not to notice. . . . It isn't over, not yet— there is still the so-called "pig run." We girls traditionally pick up our bids—invitations to join a house—then go running and squealing down frat row to our new homes—at least that's the chauvinistic fraternity version. Hundreds of frat men line the sidewalks on Saturday morning guzzling beer and hooting. . . . Last year, (a young man) tells me, one frat rented a 600-lb. hog and brought it to pig run on a leash. It had a sign written on its back that said, "Where's my bid?"

–Amy Linn, *San Francisco Chronicle,* October 2, 1978.

2   The day after a particularly vicious assault, (a woman's) lawyer urged her to file a police report. Humiliated and sporting a black eye, she drove to the police station, where her reception was less than comforting. "I walked up and said, 'I want to file a report on my husband. He beat me.' The cop said, 'Are you going through a divorce?' I said, 'Yes.' And he chuckled and said, 'Well, ma'am, these things sometimes happen during divorce proceedings, don't they?' And (she) thought, 'How do I know?' "

–Robin Abcarian, *Detroit Free Press,* July 15, 1990.

Power Inequity

1   On a Michigan campus four men—all varsity hockey players—chased and shouted threats of rape at two women as they walked home . . . the men blocked them with their car while continuing to verbally threaten them. (When the women attempted to escape into a store) the men drove their car straight at them . . . stopping just short of hitting them. While the players were sentenced and fined by the city . . . the University has neither taken an action against them nor made a statement condemning the incident.

–Sharon Holland et al., *The Michigan Daily,* January 12, 1989.

2   In Detroit, a high speed car chase resulted in a woman being thrown from an automobile, crashing through a roof, and being admitted to the hospital. The man whom police suspect of causing the crash . . . had a 12-year relationship with her. She says she left him and it appears he could not tolerate that. "See, I told you I'd kill the bitch," he told her sister after the crash.

–Robin Abcarian, *Detroit Free Press,* March 9, 1990.

Women as Property

1   I grabbed her from behind, and turned her around and pushed her against the wall. I'm 6'4" . . . and she didn't have much chance to get away from me. She tried. I pulled her back and hit her several times in the face quite hard, and she stopped resisting and she said, "All right, just don't hurt me." And I think when she said that . . . all of a sudden a thought came into my head: My God, this is a human being. . . . It was difficult for me at that time to admit that when I was talking to a woman, I was dealing with a human being, because, if you read men's magazines, you hear about your stereo, your car, your chick. . . .

–Man who attempted rape at age 17, *Ms.,* December, 1972.

2   The advertising industry has a long history of treating women as objects. The copy for a lingerie ad reads, "Here's a new way to wrap your package." Another ad labeled "Beach Bums" features a very close-up rear view of three bikini-clad women. These are a few samples of the many instances that use a women's body as just another piece of merchandise. Turning a human being into a thing is the first step in the sanction of violence.

–Jean Kilbourne, Ed.D., *Still Killing Us Softly,* Cambridge Documentary Films, 1987.

woman who does not have a male partner is inadequate (e.g., extensive media coverage has been given to the finding that professional women, who delay marriage, are less likely to find husbands). On the other hand, little concern has been expressed about older men who remain single, despite the documented evidence of higher morbidity and mortality rates among this group (Berkman & Syme, 1979).

Traditional society has primarily valued woman for her reproductive capacity and her potential as a sex object. This has led to an achievement mentality for women that has been more focused on the beauty contest than the athletic or intellectual arena. An example from a University of California–San Francisco coed about sorority rush demonstrates this attitude: "At another house there is a commotion on the roof. Four frat boys are checking us out and flashing numbers on cardboard from 1 to 10, judging our comparative assets." Another example is this ad from Iberia Airlines: "This nice little blonde from Barcelona will romance you all the way to Spain. And England. And France. And Germany. And. . . . "

Power Inequity

Despite advances in women's rights, contemporary society continues as one where men (White men in most industrialized countries) control most institutions. Women continue to earn less than men in the job market and are less likely to advance to positions of authority and power (Becker & Abel, 1978). Also, the institution of marriage often victimizes women. For example, women who hold full-time jobs outside the home typically also carry the major housekeeping and childcare responsibilities (Berk, 1985; Mason & Lu, 1988). Following divorce most women become single parents with a standard of living that is substantially less than that of their former spouse (Gerstel, 1988). The legal system imposes many barriers for women whether justice is being sought for failure to provide child support, physical abuse, or rape (Gornick & Moran, 1971; NiCarthy, 1982). Taken together, these factors reflect the lesser power held by women in comparison to men.

Women as Property

Until recent history women have legally been the property of men rather than having sovereignty over their own bodies. This circumstance still persists in much of the world and continues to influence perceptions of women in North America. The entertainment and advertising media sustain a view of women as property through the objectification of women's bodies, that is an emphasis on body parts rather than women as human beings. Powerful images convey the message that, for women, nothing less than physical perfection is acceptable. Flawless complexions, slim (and preferably odorless) bodies, are just a few examples of the unrealistic, and unhealthy, standards to which women are held. Moreover, this focus on body parts commercializes and dehumanizes women— the initial step in making them acceptable targets of violence.

In the film *Still Killing Us Softly,* Jean Kilbourne, Ed.D., identifies additional links between the objectification of and physical violence directed toward women (Lazarus, 1987). Women are depicted as vulnerable and desirous of being physically overpowered; men are portrayed as authoritative, strong figures who "know how to treat a woman." Similar images are found in popular music where women are referred to as "my bitch" and violence is an acceptable means of control and retribution. These messages, often covert, but sometimes blatant, both reflect current societal values and influence developing attitudes.

THE IMPACT OF VIOLENCE ON WOMEN IN GENERAL

A final element that must be considered when assessing the significance of the problem is that violence against women affects all women, not just those who are the immediate targets. The high prevalence of woman abuse imposes clear social constraints on women. This is reflected in the guilt that is a typical first response of an abused woman whether raped or battered. Women are not immediately angry, not outraged at the violation, but rather ashamed. Clearly, women are socialized to believe that they have incited the abuse. Society asks "What was she doing out alone so late?" or "Why does she stay if he beats her?" Girls are told "Boys will be boys, so women must be careful." Male behavior (whether attributed to sexual drives or destructive anger) is too often excused; the responsibility for avoidance rests on the woman.

The consequences of this attitude bear on every woman who lives in a society where violence against women is tolerated. It is overtly operationalized as constricting mobility and restricting patterns of interaction, but it also imposes less obvious tolls. For example, a woman who experiences sexual harassment in the workplace knows that the first question to be asked will be "What did she do to invite the proposition?" Women are expected to be able to control their social environments so that unwanted sexual advances are avoided (Merit Systems Protection Board, 1981). To be harassed, raped, or battered, especially by a man they know, too often becomes evidence of the woman's inadequacy (Tetreault & Barnett, 1987). The image society imposes is one of "loser" or "slut." Many women opt for silence rather than face a second assault in the report of the crime (Williams & Holmes, 1981). This constraint has an inevitable effect on women's expectations that their rights will be respected and justice served.

At a more universal level, a society where violence against women is a common event is acting out a profound message about the value of women to that society. In addition to the obvious impact on self-esteem, the attitude affects women's economic freedom, political power, and right to quality health care. For example, equal pay for equal work becomes a nonissue if the female worker is less valued. Also, ethical questions surrounding unnecessary hysterectomy or ownership of the birth experience are less thorny if the initial premise is to devalue the recipient of that health care.

Violence against women is an issue of power. For violence to occur there must be a perpetrator, whose behavior is not constrained by self or society, and a target, whose role is also supported by social dynamics. In the current social order many men are socialized to be aggressive, while most women are socialized to be passive (Millett, 1970; Tetreault & Barnett, 1987). Although Freud held that aggression is instinctive, empirical evidence demonstrates that violent behavior is learned. Parental practices that overtly or covertly reward aggressive behavior have been linked to increases in this behavior in children (Bandura, 1965; Newcombe, 1978). As the examples cited above demonstrate, the media also contributes to socialization for sexual inequality.

Taken together, these forces work to maintain the tacit condoning of violence against women. They fuel the masculine sense of entitlement to intrude on a woman, whether acquaintance or stranger, and they sustain the myths that allow such abuse to be tolerated rather than to give rise to broad-based societal outrage. The continuing gender inequities and epidemic proportions of violence against women underline the need for accelerated change.

NURSING ISSUES

Clearly, woman abuse is a timely and relevant area of interest for nurse researchers who study factors related to the health of women and to clinicians who provide health care. Nursing has become increasingly visible in this research effort (Burgess, 1983; Campbell, 1986; Hoff, 1990). Study of violence against women is strengthened by nursing research because of the unique perspective nursing brings to the enterprise. The profession's holistic view of person, environment, and health is needed to develop comprehensive research paradigms. Nursing also embodies a long-standing tradition of preventive care needed to explore the basic attitudes that allow woman abuse to continue.

Nurses recognize both the rising incidence of violence against women and its debilitating legacy for individual health and future family relationships. The physical and emotional sequelae of rape fit the American Psychological Association diagnostic classification of Posttraumatic Stress Disorder (Burgess, 1983). Additionally, violence against women played to its ultimate conclusion can result in suicide or homicide (Bowker & Maurer, 1987). The children of battered women are often victims themselves of abuse or neglect and may perpetuate the cycle of violence by becoming abusers or victims in their adult relationships (Kaufman & Zigler, 1987; Walker & Browne, 1985). Nursing's holistic view acknowledges that violence does not stop with the target; rather it spills over to affect family relationships, community interaction, and overall productivity. Because violence leaves a legacy of pain to be treated in future generations, this problem has long-term implications for the cost of health care. Thus, the need for greater understanding of violence against women crosses the lines of many nursing specialties to involve not only women's health nurses, but those in mental health, community health, and health policy.

Nurse scientists are able to delineate the causes and treatment of this problem. Their clinical roots enable them to confront the immediate outcomes of physical abuse, which they have often observed first-hand in emergency room or ambulatory care settings. They also recognize the more subtle consequences such as women's reluctance to require safe sex practices for fear of losing a lover/protector. The body of nursing knowledge encompasses sensitive interpersonal skills and an understanding of family dynamics. This provides the foundation for the development of reliable and precise measures of the antecedents and outcomes of abuse.

In addition to documenting the impact of violence, nursing is well positioned to develop effective intervention strategies, particularly at the primary and secondary levels of treatment. Nurses in ambulatory care settings, including school clinics, can be instrumental in challenging basic attitudes about abuse. Moreover, nurses understand the workings of the health care system. They are ideally situated to design realistic interventions and to make policy recommendations that affect priorities and standards of care.

OVERVIEW

To address effectively the issue of violence against women, research is required to discover fundamental causes of this social ill and to identify the means to eliminate it. To develop a precise, focused research agenda, an in-depth understanding of the problem from a variety of perspectives is needed. Chapters 2–5 review the literature on violence against women from four key disciplines:

- *Anthropology*—so that we might better understand why violence against women is condoned in our society and elsewhere.
- *Legal*—to assess those protections and supports that are in place and to consider those that are needed.
- *Psychology*—to illuminate what is known about the toll abuse takes on women, their future potential for intimate relationships, and on their families.
- *Nursing*—to identify how nurse researchers frame the problem and to delineate the unique contribution that nursing makes to the development of this knowledge base.

Following these reviews, Chapter 6 addresses the intersections of the different literatures. Chapter 7, the final chapter in the Research Section, outlines the priorities established by the National Institute of Mental Health.

In the second section, Chapters 8-9, implications for education are discussed. It is important for nurses to be aware of the extent and seriousness of violence against women. This is because they, too, are the products of a traditional culture and there is the risk that they will not question the prevailing attitudes that support woman abuse. Nursing education at the baccalaureate and graduate levels will be strengthened by the inclusion of content on woman abuse. Strategies to accomplish this are recommended.

The third section, Chapters 10-17, deals with implications for nursing practice. It is essential that nurses in practice settings know about factors that increase women's risk of violence; that they recognize cues that signal abuse; and that they be prepared to intervene in a sensitive and empowering way. The end of this section explores ways that the health care system can be organized to break the cycle of violence and to provide specific strategies for prevention.

REFERENCES

Ann Arbor News. (1990, January 8), p. 15.

Appleton, W. (1980). The battered woman syndrome. *Annals of Emergency Medicine, 9,* 84–91.

Avery, B. (1990). Breathing life into ourselves: The evolution of the National Black Women's Health Project. In E. C. White (Ed.), *The black woman's health book* (pp. 4–10). Seattle: Seal Press.

Bandura, A. (1965). Influence of model's reinforcement contingencies on the acquisition of limited responses. *Journal of Personality and Social Psychology, 1,* 589–595.

Bardwick, J., (1980). *Women in transition: How feminism, sexual liberation, and the search for self-fulfillment have altered our lives.* London: Harvester Press.

Becker, J. V., & Abel, G. (1978). Men and the victimization of women. In J. Chapman & M. Gates (Eds.), *The victimization of women* (pp. 29–52). Beverly Hills: Sage.

Becker, J. V., Skinner, L. J., Abel, G. G., & Chichon, J. (1986). Level of postassault sexual functioning in rape and incest victims. *Archives of Sexual Behavior, 15,* 37–49.

Belenky, M., Clinchy, B., Goldberger, N., & Tarule, J. (1986). *Women's ways of knowing: The development of self, voice, and mind* (pp. 155–189). New York: Basic Books, Inc.

Berk, S. (1985). *The gender factory: The apportionment of work in American households.* New York: Plenum.

Berkman, L. F., & Syme, S. L. (1979). Social networks, host resistance, and mortality: A nine-year follow-up study of Alameda County residents. *American Journal of Epidemiology, 109,* 186–204.

Billingham, R., & Henningson, K. (1988). Courtship violence. *Journal of School Health, 58,* 98–100.

Boston Women's Health Collective. (1984). *The new our bodies, ourselves* (pp. 99–117). New York: Simon & Schuster.

Bowker, L., & Maurer, L. (1987). The medical treatment of battered women. *Women and Health, 12,* 25–45.

Brownmiller, S. (1975). *Against our will: Men, women, and rape* (pp. 313–386). New York: Simon & Schuster.

Burgess, A. (1983). Rape trauma syndrome. *Behavioral Sciences and the Law, 1,* 97–112.

Campbell, J. (1986). Nursing assessment for risk of homicide with battered women. *Advances in Nursing Science, 8,* 36–51.

Chapman, J., & Gates, M. (eds.). (1978). *The victimization of women.* Beverly Hills: Sage.

Dobash, R. E., & Dobash, R. P. (1978). Wives: The "appropriate" victims of marital violence. *Victimology: An International Journal, 2,* 426–442.

Eichler, A., & Parron, D. (Eds.). (1987). *Women's mental health agenda for research.* Rockville, MD: National Institutes for Mental Health.

Finkelhor, D. (1984). *Child sexual abuse: New theory and research.* New York: Free Press.

Gayford, J. (1975). Wife battering: A preliminary survey of 100 cases. *British Medical Journal, 1,* 194–197.

Gerstel, N. (1988). Divorce, gender, and social integration (1988). *Gender and Society, 2,* 343–367.

Gornick, V., & Moran, B. (1971). *Women in sexist society: Studies in power and helplessness.* New York: New American Library.

Hanneke, C. R., Shields, N. M., & McCall, G. J. (1986). Assessing the prevalence of marital rape. *Journal of Interpersonal Violence, 1,* 350–362.

Hoff, L. A. (1990). Human abuse and nursing's responses. In *Anthropology and Nursing.* P. Holden (Ed.). London: Routledge.

Horning, C., McCullough, C., & Sugimoto, T. (1981). Status relationship in marriage: Risk factors in spouse abuse. *Journal of Marriage and the Family, 43,* 675–692.

Hotaling, G., Finkelhor, D., Kirkpatrick, J., & Straus, M. (Eds.). (1988). *Family abuse and its consequences.* Newbury Park, CA: Sage.

International Congress on Women's Health Issues Proceedings. (1988, November). Tampa. FL.

International Congress on Women's Health Issues Proceedings. (1990, November). Palmerston North, New Zealand.

Kaufman, J., & Zigler, E. (1987). Do abused children become abusive parents? *American Journal of Orthopsychiatry, 57,* 186–192.

Kilpatrick, D. G., Best, C. L., Veronen, L. J., Amick, A. E., Villeponteaux, L. A., & Ruff, G. A. (1983). Mental health correlates of criminal victimization: A random community survey. *Journal of Consulting and Clinical Psychology, 53,* 866–873.

Klein, F. (1984). Violence against women. In *The new our bodies, ourselves.* New York: Simon and Schuster.

Koss, M. P. (1990). The women's mental health research agenda. *American Psychologist, 45*(3), 374–380.

Koss, M. P. (1985). The hidden rape victim: Personality, attitudinal, and situational characteristics. *Psychology of Women Quarterly, 9,* 193–212.

Koss, M., Gidycz, C., & Wisniewski, N. (1987). The scope of rape: Incidence and prevalence of sexual aggression and victimization in a national sample of higher education students. *Journal of Consulting and Clinical Psychology, 55,* 162–170.

Lazarus, M. (1987). *Still killing us softly: Advertising's image of women.* Cambridge Documentary Films.

Malamuth, N. (1981). Rape proclivity among men. *Journal of Social Issues, 37,* 138–155.

Mason, K., & Lu, Y. (1988). Attitudes toward women's familial roles: Changes in the U.S. 1977–1985. *Gender and Society, 2,* 39–57.

Merit Systems Protection Board. (1981). *Sexual harassment in the federal workplace: Is it a problem?* Washington, DC: U.S. Government Printing Office.

Millet, K. (1970). *Sexual politics* (pp. 215–312). New York: Avon.

Newcombe, A. (1978). Some contributions of the behavioral sciences to the study of violence. *International Social Science Journal, 30,* 750–768.

NiCarthy, G. (1982). Getting free: A handbook for women in abusive relationships (pp. 80–97). Seattle: Seal Press.

Public Health Service. (1985). *Women's health,* Vol. 2. Report of the PHS Task Force on Women's Health Issues, Washington, DC: Department of Health and Human Services Publication #85–50206.

Russell, D. (1983). The incidence and prevalence of intrafamilial and extrafamilial sexual abuse of female children. *Child Abuse & Neglect, 7,* 133–146.

Russell, D. & Van de Ven, N. (eds.). (1976). *Crimes against women: Proceedings of the International Tribunal.* Millbrae, CA: Les Femmes.

Sanday, P. R. (1981). The socio-cultural context of rape: A cross-cultural study. *Journal of Social Issues, 37,* 5–27.

Stark, E. et al. (1981). *Wife abuse in the medical setting.* Rockville, MD: The National Clearinghouse on Domestic Violence.

Straus, M., Gelles, R., & Steinmetz, S. (1980). *Behind closed doors.* Garden City, NJ: Anchor Books.

Tetreault, P. A., & Barnett, M. A. (1987). Reactions to stranger and acquaintance rape. *Psychology of Women Quarterly, 11,* 353–358.

United States Department of Commerce. (1989). *Statistical abstract of the United States.* Washington, DC: United States Department of Commerce.

United States Department of Justice. (1982). *President's Task Force on Victims of Crime: Final report.* Washington, DC: U.S. Government Printing Office.

Walker, L. E., & Browne, A. (1985). Gender and victimization by intimates. *Journal of Personality, 53,* 179–195.

Williams, J., & Holmes, K. (1981). *The second assault: Rape and public attitudes* (pp. 18–22). Westport, CT: Greenwood Press.

Chapter 2

An Anthropological Perspective on Wife Battering

Lee Ann Hoff

INTRODUCTION

This chapter addresses several issues that intersect anthropology, nursing research, and approaches to studying a sensitive topic with a disadvantaged population—battered women. First, the anthropological perspective is discussed including some issues faced by the anthropological researcher and the adaptation of ethnographic research methods to contemporary situations such as domestic violence. A brief overview of the cross-cultural incidence of wife abuse is also presented. Illustrations are drawn from the author's field research with battered women and their social network members and the process of uncovering values and beliefs about women and violence that are embedded in everyday language and in public policy regarding battered women. Finally, the complementarity of clinical nursing expertise and training in ethnographic research methods is addressed. This is revealed in the secondary therapeutic effects of

This chapter is dedicated to women survivors of abuse worldwide.

the research process and suggests that stronger liaisons between nursing and anthropology can benefit both fields.

Wife-Beating as a Public Issue

While anthropology has much to offer in the explication of wife battering, the current worldwide attention to this issue can hardly be traced to the discipline of anthropology, or to nursing for that matter. In nursing, Ann Burgess (Burgess & Holmstrom, 1974) is a notable exception to this pattern, while this book symbolizes powerfully that we have come a long way in a few years.[1] Among social scientists, feminist anthropologists were among the earliest and most influential in their critique of gender-based theoretical models in mainstream anthropology, which contribute to women's historical and contemporary oppression. Now this feminist vision is accepted commonly as central to understanding the violent abuse of women (Reiter, 1975; Sacks, 1975; Leacock, 1975; Rosaldo & Lamphere, 1974).

And so, it is neither nursing, or anthropology, but rather, the women's movement worldwide that is primarily responsible for bringing the issue of violence against women to public attention (Hoff, 1990a; Schechter, 1982). From the triple perspective of nursing, anthropology, and feminism, the need to build bridges and bring the best of all three perspectives to bear on this urgent topic is clear. And indeed, while child abuse and other types of violence all need attention, wife-beating is the most common type of violence.

Language, Analysis, and Wife-Beating

Next, a preliminary note about language. Historically, language and linguistics have been integral to the anthropological enterprise, as in "language is a window to culture." Feminist analysis[2] extends this relationship, insisting that language, politics, and gender relations are inextricably linked (Morgen, 1989). Applied to the topic of violence against women, using the term *spouse* instead of *wife* successfully deflects from the reality that most abused spouses are in fact wives. Use of the inclusive term spouse has the effect of decontextualizing

---

[1]In another paper (Hoff, 1991) nursing's response to victims has been analyzed from an historical and critical perspective. While nurses have been generally invisible as activists on behalf of victims, it is crucial to consider the number of features that nurses—predominantly women—have in common with victims such as battered women. Nurses and battered women, for example, share a sociocultural origin of their problems in the devaluation of women and women's work. The public's response to their plight is often indifference or blame. In turn, both groups tend to internalize society's judgment as self-blame. Ignoring these commonalities can result in nurses colluding inadvertently in "blaming the victim"—in this case themselves—much as battered women do when they are isolated and act without benefit of sensitivity to the historical realities of their situation.

[2]The term *feminist* does not imply a monolithic viewpoint on gender issues. Feminist perspectives are broadly classified as liberal, socialist, radical, and psychoanalytic. While all feminists are concerned about women's equality, they differ—sometimes widely—about how such equality is to be achieved and about their vision of an egalitarian society (see Segal, 1987; Reiter, 1975; Eisenstein, 1979; Stacey, 1986). This paper favors nonseparatist, socialist feminism.

the topic from relations of domination that characterize most marital bonds worldwide. Therefore, wife abuse is used exclusively in this chapter with the meaning of *wife* expanded to include an unmarried woman in a sexually intimate relationship.

Similarly, the term *family violence* tends to obscure the reality that it is individuals who act violently toward others, mostly within family contexts. The term *family violence* makes it easier to construe theories such as family systems pathology as the root cause of violence (Bograd, 1984). These theoretical constructions move us along from individual victim-blaming to family-blaming. We can thus avoid confronting the dynamic relationship between *individual* acts of violence, *socially* approved violence, and *culturally* embedded values regarding women, children, and elders that create a climate for deviant personal behavior (Hoff, 1991).

Attention to language thus highlights the distinction between feminist and mainstream perspectives regarding values and objectivity. Feminists and critical theorists assume that all research and the theories guiding it are value-laden (Therborn, 1980; Young, 1980). This includes the very choice of methods itself and those traditional methods purported to be value-free because of the presumed greater objectivity of quantitative approaches to data-gathering and analysis. The difference for feminists is not the relative merits of qualitative and quantitative approaches, but rather, the emphasis placed on making one's values explicit, regardless of method (Oakley, 1981; Hoff 1991).

Another linguistic window to understanding violence is one's approach to the issue of causality. Most mainstream analysts look for the *cause* of violence, emphasizing variable analysis; in contrast, critical theorists and most feminists emphasize the sociocultural *context* of violence, and focus on an *interpretive* analysis of the highly complex factors associated with wife-beating (Truzzi, 1974; Dobash & Dobash, 1979; Hoff 1991).

THE ANTHROPOLOGICAL PERSPECTIVE: WHAT IS IT?

The anthropological perspective includes a way of viewing the world and approaches to studying that world. Because this perspective is vast and complex, this discussion focuses on those facets particularly relevant to wife-battering. Among the social sciences, anthropology often assumes an integrating role, drawing on concepts from history, economics, politics, linguistics, religion, and biology, and on material artifacts to understand a people or subunits within a culture. Anthropology thus parallels nursing in its integrating role among the health sciences (Osborn, 1976). Often this is referred to as a holistic perspective: seeing the individual in relation to the whole, in sociocultural *context*. Nursing and anthropology also complement each other in remaining open to a variety of approaches to understanding health/illness behavior, culture, and related meanings of phenomena such as violence to a society's members.

Regarding various subtopics in anthropology, approaches to both theory and method guiding research can be usefully distinguished by the prepositions "in" or "among," and "of." For instance, by an anthropology *in* nursing (or medicine) is meant that the anthropologist enters the nursing or medical practice domains and applies anthropological concepts to nursing and medical situations as they exist. One example of anthropology *in* nursing is the study of the cross-cultural response to pain. In a second example, an already prepared nurse seeks additional training in anthropology as an adjunct to culturally-sensitive practice or research.

In contrast, an anthropology *of* nursing focuses on the profession *in itself* as the domain of inquiry (Hoff, 1988); e.g., although no hospital can remain open without nurses, the majority of health care workers, how do we explain nursing's 100-year pattern of domination by hospitals and medicine? (Of course, more people than anthropologists may wish to study this question.)

Applied to violence, an anthropology *of* violence asks, for example, what counts as violence, from the perspective of the victim, the witness, and the performer (Riches, 1986, p. 3). What counts as evidence of battering? And how does individual violent behavior relate to broader structural and cultural issues (e.g., Counts, 1987)? Network-focused research has examined what counts as help during a battering crisis (Hoff, 1991). In general, an anthropology *of* a particular topic or phenomenon assumes a more critical perspective of the issue, while the "in" approach more often examines the topic of violence in a narrower framework, often eschewing the structural and cultural factors feeding the problem, in a deliberate, apolitical stance on the issue.

Considering anthropological research methods further, although often associated with qualitative approaches, it is too simplistic to pigeonhole anthropology along quantitative/qualitative dimensions. Currently, some anthropologists are turning increasingly to quantitative techniques to analyze cross-cultural data. Even historians and ethicists are adopting this approach. (This pattern can be traced to the strong quantitative bias in all academic disciplines, which is not necessarily related to the nature of the research question.) The particular focus of quantitative analysis of ethnographic data shows patterns and similarities across societies. The works of Levinson (1989), Campbell (1985), and Masamura (1979) illustrate this method applied to wife-beating.

A major advantage of such cross-cultural surveys is to establish scientifically the worldwide incidence of wife-beating. The most recent of these surveys used coded material from 800,000 pages of ethnographic sources (known as the Human Relations Area Files, HRAF) (Levinson, 1989). Levinson statistically analyzed a subset of this material, 90 societies, and found that in 15 of these societies, "family" (sic) violence was rare or entirely absent. This approach, used by an anthropologist, is close to the sociological tradition of analyzing larger data bases quantitatively; but it is also fraught with the same limitations of statistical analysis, namely, loss of context and meaning in aggregate data.

Nevertheless, Levinson's findings, if valid, would represent a ray of hope. That is, uncovered factors that predict low or no violence could be used as a basis for social change.

Levinson concludes that family violence does not occur in societies in which family life is characterized by "cooperation, commitment, sharing and equality" (p. 104). Thus, for example, among the Bang Chaners of Central Thai, a society of 10 million people with no apparent wife-beating, he cites three psychosocial patterns:

1 A social goal of avoiding disputes, along with a range of nonviolent techniques to deal with aggressive feelings.

2 The belief that all people are entitled to respect regardless of role, status, or power.

3 The virtual absence of the division of labor by sex in the household (p. 107).

Levinson ends his research report on an upbeat note remarkably similar to that of feminist activists: Despite the worldwide prevalence of wife-beating, the Bang Chaners of Central Thai are living proof that *it doesn't have to be that way.* Particularly relevant to the Bang Chaners is the combination of factors associated with nonviolence and the absence of the division of labor by sex. This finding corresponds with recent feminist analysis (especially Ruddick, 1989; Chodorow, 1978; and Keller, 1983) of women's primary role in childrearing and its relationship to a number of other gender-based oppressions and world problems (Goodman & Hoff, 1990).

However, Levinson's findings contradict evidence from Conners (in press) and other United Nations-based sources that assert that wife-beating is "prevalent in all societies and crosscuts all racial, cultural and socioeconomic lines" (Heise, 1989). In part this can be explained by the fact that feminist and United Nations-based groups are more concerned with human rights than with scientific accuracy when claiming the virtual universality of wife-beating.

But Levinson's findings of no or rare violence in 15 societies in his sample is more likely due to the *source* of his data, the HRAF, which are questioned on validity and reliability grounds in many anthropological circles. How much more, then, might we question the validity of these files regarding the presence of violence? The validity critique is more serious here when considering that research for most of the ethnographies in the files was done well before public consciousness about violence, particularly violence against women. Furthermore, the majority of these ethnographies were produced by male researchers who likely would not have concerned themselves with violence against women when the general public seemed not to be concerned—not to mention being part of the patriarchal social structure that appeared to condone wife-beating, and still does so implicitly through policy formation (to be discussed below).

Campbell's (1985) cross-cultural analysis, also using primarily the HRAF, tried to correct for this bias by using only data from ethnographies written *by* women who used *women* as primary informants. She, like Levinson, found in several of the societies studied that wife-beating was reported as absent or rare (p. 1979). Campbell's results, however, cannot be compared with Levinson's as he did not control for gender of the ethnographer. While these cross-cultural surveys and correlational studies add to our overall knowledge about the frequency and severity of wife-beating, they leave unanswered many questions more suited to in-depth study by the traditional anthropological method, ethnographic analysis, to highlight the uniqueness and differences among societies.

For decades, the hallmark of anthropological method has been fieldwork and ethnography, or immersion in the cultural milieu of the population being studied, with systematic observation, recording, and analysis of what is revealed in everyday life. Practically, this means that the anthropologist occupies a marginal position in the culture studied. The researcher is at once both in and out of the culture, a participant-observer. The assumption is that one cannot truly understand the other's point of view apart from immersion in it. On the other hand, total immersion, or "going native," results in loss of the objectivity desired for scientific analysis.

Historically, anthropology has a mixed record vis-à-vis this approach to uncovering beliefs and patterns of behavior and understanding a society and its members. The romantic notion of the anthropologist in a remote African village or Pacific Island is now largely passé. Rather than disinterested objective observers and recorders of cultural patterns, some anthropologists entered foreign cultures with their own cultural blinders and came to be seen as arms of the colonial administration, and thus participants in the exploitation of disadvantaged peoples. This, along with development patterns and the rise of nationalism, has led to the adaptation of traditional anthropological fieldwork methods to contemporary situations such as domestic violence in urban settings.

When applying the anthropological perspective to violence against women in contemporary U.S. society, some sticky questions arise: How does one immerse oneself in the domestic scene in which violence against women occurs without invasion of privacy; and how does one assume the role of outside objective observer in one's own culture? Since most violence among family members occurs behind closed doors, clearly the researcher will rarely observe the violence firsthand, nor is it necessary to do so. As for the role of observer in one's own culture, the task is difficult but not impossible if the normal canons of research are observed with special vigilance. Most important, though, resolution of these questions requires continual alertness to our own cultural biases, and careful attention to the *essence* of ethnographic method so that its key features can be applied in a traditional fashion. Traditionally, ethnographic research (using participant-observation and in-depth interviewing especially) pays particular attention to discerning the *meaning* of the informant's experience, in this case, violence over the life span, and making sense of that experience in sociocultural perspective. Thus, if immersion in the other's culture is ethically prohibited or otherwise impractical, it is still possible to elicit another's view of the phenomenon under study by more limited involvement.

Specifically, the researcher samples enough aspects of the person's everyday life over time to provide an authentic picture of that person's world and how it is influenced by cultural beliefs and social norms, such as values and policies about women, gender roles, marriage and the family, and violence. For example, the researcher observes during playtime, mealtime, family gatherings, a morning at the laundromat, outings, etc. The validity of findings from this method is embedded in the understanding achieved through *depth* and *extent* of involvement, rather than through statistical sampling techniques.

In my own fieldwork, I went a step beyond the traditional role of eliciting data from key informants and engaged the women as active collaborators in the research process (Hoff, 1991). This included obtaining their feedback on research approaches and a draft of the report. On ethical grounds, I recommend this tactic to all researchers working with disadvantaged groups as a means of providing them a voice and empowerment through the research process (Adams, 1981). This strategy assumes, of course, the premise already suggested, namely, that no research method is value-free, including purportedly objective strategies such as statistical analysis of random survey findings. Thus, for example, when Straus, Gelles, and Steinmetz (1980) found in their national random sample that women's violent acts in the marital relationship equal those of men, these objective findings took on an entirely different meaning when considered in context. That is, most violence by women in that sample was in self-defense, and seldom did it result in physical injury as was the case with male violence. Unfortunately, by the time this was made clear, the statistical "evidence" had already been used politically to question the need for battered women's shelters.

When quantitative techniques are used by anthropologists, particular attention should be paid not to sacrifice meaning and context to statistical significance. For example, in my research with battered women and their network members, I developed a Likert-type values index to uncover beliefs about marriage, the family, women, and violence. The findings were analyzed along a traditional/feminist continuum. But unlike the traditional administration of a Likert scale, I used the items as a guide to in-depth, tape recorded interviews, some excerpts of which provided empirical data for ethnomethodological analysis, specifically Presupposition Analysis and Membership Categorization Device. This is discussed in detail in the next section.

ANTHROPOLOGICAL RESEARCH ON WIFE-ABUSE: A CASE ILLUSTRATION

This section includes three parts: 1) A brief summary of the larger study; 2) ethnographic data about a battered woman called Ruth (not her real name) and her interaction with formal network members, specifically a public housing director and a state legislator; 3) an ethnomethodological analysis of the ethnographic data. This analysis illustrates the tradition of *interpretive*, not causal analysis.

Summary of Original Study

This study (Hoff, 1990) examines the influence of values and social support on battered women, as expressed through a woman's social network. Social network issues were examined with 9 battered women and 131 network members, using qualitative methods in a naturalistic urban setting for approximately 1 year. Values and network factors were examined in a life-history perspective for their influence on the women before, during, and after their experience of violence. The conceptual framework for data analysis drew on these sources: critical theory; the sociology of knowledge; ethnomethodology; feminist and anthropological analysis of kinship, ritual, and belief systems; symbolic interaction; crisis theory; and network concepts.

Outcomes of the study demonstrate links between individual battered women, their social networks, and the larger society. Victim-blaming and self-blame of battered women are traced to traditional ideology about women, marriage, and the family, and concomitant privatization and medicalization of violence. Such beliefs and practices appear to be supported by male-dominated social and political structures that sometimes create a context in which violence against women flourishes with social approval. Adding to this complex interactional process are childrearing patterns that produce tendencies toward competition and separation for boys, and cooperation and nurturance for girls, thus laying the foundation for later conflict between the sexes. The attempts of natural network members to help battered women were insufficient, underscoring the public aspects of this problem. Yet, formal network support was gravely lacking.

Methodologically, this study reveals that a collaborative approach (in contrast to traditional strict boundaries between researcher and the researched) enhances its usefulness to the participants and others. It also narrows some gaps between theory and practice and between mainstream and feminist researchers. Finally, a collaborative approach addresses some of the ethnical issues in researching sensitive topics with socially disadvantaged groups.

The consequences of violence (e.g., homelessness and poverty) for children, the women, and all of society have several practice implications:

1   Public education to prevent violence.
2   Consciousness-raising toward egalitarian ideology about the nature and role of women as a prelude to redefining and changing oppressive social arrangements.

3 A redirection of public policy and human service practice to hold assailants rather than their victims accountable for their violence.

4 The need of nurses and others to combine crisis intervention with long-term social action strategies to assist victimized women and hasten the end of worldwide wife-abuse.

Ethnographic Case Summary

The following ethnographic data are excerpted from the larger study (Hoff, 1990). The time frame for Ruth's interaction with two public officials is *after* crises around acute battering episodes, but *during* crises around homelessness that continued for months after Ruth left both her husband and a battered women's shelter. In this study, individuals such as these public officials were defined as formal social network members, persons theoretically available to a citizen whose natural social network members (family, friends, neighbors) were unable to meet the needs of a person in crisis.

After leaving her husband, Ruth's problems with housing went on and on. She spent the maximum time in two shelters, but when she requested emergency housing assistance, she was refused. Following appeal of this decision by Ruth's attorney, the judge ordered another review of the case. The researcher observed and summarized these highlights of Ruth's hearing with the Director of Occupancy of the Housing Authority:

> Ruth described in detail how she had been brutally beaten and choked by her husband while pregnant, ordered out of their apartment, and threatened with her life if she didn't go. Her mother testified to her knowledge of her daughter's beating over several years, and that she was unable to support Ruth and her child in her own home, despite her sympathy and emotional support of Ruth. The Housing Director explained that his office had thoroughly discussed the issue of battering as an eligibility requirement for emergency housing placement. He also explained that to be placed on the emergency list, a person must be homeless "through no fault of one's own."
>
> In a hesitant, cautious explanation, the Housing Director appeared to have caught himself with the conclusion that since battering was deliberately excluded as a criterion after long, thoughtful discussion, a woman homeless for this reason must be so through her own fault. He seemed embarrassed at this point with Ruth directly before him, and attempted an apology, suggesting that he hoped Ruth would not get the impression that the Housing Authority thinks that battered women are to blame for their battering and homelessness.
>
> After two hours of testimony by Ruth, her mother and her attorney, the hearing was concluded with the Director's statement that her eligibility for emergency priority would be reconsidered after they received written evidence of her homelessness resulting from domestic conflict. The specific evidence requested was police and medical records. The evidence that Ruth and her mother had just given basically did not count (p. 196).

Meanwhile, the problem of homelessness in the northeastern United States had become so acute that public hearings were scheduled to air the problem before the Committee on Human Services of the State Legislature. Shelter staff knew of Ruth's housing problems and therefore contacted her to consider testifying at the public hearing of the State Committee. She agreed to prepare a two-minute statement with the help of a shelter volunteer and arranged to have the volunteer present Ruth's testimony in the event she was not through with a previously arranged doctor's appointment. Ruth, in fact, was unable to appear, and the volunteer began to read the following testimony after introducing herself as Ruth's advocate and noting Ruth's inability to appear due to a medical appointment around immanent delivery of her child. It read:

> I left my husband several times after he beat me but went back because he was in the service and always promised to change, and we had a little girl. Then one night last June I thought he'd kill me. We were out walking and arguing about me being pregnant. He pushed me toward the cars so I'd get run over. I resisted, so he threw me in the bushes. Then he pushed me up against an electric power outlet. He choked me and kept hitting me in the stomach and insisting that I have an abortion. I didn't want an abortion. We went to the police station and they told me to come back in the morning and file a complaint. I started to bleed and was afraid I'd lose my baby. The next day my husband told me to get out of the apartment and threatened to kill me if I didn't go. So I left and went to a shelter for battered women in Middletown and started looking for an apartment. When my 10 weeks was up there I moved in with a staff member for a couple months and kept on looking for an apartment. I applied at nine housing authorities. One had a 10-year waiting list.
>
> After two months I had to leave the staff member's house so I went to another battered women's shelter and had to take a leave of absence from college. This shelter told me I had to leave after six weeks. I'm getting more and more discouraged because it seems like no matter what I do nothing works out. I'm due to have my baby on January 25 and I'm worried about how I'll manage. The Middletown Housing Authority told me that domestic violence was not a good enough reason for getting on the Emergency Housing list. I don't understand that. My lawyer is appealing that decision, but I'm afraid I still won't have a place by the time my baby comes, no matter what my lawyer does.
>
> I crashed at my sister's house for a couple nights, then had to leave. I went to the city shelter and stayed two nights. I couldn't stand it . . . alcoholic men screaming all night long and a matron standing and watching me undress and take a shower like I'm a criminal or something. I had to take my little girl out of school because I never know where I'll be from one night to the next. I hope I find a place to stay before my baby is born (p. 197).

Unlike others who testified, Ruth's advocate was unable to complete the two-minute presentation because of interruptions by the presiding committee chairman. The following are the excerpts of the volunteer's protest letter recounting the interaction around this testimony:

Twice you interrupted her testimony . . . pounded your gavel, and made it appear that I was usurping the time of other, more worthy people. After publicly denigrating Mrs. R's testimony, you implied that I had inappropriately used the public hearing time. . . . Ironically, this is just what happens to battered women: They are brutally beaten and then told that it is their fault. . . . What makes your response even more ironic during a hearing on homelessness is that the only reason Mrs. R. is homeless is because domestic violence—even when it is life-threatening—is not a legitimate reason for a woman and her children to receive emergency housing in this state. . . . Mrs. R's story is only a single example of indifference faced by battered women who try to free themselves from violent marriages—indifference and scorn from police, courts, housing authorities, and others. There are thousands like her. At today's hearing several people referred to the problem of homelessness as obscene, a crime in the richest country on the face of the earth. It is also obscene to continue to blame homeless battered women for their plight and not grant them the same attention accorded people who are homeless for other reasons. . . (p. 198).

Ethnomethodological Analysis

Ruth's interaction with these formal network members links empirically the relationship between public policy and the personal distress of a battered woman. Her experience and that of her advocates with public authorities provide evidence of the process of maintaining the definition of violence against women as a private rather than public issue.

It could be argued that the committee chairman's rejection of Ruth's testimony as her advocate tried to deliver it was a result of the accidental circumstance that he happened not to be listening when the advocate introduced the testimony. Yet even after the relevance of the testimony was reexplained, the response was the same, with the additional exhortation about not misusing the committee's valuable time when many homeless people were waiting to testify. It could be argued further that had Ruth been present in person with her ninth month of pregnancy highly obvious, the committee chairman's response would have been more sympathetic. This argument fails as well, since the testimony on its own merits as audibly presented was discounted as irrelevant to the issue of homelessness. Also, without a full-term pregnant woman present, the public policy regarding homeless battered women can be analyzed independent of the emotional response most persons might have to a visibly pregnant woman.

For such analysis, the interaction between the advocate and the committee chairman was interpreted by drawing on the ethnomethodological perspective (Douglas, 1970; Sacks, 1967; Coulter, 1979a; Smith 1987). Applied to the study of violence, ethnomethodology analyzes rules of conduct and methods of reasoning employed by victims and perpetrators of violence; that is, ethnomethods, those of the people. It focuses on how battered women make sense out of their own and others' behavior, on what counts for them as support, and what counts as a public matter for institutional representatives of a woman's social network.

Such analysis presupposes that the cultural rules and common sense logic used by battered women and others are publicly—and therefore, empirically—available for analysis in language and other interaction. These data of interaction can thus make publicly visible the beliefs, attitudes, and structure that characterize a particular linguistic community or society. It fills in gaps left by political and ideological discourse, and by casual analysis of deviance, stress, and coping (Cicourel, 1981; Knorr-Cetina & Cicourel, 1981; Coulter, 1979b; Young, 1980).

Two ethnomethodological techniques were used in this study. The first technique, *Presupposition Analysis*, assumes that people's beliefs and attitudes are revealed in what they say and do (Coulter, 1979a). This technique is illustrated in the following empirical examples from the general study: "He beat me because he didn't like what I cooked . . . it was my own fault." This statement presupposes a woman's belief that she is responsible for the violence of her assailant. After beating up his wife, a husband says: "I'll take you to the police station and tell them how stupid you are." This statement and action presuppose a man's confidence that the police will not hold him accountable for his violence, that he will "get by."

The second technique, *Membership Categorization Device* (MCD), refers to the organized ways humans describe and understand people and their activities (Sacks, 1974; Benson & Hughes, 1983). One categorization device is the notion of *Relational Pair* (RP); for example, parent/child; male/female; deserving homeless/undeserving homeless; homeless through no fault of own/homeless through own fault.

In Ruth's interaction with formal social network members the RPs are deserving homeless/undeserving homeless and homeless through no fault of own/homeless through own fault. The Housing Authority's omission of battering as a criterion qualifying one as "homeless through no fault of one's own" implies that public officials categorize the homeless into the RP of deserving/undeserving. The legislative committee chairman's twice repeated cutting out procedure and subsequent remarks (e.g., lecturing about misuse of a public hearing on homelessness) presupposed his belief that battered women belong to the category of "undeserving" and "through their own fault."

This interpretation suggests that the committee chairman was not merely displaying bad manners or impatience. Rather, his reasoning is displayed in his words, while the power of his beliefs and his authority was symbolized in his use of the gavel to reinforce the public policy regarding the needs (or, according to this logic, the non-needs) of homeless battered women. Or, since battered women do have needs, this interaction underscores the belief that they are not a concern of this public official (and probably others), not even someone with the term *human services* in his title.

This display is similar to the purported objective reasoning of the housing director in his testimony about the long and thoughtful discussion held on the issue of homeless battered women. This decision, coupled with the eligibility clause, "homeless through no fault of their own," and dramatically reinforced in a public hearing, leads to this inescapable conclusion: At least one public official (and likely more) in this otherwise liberal state apparently believes that battered women and their children are homeless because of their own fault and therefore do not qualify for emergency housing assistance, even if such housing were physically available.

These policies, fully enforced in the early 1980s, support the belief that if women are beaten it is because they deserve it; and if they escape with their lives or are thrown out they also deserve their homelessness. These policies also support feminist conclusions based on political analysis of the centuries of exclusion of women speaking in the public arena. The testimony of women is discounted even when they are in desperate physical need and when the context is specifically designated as a public hearing with the assumption of a citizen's right to be heard there (Elshtain, 1981; Okin, 1979). Data from this study suggest that sexist values are linked not only to violent attacks on women, but also—by informing and supporting archaic public policies—contribute to the continuing misery of these women long after they have managed to escape violent relationships—usually with little or no help from formal network members.

In summary, these ethnographic data offer empirical evidence to link micro and macro factors affecting wife abuse and its aftermath. That is, public officials' behavior pointed to their belief that Ruth's problem was a personal matter only, in spite of overwhelming evidence from this and other studies (e.g., Dobash & Dobash, 1979; Pagelow, 1981) that battering is rooted in the social inequality of women. These social origins support a definition of violence against women as a public issue with wide implications for nurses and most health workers who traditionally have focused on individual behaviors.

CONCLUSION

This discussion has presented several key issues regarding the anthropological perspective, with particular emphasis on its relevance for researching and understanding the topic of wife abuse. Nurses' effective use of this perspective certainly does not require full-fledged training as an anthropologist, just as our use of surveys and other quantitative methods does not require becoming a sociologist or statistician. I propose, however, that the nursing profession and our clients could benefit greatly if much more attention were paid to this perspective than has been common. Nurses, perhaps more than any other group of researchers, have the most amazing access to people, their patterns of interaction, and the unique meanings and values they attach to events and people in their lives.

Combining the anthropological fieldwork method with my psychiatric nursing and crisis expertise, I was able to enhance cross-fertilization between these two fields, and hopefully have added something to each in the process. For example, without my clinical training as a therapist, dealing with the dependency relationships, that every fieldworker knows, would have been harder. There might have been greater danger of "going native" (dropping the research role and joining the culture studied). Without my crisis expertise, the likelihood of a possible homicide by one of the women I worked with might have been increased. The combination of ethnographic and clinical skills helped me to sort out the therapeutic side effects of the research process. My theoretical knowledge in both the anthropology and crisis fields aided my broadening of each around such concepts as "rites of passage" (Hoff, 1989, 1990).

From my experience and that of other nurse-anthropologists, I can only recommend more frequent liaisons between nurses and anthropologists, especially those with a feminist perspective. Such liaisons provide the fruitful promise of deeper understanding of battered women, and progress toward eventually eliminating the worldwide plague of violence against women.

REFERENCES

Adams, R. N. (1981, Summer). Ethical principles in anthropological research: One or many? *Human Organization: Journal of the Society for Applied Anthropology, 2,* 155–160.

Benson, D., & Hughes, J. A. (1983). *The perspective of ethnomethodology.* London: Longman.

Bograd, M. (1984). Family systems approaches to wife battering: A feminist critique. *American Journal of Orthopsychiatry, 54,* 558–568.

Burgess, A. W., & Holmstrom, L. L. (1974). In M. D. Bowie (Ed.), *Rape: Victims of crisis.* Robert J. Brady Company.

Campbell, J. (1985). Beating of wives: A cross-cultural perspective. *Victimology: An International Journal, 10,* 174–185.

Chodorow, N. (1978). *The reproduction of mothering: Psychoanalysis and the sociology of gender.* Berkeley: University of California Press.

Cicourel, A. V. (1981). Notes on the integration of micro- and macro-levels of analysis. In K. Knorr-Cetina & A. V. Cicourel (Eds.), *Advances in social theory and methodology* (pp. 51–80). London and Boston: Routledge & Kegan Paul.

Conners, J. F. (1989). *Violence in the family: Causes and consequences.* Prepared for the Division for the Advancement of Women, Centre for Social Development and Humanitarian Affairs. Vienna: United Nations.

Coulter, J. (1979a). Beliefs and practical understanding. In G. Psathas (Ed.), *Everyday language: Studies in ethnomethodology* (pp. 163–186). New York: Irvington Publishers.

Coulter, J. (1979b). *The social construction of the mind.* Totowa, NJ: Rowman and Littlefield.

Counts, D. (1987). Female suicide and wife abuse: A cross-cultural perspective. *Suicide & Life-Threatening Behavior, 17,* 194–204.

Dobash, R. P., & Dobash, R. E. (1979). *Violence against wives: A case against the patriarchy.* New York: Free Press.

Douglas, J. D. (Ed.). (1970). *Understanding everyday life.* Chicago: Aldine.

Eisenstein, Z. R. (Ed.). (1979). *Capitalist patriarchy and the case for socialist feminism.* New York: Monthly Review Press.

Elshtain, J. B. (1981). *Public man, private woman: Women in social and political thought.* Princeton, NJ: Princeton University Press.

Goodman, L. M., & Hoff, L. A. (1990). *Omnicide: The nuclear dilemma* (pp. 118–125). New York: Praeger.

Heise, L. (1989). International dimensions of violence against women. *Response: To the Victimization of Women and Children, 12,* 3–11.

Hoff, L. A. (1988, July). *Anthropology and nursing* [paper]. Symposium of the Anthropology of Nursing. 12th International Congress of Anthropological and Ethnological Sciences (ICAES). Zagreb, Yugoslavia.

Hoff, L. A. (1989). *People in crisis* (3rd ed.). Redwood City, CA: Addison-Wesley.

Hoff, L. A. (1990). *Battered women as survivors.* London: Routledge.

Hoff, L. A. (1991). Human abuse and nursing's response. In P. Holden (Ed.), *Anthropology and nursing* (pp. 130–147) London: Routledge.

Keller, E. F. (1983). Gender and science. In S. Harding & M.B. Hintikka (Eds.), *Discovering reality* (pp. 187–205). Dordrecht, Holland and Boston, MA: D. Reidel.

Knorr-Cetina, K., & Cicourel, A. V. (Eds.) (1981). *Advances in social theory and methodology.* London and Boston, MA: Routledge & Kegan Paul.

Leacock, E. (1975). Class, commodity, and the status of women. In R. Rohrlich-Leavitt (Ed.), *Women cross-culturally: Change and challenge.* The Hague: Mouton.

Levinson, D. (1989). *Family violence in cross-cultural perspective.* Newbury Park, CA: Sage.

Masumura, W. T. (1979). Wife abuse and other forms of aggression. *Victimology: An International Journal, 4,* 46–59.

Morgen, S. (Ed.). (1989). *Gender and anthropology: Critical reviews for research and teaching.* Washington, DC: American Anthropological Association.

Oakley, A. (1981). Interviewing women: A contradiction in terms. In H. Roberts (Ed.), *Doing feminist research* (pp. 30–61). London: Routledge & Kegan Paul.

Okin, S. M. (1979). *Women in western political thought.* Princeton, NJ: Princeton University Press.

Osborn, O. (1976). Anthropology and nursing: Some common traditions and interests. In P. J. Brink (Ed), *Transcultural nursing: A book of readings* (pp. 6–15). Englewood Cliffs, NJ: Prentice-Hall.

Pagelow, M. D. (1981). *Woman-battering: Victims and their experiences.* Beverly Hills, CA: Sage.

Reiter, R. R. (Ed.). (1975). *Toward an anthropology of women.* New York: Monthly Review Press.

Riches, D. (Ed.). (1986). *The anthropology of violence.* Oxford and New York: Basil Blackwell.

Rosaldo, M. D., & Lamphere, L. (Eds.). (1974). *Woman, culture & society.* Stanford: Stanford University Press.

Ruddick, S. (1989). *Maternal thinking: Toward a politics of peace.* Boston, MA: Beacon Press.

Sacks, H. (1967). The search for help: No one to turn to. In E. Shneidman (Ed.), *Essays in self destruction* (pp. 203–223). New York: Aronson.

Sacks, H. (1974). On the analyzability of stories by children. In R. Turner (Ed.), *Ethnomethodology* (pp. 216–232). Harmondsworth, England: Penguin.

Sacks, K. (1975). Engels revisited: Women, the organization of production, and private property. In R. R. Reiter (Ed.), *Toward an anthropology of women* (pp. 211–234). New York and London: Monthly Review Press.

Schechter, S. (1982). *Women and male violence.* Boston, MA: South End Press.

Segal, L. (1987). *Is the future female? Troubled thoughts on contemporary feminism.* London: Virago Press.

Smith, D. E. (1987). *The everyday world as problematic: A feminist sociology.* Boston, MA: Northeastern University Press.

Stacey, J. (1986). Are feminists afraid to leave home? The challenge of conservative pro-family feminism. In J. Mitchell & A. Oakley (Eds.), *What is feminism: A reexamination.* New York: Harper & Row.

Straus, M. A., Gelles, R. J., & Steinmetz, S. K. (1980). *Behind closed doors: Violence in the American family.* New York: Anchor Books.

Therborn, G. (1980). *The ideology of power and the power of ideology.* London: Verso.

Truzzi, M. (Ed.). (1974). *Verstehen: Subjective understanding in the social sciences.* Reading, MA: Addison-Wesley.

Young, A. (1980). The discourse on stress and the reproduction of conventional knowledge. *Social Science and Medicine, 14B,* 133–146.

Chapter 3

A Legal Analysis of Domestic Violence Against Women

Diane K. Kjervik

The plight of the battered woman is most obvious in the failure of the legal system to respond to her needs. Under the banner of equality of choice, respect for privacy, and even-handed consideration of the evidence, police, courts, and legislatures have ignored the criminal brutality inflicted on women by intimate partners. Even recently enacted changes in the law brought about by pressure from feminist groups have failed to address adequately this failure. This chapter will review legal problems that exist for battered women, legal attempts to remedy the problems, and a feminist jurisprudential analysis of potential remedies that would be more likely to bring meaningful change.

Any discussion of the law must recognize the ethical assumptions underlying legal decisions. As will become clear, the feminist analysis of legal approaches demands recognizing, questioning, and restructuring these fundamental assumptions when necessary. Throughout this chapter, ethical questions

This chapter is dedicated to Pamela Guenther of Colorado, who was shot and killed by her husband who had abused her for 15 years. Reported on PBS's *Frontline* program entitled "My Husband is Going to Kill Me," February 20, 1990.

will be raised along with the legal analysis. The purpose of this approach is to make visible what otherwise remains hidden, as the suffering of the battered woman has for so many years.

THE BATTERED WOMAN SYNDROME AS A LEGAL ARGUMENT

The response of the abused woman to her situation has been described as the battered woman syndrome that describes three stages through which a battering relationship proceeds over time (Walker, 1984). In the first stage, tension builds and small incidents of verbal and physical insults occur. Second, the physically violent episode takes place often causing serious injury to the woman. Finally, the cycle is reinforced by the loving contrition that the batterer gives the woman. As a result of this behavioral pattern, the woman learns to be passive and submit to further abuse. The basis for the conceptual development of this syndrome is the need to explicate the female victim's perspective on violence especially in the situation where she defends herself from abuse. Feminist scholars believe that it is important to clarify women's experiences that have lain dormant for years due to misinformation, stigmatization, and disparagement of women.

Legally, the battered woman syndrome expresses the context in which the woman strikes back against her abuser. As Lenore Walker points out, in terms of self-defense, there is a fundamental difference between the way that battered women tell what happened to them and what the court expects of them under evidentiary rules (Walker, 1986). She notes that the law expects discrete events to be recounted separately from emotional or contextual expression. Therefore, it is important for the court to allow an expert witness to testify about the context of the woman's response, that is, the battered woman syndrome. A feminist goal is to alter rules of evidence so that this evidence will be allowed as part of a woman's self-defense argument.

LEGAL PROBLEMS OF BATTERED WOMEN

The legal problems faced by battered women include those of all women who seek separation and divorce from their husbands such as spousal maintenance (alimony), child support, and child custody. However, an ironic twist can occur when a battered woman's response to living with violence, that is, the battered woman syndrome, is used as a sword against her instead of a shield on her behalf. For instance, Mary W.'s parental rights to her five children were removed by a court in West Virginia, because Mary W. had been a victim of domestic violence, and the court argued she had failed to protect her children from physical and sexual abuse. In reversing the lower court's ruling and remanding for further hearings, the Supreme Court of Appeals in West Virginia asked whether Mary W. knowingly allowed or condoned the abuse and whether she took action to either protect the children or the abuser. The court concluded that Mary W. did not knowingly allow the violence. She had removed the children from the home, reported the abuse to the Department of Human Services, and she tried to stop the sexual abuse in spite of the fact that she was beaten and threatened with a knife (In re Betty J. W., 1988).

The lower court's judgment reflects the persistent presence of the societal value of blaming and punishing the victim of abuse rather than facilitating the support she needs. Victim blaming is founded upon the spurious legal and ethical premise that victim and abuser are both adults and therefore have equal power to affect change. Thus, the principle of justice supposedly operates to create fairness. What remains invisible is the status of the respective groups, that is, women and men, as this relates to the individual situation of victim and abuser.

In addition to questions of child custody, battered women also face the critical issue of stopping the violence inflicted upon themselves and their children. Most states have statutory provisions for restraining orders to stop the abuser from contacting the victim (Brown, 1988). However, their effectiveness is limited for several reasons. First, economically, abused women often cannot afford the court and attorney costs involved in obtaining the restraining order. This reduces access to restraining orders (Brown, 1988). Second, enforcement by the police and the criminal justice system is inadequate.

Research has shown that the most effective way of stopping domestic violence is arresting the perpetrator (Brown, 1988; Gundle, 1986). However, police do not arrest appropriately even when the law requires mandatory, warrantless arrest where probable cause of domestic violence exists. For instance, in Connecticut, police were arresting both victim and perpetrator presumably because it was difficult to draw the distinction between initial violence and violence used by the victim in self-defense (Brown, 1988). In Oregon, the first state to require the police to arrest in certain domestic violence situations, a commission appointed by the governor found that police officers were continuing to treat domestic violence as necessitating "crisis intervention" rather than "crime intervention" (Gundle, 1986). One third of all law enforcement agencies had not changed their policies at all despite the change in the law.

In a study mandated by the Minnesota Supreme Court, it was reported that despite the progressive domestic abuse state statutes, victims did not receive criminal or civil relief required under the statutes. For instance, although protective orders were frequently issued, they were rarely enforced, and although numerous criminal arrests were made, prosecutors dismissed charges using their discretionary power to do so (Minnesota Supreme Court, 1989). Balos and Trotzky (1988) reported that in two Minnesota counties, only 22% of the cases where protective orders were violated resulted in arrests, despite the fact that the law mandates arrest. Of the 68 arrests made, only 2 resulted in felony convictions, 1 felon being sentenced to 3 years probation and the other 43 months in prison (Balos & Trotzky, 1988). Similar to the practice in Connecticut, in some parts of Minnesota, judges were ordering mutual orders for protection even when only one person had petitioned for the order and there was no evidence of mutual abuse (Minnesota Supreme Court, 1989).

LEGAL ATTEMPTS TO REMEDY INADEQUACIES

Brown (1988) suggests several ways that temporary restraining orders can be made more effective. In terms of economic access, he reports that several states require the batterer to pay court costs, or require no court costs to the one seeking the order. Some jurisdictions allow orders for spousal maintenance, child support, restitution for injuries from battering, or mandatory counseling for the batterer to be included in the restraining order. The effectiveness of these approaches is still being studied, but some improvement in the batterer's attitudes and/or behavior after counseling has been reported informally by Michael Norko, a psychiatrist in the New Haven family violence program (Brown, 1988).

In Oregon, Henrietta Nearing brought a civil court action against police for refusing to enforce Oregon's mandatory arrest provision. Police failed to arrest the abuser who violated the restraining order seven times 2½-month period despite being called three times by Nearing. The trial court found for the police and the Appeals Court agreed, but the Oregon Supreme Court reversed that judgment. It held that police who knowingly fail to enforce a judicial order issued under the Abuse Prevention Act are potentially liable for harm to the victim who could have benefited from the order (*Nearing v. Weaver,* 1983).

Subsequent to the Nearing decision, police practices have changed dramatically. Arrests are more routinely made where probable cause of violence or violation of a restraining order exists. Attitudinal changes have resulted such as fewer men bragging about pushing their wives around, fewer women feeling shame about reporting violence, and more women being willing to talk about problems openly (Gundle, 1986).

This case raises the interesting question of why in the situation of domestic violence, women have to bring court actions to force police to act according to laws on the books. It is as though women have to use force to obtain the force they need to prevent violence. What justice is there in expecting the victim to carry this heavy burden while the aggressor can hide behind police and prosecutorial inaction?

A case in the state of Washington demonstrates the use of evidence of the battered woman syndrome by the prosecution who brought charges of rape against Darrell Ciskie (*State v. Ciskie,* 1988). After having been intimate with "C. H." for a year, Darrell Ciskie began to show fits of anger and to harass C. H. In spite of her efforts to slow down the relationship, C. H. continued to see Ciskie, and four rapes allegedly occurred between January and October,

1983. After each episode, Ciskie would apologize. Threats with knives, strikes in the face, forcible fellatio and sodomy, and extreme verbal abuse were used to force sexual activities. Ciskie's attorney argued that C. H.'s concerns were "overstated" and "carefully rehearsed," that she bruised easily, and that sexual relations were consensual. The trial court allowed evidence of battered woman syndrome to help the jury understand the behavior and mental state of the victim, and the defendant was convicted of first, second, and third degree rape. The Supreme Court of Washington supported the conviction and the use of battered woman syndrome testimony.

Whether more informal methods of dispute resolution would be effective in domestic violence cases is open to question. Alternative dispute resolution, a form of mediation, could become a form of cheaper, yet second class justice, in which participants have no assurance that the mediator or arbitrator will have any greater understanding of power inequities than judges have (Edwards, 1986). The purpose of mediation would be thwarted in a situation where, for instance, the batterer would have to be forced out of the home (Edwards, 1986).

BATTERED WOMEN WHO KILL

One of the most controversial legal questions today is the use of testimony regarding the battered woman syndrome as part of a self-defense argument on behalf of a battered woman who has killed her abuser. Without this evidence the picture of the battered woman as one who willingly places herself in jeopardy exists.

Coffee (1986–1987) reports on those states confronted by the question of the admissibility of expert testimony about the battered woman syndrome. Seven states have allowed the testimony to be admitted unconditionally: Georgia, Kansas, Maine, New Hampshire, New York, Pennsylvania, and Washington; five states and the District of Columbia have allowed the testimony conditioned upon such concerns as sufficient knowledge of the expert or state of the art concerning the syndrome: Florida, Illinois, New Jersey, North Dakota, and South Carolina; and four states have determined that evidence of battered woman syndrome is inadmissible for varying reasons: Louisiana, Texas, Wyoming, and Ohio.

Admissibility of expert testimony is typically subject to a three-prong test:

1 The subject matter must be so distinctly related to a given profession that it is "beyond the ken" of the average lay person.

2 The expert must have sufficient skill or experience in the field to aid the judge and jury.

3 The state of art or science in the area must permit a reasonable opinion by the expert (Coffee, 1986–1987).

While nurses who act as expert witnesses must be prepared to have their own credentials scrutinized, they would be assisted immensely by nursing research that has developed the science of battered woman's syndrome so that the third test could be met successfully. Where the science is newly evolving, persons appearing as witnesses can present misleading information to the jury. For instance, Lenore Walker, who has served as an expert on the battered woman syndrome in numerous cases, reported that in one case where her testimony was ruled inadmissible, a male sociologist and a male political scientist had testified that her National Institute of Mental Health-funded research was biased because of Walker's feminist views (Schneider, 1986). Walker also reports that when testimony of battered woman syndrome is allowed, conviction rates are very low, that is, of the 33 cases where she presented testimony, only 4 women were convicted, one fourth were acquitted, 40% were convicted of lesser charges and placed on probation (Walker, 1986).

Absent adequate expert testimony on the battered woman syndrome, the courts' old prejudices remain as happened in the Wyoming case against Carol Griffin, who was convicted of voluntary manslaughter. The court's opinion reflects its limited understanding of battered women:

> Appellant hardly qualifies for what the literature describes as a battered wife. She was not afraid to contact the police, having done so on five prior occasions. Each time the police came to their residence, there was an argument between the parties over who had done what, who was at fault; and in each instance appellant was enormously drunk. She had pushed Clyde Griffin out of the house on several occasions, fought with him, and cut him with a broken bottle and knife, had employed a lawyer and entered into two separation agreements. The parties were separated at the time of the shooting. She had been married four times prior to this marriage to the deceased, three of those marriages ending in divorce. She knew how to get out of her marriage without killing Clyde Griffin. She could hardly have believed it necessary to kill him to terminate their relationship. (*Griffin v. State,* 1988, pp. 248–249)

Even when adequate testimony regarding the battered woman syndrome is presented, courts may refuse to accept the self-defense argument because they do not find imminence in the threat of harm by the abuser, where, for instance, as in Judy Norman's case, her abusive husband was asleep when she shot and killed him (*State v. Norman,* 1989). Judy Norman had been married to her husband for five years when he began getting drunk and slapping, punching, kicking, striking her, and throwing glasses, bottles, and other objects at her. He had also put lighted cigarettes out on her body, threw hot coffee on her, broke glass on her face, forced her to sleep on the floor, and also to prostitute herself for the family income. This abuse went on for 20 years, and on those occasions that Norman left her husband, he followed her and forced her to return. The day before the killing, Norman had been beaten all day and went to a mental health center to find out about committing her husband. Later she confronted him with this possibility and he said he would kill her before anyone got to him. He continued beating her, not allowing her to bring food into the house for the children, calling her a "dog" and forcing her to sleep on the floor. When he fell asleep, she took the children to a relative's house and returned to the house with a pistol and shot her husband. Norman was convicted of voluntary manslaughter and sentenced to 6 years in prison by the trial court, but on appeal, the case was remanded for a new trial.

However, the North Carolina Supreme Court reversed the decision of the Appeals Court saying that the evidence did not support a finding that Norman killed her husband in reasonable fear of imminent death. Two expert witnesses, William Tyson, a psychologist, and Robert Rollins, a psychiatrist, testified that Norman fit the profile of the battered woman syndrome and believed herself to be doomed to torture and abuse and she believed that death was inevitable. A majority of jurisdictions agree with the North Carolina use of an objective test, that is, what a reasonable person would have believed in these circumstances; a minority of jurisdictions use a subjective test, that is, what the defendant believed (Bunyak, 1986). While the objective test may sound fair, it is based upon male standards as to what reasonableness means, ignoring such matters as upbringing, relative size and strength as these relate to a female's perception of danger (Bunyak, 1986).

In both *State v. Kelly* (1984) and *Commonwealth v. Craig* (1990), courts found evidence of the battered woman syndrome admissible. In the *State v. Kelly* (1984) case, the American Psychological Association filed an amicus brief in support of admissibility and detailing the scientific reliability of the syndrome (Schneider, 1986). Schneider cautions that use of testimony on the battered woman syndrome can reinforce negative myths about the sickness or frailty of women, and therefore, should be used as an argument for justification of homicide rather than an excuse for homicide (Schneider, 1986). She criticizes the *State v. Kelly* (1984) opinion as looking too much at why Gladys Kelly did not leave rather than the reasonableness of why she acted. Use of the testimony can provide justification for group behavior rather than looking at one woman's frailty. Use of premenstrual syndrome as a defense to a crime raises similar dilemmas (Chait, 1986).

Ewing (1987) reports a compilation of qualitative studies of battered women who kill summarizing a comparison between the profile of the battered woman who kills and one who does not as follows:

> Overall, it seems that the battered woman who kills her batterer has been battered more frequently and has suffered more serious injuries in the course of more rapidly escalating physical abuse. She is more likely to have been raped and sexually abused, threatened with death, and menaced with weapons. Her children are more likely to have been abused by her batterer. She is more likely to be an alcohol or drug abuser. In addition, it seems that the battered woman who kills may be somewhat older, somewhat less educated, and more socially isolated than the battered

woman who does not kill—characteristics which, coupled with more frequent threats of reprisal for leaving, make it more difficult for her to leave her batterer. (Ewing, 1987, p. 40)

Ewing (1987) disagrees with the use of battered woman syndrome as a defense because of legal and policy reasons such as overbreadth of definition and possibly violation of the equal protection clause. He suggests instead a doctrine of psychological self-defense that would apply to all battered spouses, regardless of gender. Ewing essentially would argue that the killing is justified when committed to protect one from extreme forms of psychological injury, namely, "gross and enduring impairment of one's psychological functioning which significantly limits the meaning and value of one's existence" (Ewing, 1987, p. 79). Ewing points to many objections courts might raise to this approach such as an increase in domestic violence, spurious claims of self-defense, and difficulty in implementation. So far courts have not used the Ewing approach, but his approach raises important questions about injury that can be done to the will of a battered spouse and resulting damage to her capability to consent or refuse. However, the approach runs into Schneider's (1986) criticism about emphasis on the woman's incapacities rather than the reasonableness of her choice.

FEMINIST ANALYSIS

Feminist analysis of domestic violence begins with the nature of law and what it tries to accomplish. If, as Shaughnessy (1988) argues, law is "regulated force" and lawyers who are agents of law exercise power, then the intersection of gender and law rests primarily on the concept of power. Oppression of females in our society involves the use and abuse of power that law can either remedy or exacerbate. Legal arguments on behalf of battered women are therefore bolstered by emphasis upon oppression rather than an exclusive examination of victimization. As Schneider suggests, feminist legal approaches should take account of battered women's experiences of being acted upon (victim) and acting (responding to the oppressor) (Schneider, 1986).

In order to make just decisions, courts, legislatures, and executive agencies who are arbiters of power need to begin with a recognition of power inequities not only between parties before them, but also between the legal entity and the party. As Kjervik and Grove (1988) have argued, responsibility for remedying power inequities should be in the hands of the person with power. Courts, for instance, should recognize their power and the subjectivity of their judgments and then act to establish the objectivity that surpasses their own attitudes and emotions.

Flowing from the power that legal tribunals have are interpretations of privacy (the man and his castle), credibility of the battered woman testimony, and responsibility of victim and abuser for the violence in the relationship. Privacy can become an opportunity to abuse power inequities. As Zimring (1987) states, " . . . privacy can metastasize into a Hobbesian arena where the strong prey on the weak and the weak on the weaker still. Life's greatest moments occur behind closed doors. So, too, do some of modern life's most outrageous exploitations" (p. 521). The law has been willing to be involved in domestic matters of child abuse and abuse of vulnerable adults, and likewise needs to be involved with assaults on battered women occurring behind closed doors.

Battered woman syndrome testimony can enlighten courts and legislators on the response victims experience from attacks upon their bodies and their self-will. The value our society places on privacy can contribute to the battered woman's sense of invisibility and isolation. As Scales (1986) points out, feminist lawyers must find what is invisible, make it visible, and explore ways to make appropriate parties responsible for necessary changes. When the battered woman's situation becomes visible, her veracity is challenged. The purpose of expert testimony is to lend credibility to the battered woman's explanation of events by placing in context her actions as necessary for survival (Schneider, 1986). Allowing her to tell her story empowers her to respond to allegations that she behaved irresponsibly when instead she was responding to the behavior of her partner. When there are challenges to domestic abuse statutes, courts can use the opportunity to refine the nature of the violence addressed by the statute. For instance, in *State v. Kameenui* (1988), the Supreme Court of Hawaii ruled that the term *physical abuse* was not vague, that is, a reasonable person knows what this term means, and the statute was not overbroad. In other words, the right of privacy does not extend to an abuser who hits someone in the home. Convictions of the two men who had beaten their wives were upheld by the court.

Feminist jurisprudence demands adequate psychological and epistemological sophistication in law (Scales, 1986). Feminist scholars have used Gilligan's (1982) ethic of caring to criticize legal methods such as the adversarial approach to conflict resolution (Menkel-Meadow, 1985) and the individual rights focus (Scales, 1986). With a responsibility focus rather than rights, basic tenets of law including those embodied in the U.S. Constitution can be questioned and re-interpreted (Menkel-Meadow, 1985). Court rulings or legislative decisions can be examined for preservation of important community relationships rather than individual rights and autonomy.

Perhaps the strongest message of the feminist perspective on law is to question what is assumed to be neutral or objective, because the invisible but powerful male norm allows male assumptions to control decisions. Fairness, as Scales (1986) points out, necessitates a look at real human predicaments, one of which is subjectivity in human decision making. If the law's purpose is to decide the moral crux of matters, its decision makers must recognize their own subjectivity and move beyond it.

CONCLUSION

This chapter has analyzed current legal issues facing battered women. In some states, legislatures have been willing to respond to the need of battered women for protection from abusers by enacting legislation mandating warrantless arrest. However, these arrests often are not made and if taken to court, charges against the abuser often are dropped. Some state courts have been willing to award damages to a battered woman for lack of enforcement of protective orders, convict men who have battered their wives, and allow expert testimony on the battered woman syndrome as evidence of self-defense where a battered woman has killed her abuser. Still, many states do not provide these protections. The legal system needs to examine its own subjective assumptions about gender roles and find ways to empower the women who have been brutalized psychologically and physically by intimate partners.

REFERENCES

Balos, B., & Trotzky, K. (1988). Enforcement of the domestic abuse act in Minnesota: A preliminary study. *Law and Inequality, 6,* 83–125.

Brown, G. R. (1988). Battered women and the temporary restraining order. *Women's Rights Law Reporter, 10,* 261–267.

Bunyak, J. R. (1986). Battered wives who kill: Civil liability and the admissibility of battered woman's syndrome testimony. *Law and Inequality, 4,* 603–636.

Chait, L. R. (1986). Premenstrual syndrome & our sisters in crime: A feminist dilemma. *Women's Rights Law Reporter, 9,* 267–293.

Coffee, C. L. (1986–1987). A trend emerges: A state survey on the admissibility of expert testimony concerning the battered woman syndrome. *Journal of Family Law, 25,* 373–396.

Commonwealth v. Craig, 1990 WL 2760 (Ky., 1990) (slip copy).

Edwards, H. T. (1986). Alternative dispute resolution: Panacea or anathema? *Harvard Law Review, 99,* 668–684.

Ewing, C. P. (1987). *Battered women who kill: Psychological self-defense as legal justification* (pp. 77–94) Lexington, MA: Lexington Books.

Gilligan, C. (1982). *In a different voice: Psychological theory and women's development* (pp. 6–23). Cambridge, MA: Harvard University Press.

Griffin v. State, 749 P.2d 246, 248 (Wy. 1988).

Gundle, R. (1986). Civil liability for police failure to arrest: *Nearing v. Weaver. Women's Rights Law Reporter, 9,* 259–265.

In Re Betty J. W., 371 S.E. 2d 326 (W. Va. 1988).

Kjervik, D. K., & Grove, S. (1988). A legal model of consent in unequal power relationships. *Journal of Professional Nursing, 4,* 192–204.

Menkel-Meadow, C. (1985). Portia in a different voice: Speculations on a women's lawyering process. *Berkeley Women's Law Journal, 1,* 39–63.

Minnesota Supreme Court. (1989). *Task force for gender fairness in the courts.* St. Paul, MN: Minnesota Supreme Court.

Nearing v. Weaver. 295 Or. 702, 670 P.2d 137 (1983).

Scales, A. C. (1986). The emergence of feminist jurisprudence: An essay. *Yale Law Journal, 95,* 1373–1403.

Schneider, E. M. (1986). Describing and changing: Women's self-defense work and the problem of expert testimony on battering. *Women's Rights Law Reporter, 9,* 195–222.

Shaughnessy, J. M. (1988). Gilligan's travels. *Law and Inequality, 7,* 1–27.

State v. Ciskie, 110 Wash. 2d 263, 751 P.2d 1165 (1988).

State v. Kameenui, 753 P.2d 1250 (Ha., 1988).

State v. Kelly, 97 N.J. 178, 478 A.2d 364 (1984).

State v. Norman, 324 N.C. 253, 378 S.E.2d 8 (1989).

Walker, L. E. (1984). *The battered woman syndrome* (pp. 55–70). New York: Springer.

Walker, L. E. (1986). A response to Elizabeth M. Schneider's "Describing and changing: Women's self-defense work and the problem of expert testimony on battering." *Women's Rights Law Reporter, 9,* 223–225.

Zimring, F. E. (1987). Legal perspectives on family violence. *California Law Review, 75,* 521–522.

Chapter 4

A Psychological Model for Analysis of Outcomes Related to Trauma

Theresa F. Mackey

Despite advances made in victimology, many clinicians and researchers often fail to understand the long-term consequences of child abuse, spouse abuse, incest, rape, and terrorism against women (Carmen, Reiker, & Mills, 1984; Foley & Grimes, 1987; Finkelhor, 1979; Finkelhor & Browne, 1986; Forward & Buck, 1989; Kilpatrick, Saunders, Veronen, Best, & Von, 1987; Rutter, 1989; Summit, 1983; Terr, 1983a). Health professionals also often fail to conceptualize the victim-to-patient process (Reiker & Carmen, 1986) that results from victims' accommodating the judgments others make about their abuse, their true feelings, the meaning of their abuse, and the profound disconfirmation of their realities. In this process survival is dependent on denial of the self coupled with congruence with the norms and expectations within a dysfunctional system, and love is conditional. Further, this process extends to the work environment where adults who were raised in abusive or dysfunctional family environments replicate these systems in their work setting (Goncalves, 1990). In these dysfunctional systems sexual exploitation, assault, harassment, and discrimination are variations of the phenomena.

The purpose of this chapter is to provide a guide for understanding the response of female children and adults to violence from a psychological perspective of the trauma and its wake. Theoretical, research, and clinical literature on child sexual abuse, rape, and sexual assault served as the primary content area reviewed; to a lesser extent physical abuse, domestic violence, and elder abuse were also reviewed. The emphasis of this paper is on the response of women to violence, not treatment efficacy. A conceptual model of factors influencing response to a traumatic event, and the pathways of outcome is presented as well as results of relatively recent research and literature that illustrate components of the model. Next, conclusions and implications are presented for consideration.

In preparation for writing this paper, a keyword search of the literature was conducted on concepts such as adjustment, recovery, and adaptation in order to discern the state of the science on trauma resolution. Other keywords were crossed with these concepts—that is, sexual abuse, rape, domestic violence, eating disorders, and substance abuse. What emerged was an association of childhood trauma with multiple outcomes, and a host of problems: Confusion in discriminating between diagnoses (e.g., a borderline personality disorder and posttraumatic stress disorder); failure to detect and provide trauma-specific treatment versus, for example, treatment for chronic depression; and failure to dual-diagnose *and* treat both conditions.

As a result of this keyword search, the wake of trauma became painfully clear: *Adult women are first female children who as children are violated and abused by others.* This glaring reality is too often ignored as we provide care to children or adults—and I emphasize the difference because, in my experience, too often "the child within" the adult is neglected. The damage wrought by violence in childhood is carried forward to adulthood with disastrous consequences for women in the destruction of life and its quality. *Abuse of female children is violence against women.*

Not all women are victims of childhood trauma, and that also will affect how these women resolve a traumatic event in adulthood. However, given the prevalence of childhood abuse (see Chapter 1), being female is a high risk factor for abuse or violence in childhood and later life. This observation prompted Carmen, Russo, and Miller (1981) to state, "the frequency with which incest, rape, and marital violence occur suggests such events might well be considered normative developmental crises for women" (p. 1321). Assessment and intervention in any form of violence on an adult female must take into consideration:

1   Whether or not she has experienced childhood physical or sexual abuse (or both).

2   Whether she is a battered woman or previously raped (or both).

3   The presence of a history of any trauma—natural disasters, burglary, witness to homicide, political torture.

4 What pre-event resources and demands enable her to more or less process that trauma within herself.

5 What post-event contexts or environment influence her processing of that trauma.

So, while I had expected to focus primarily on the sequelae of rape, the literature that emerged from my study about recovery from trauma turned my path in another direction: pre-event high risk factors. *Children who are victims of violence, or who are close to victims of violence, are at high risk for long-term difficulties and subsequent violence.*

The position asserted here is that we must attend to the *life-span* continuum of violence against women. Understanding the pathways of response to a trauma over the lifespan is *essential* if we are to understand and effectively intervene in the wake of that trauma, and to promote the health and well-being of our clients. To facilitate this process a Person × Event × Context or environment conceptual model of trauma and its wake is proposed (see Figure 1), and the components of the model are depicted in Tables 4-1–4-4. First, an overview of the conceptual model is presented, and then a discussion of the components of the model based on literature in the field is presented.

A CONCEPTUAL MODEL OF TRAUMA AND ITS WAKE

The following section presents an overview and introduction to the conceptual model of trauma and its wake. The first triangle of the model references precondition, person, and environment (see Table 4-1). This component depicts the importance of our understanding childhood development if we are to comprehend how children process a traumatic event, like sexual abuse (e.g., Hartman & Burgess, 1986, 1988), and how that processing in childhood is carried forward over the course of a lifetime, such as that reported by adult survivors of incest. This course includes the progression from victim-to-patient so poignantly depicted in the movie *Nuts* and in the literature in victimology (e.g., Bass & Davis, 1988; Carmen, Reiker, & Mills, 1984; Reiker & Carmen, 1986; Siegel & Romig, 1988).

Common sense tells us that the development of a child who lives in the midst of domestic violence, or witnesses his or her mother's homicide, is interrupted and different from that of a child who has no victimization history. Each of these children enters adulthood with different personal resources with which to transit the balance of their lives. Further, not only does the presence or absence of a traumatic event intersect with the person's age-specific development, but this development is also influenced by contextual or environmental factors, such as social inequality (National Institute of Mental Health, 1986), that simultaneously create barriers to service access and quality treatment (Carmen, Russo, & Miller, 1981). Other factors influencing development are a

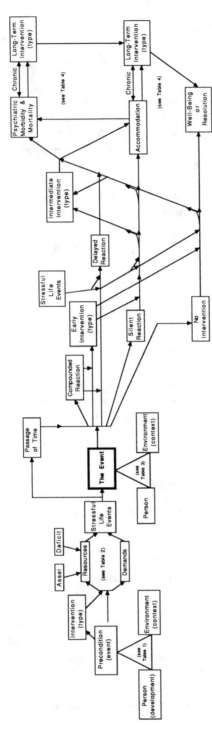

Figure 4-1 Violence against women: A conceptual model of trauma and its wake*.

*Based on: Antonovsky, A. (1987). *Unraveling the mystery of health.* San Francisco: Jossey-Bass; Burgess, A. W. (1983). Rape trauma syndrome. *Behavioral Sciences and the Law,* 1(3), 97–112; Figley, C. (Ed.) (1985, 1986). *Trauma and its wake,* Vol I, II. New York: Brunner/Mazel, Publishers; Fink, S. (1989). *Family care of the elderly: Factors affecting the well-being of caregiving families.* Unpublished manuscript; Foley, T. (1984–1987). *Family response to rape.* NIMH Grant #5K08-MH00557; Green, B., Wilson, J., & Lindy, J. (1985). *Conceptualizing post-traumatic stress disorder: A psychosocial framework.* In C. R. Figley (Ed.), *Trauma and its wake: The study and treatment of post-traumatic stress disorder.* New York: Brunner/Mazel, Publishers; Koss, M. & Burkhart. B. (1989). A conceptual analysis of rape victimization. *Psychology of Women Quarterly.* 13:27–40; McCann, I., Sakheim, D. & Abrahamson, D. (1988). Trauma and victimization: A model of psychological adaptation. *The Counseling Psychologist,* 16(4), 531–594; van der Kolk, B. (1987). *Psychological trauma.* Washington, DC: The American Psychiatric Press; Walker, A. (1989). The psychobiology of trauma. In J. Wilson (Ed.), *Trauma, transformation and healing: An integrative approach to theory, research and post-traumatic therapy.* New York: Brunner/Mazel, Publishers; Wilson, John P. (1989). A person-environment approach to theory, research and post-traumatic-stress reactions. In J. Wilson (Ed.), *Trauma, transformation, and healing: An integrative approach to theory, research, and post-traumatic therapy.* New York: Brunner/Mazel Publishers. See Tables 1-4 for component details.

Table 4-1   Developmental Factors and Antecedents Influencing Resolution of Subsequent Traumatic Life Events

Precondition (event) ×	Person (development) ×	Environment (context)
Child sexual abuse	Biological	Sex-role socialization
Child physical abuse	Health status	Family Process, or
Witness	Genetic factors,	functioning
Homicide	Predisposition	Differentiated
Domestic violence	Developmental disability	vs. enmeshed
Rape	Psychophysiology	Domestic violence
Terrorism, accident, other	Cognitive	Substance abuse
Psychological abuse	Schema: self, others	Culture
No victimization/	Information processing	Social inequality
abuse history	Structure	Poverty
	Normal development vs.	Discrimination
	trauma impaired	Education
	dissociative phenomena,	Health care
	attention deficit	Employment
	Coping style	Spiritual/moral
	Mood/emotions	Social support
	Affect regulation	Family burden
	Behavior	
	Social functioning	
	Task performance	
	Skill/ability	
	Trauma responses	
	Conduct disorder	
	Coping style	
	Assertive	
	Self-sacrificing	

functional or dysfunctional family system (Forward & Buck, 1989; Foley & Grimes, 1987; Mellody, Miller, & Miller, 1989), sex-role socialization (Frieze, Parsons, Johnson, Ruble, & Zellman, 1978; Schechter, 1982; Weitzman, 1979); and society's betrayal of the child by the hidden cruelty in childrearing that breeds the roots of violence (Forward & Buck, 1989; Miller, 1984, 1986). Finally, the availability of treatment is a factor. Whether the child and family receive treatment for the trauma sustained, and the nature of the treatment received, also influence the post-event development of the child into adulthood.

The second component of the model, depicted in an octagonal shape, references resources available to a woman, enabling her to live and cope with daily life (see Table 4-2). Resources may be both an asset and a deficit (Antonovsky, 1987). For example, a woman may perceive her financial resources to be adequate; however, when faced with paying the costs of health care and therapy following a traumatic event, she may face an insurance company that either refuses to pay the costs of a professional skilled in treating post-trauma sequelae (e.g., a nurse) or allows only a short period of treatment.

The concepts of social support and coping are domains of study in themselves and beyond the scope of this chapter. These concepts are entered under resources, as empirical evidence suggests a positive relationship between mental and physical health and social networks and social support on the one hand (Israel & Rounds, 1987), and between coping strategies and adjustment to subsequent traumas on the other (Silver & Wortman, 1980; Taylor, 1983).

The concept of demands takes into consideration variation in the responsibilities of daily life faced by women—demands that influence their mental and physical health. For example, the multiple roles of women (e.g., parent, partner, caregiver, wage-earner) act as stressors affecting their mental health and ability to cope with stressful life events (SLEs) (Baillie, Norbeck, & Barnes, 1988; NIMH, 1986).

The third component of the model accounts for the influence that SLEs may have on a woman's health status. Early research indicated that the type and number of stressful life events a person experienced was associated with physical and psychiatric illnesses (Holmes & Rahe, 1967). More recently, empirical data indicates that the total number of events identified by the respondent as negative or "bad" are predictive of higher morbidity (Nobeck & Tilden, 1983). Revised prior life event scales now include traumatic events, such as a prior rape or domestic violence (Norbeck, 1984), in order to detect intervening effects of a prior trauma on the most recent trauma being assessed.

The fourth component of the model (referenced by arrows on the flow chart) addresses time, treatment possibilities, and subsequent traumatic events that may arise. The model indicates that at this point in time:

1 A woman enters with or without a history of childhood trauma.
2 She has been treated or untreated for a trauma.

Table 4-2   Resources and Demands Influencing Well-Being

Resources (assets and/or deficits)	Demands
Social support	Role strain
Coping	Partnership/marriage
Preexisting personality, cognitive structure	Career/work, parenting
	Community/neighborhood
Genetic predisposition	Life cycle
Socioeconomic status	Caregiver burden
Health status	Daily hassles
Family and/or dyadic	
Environment/functioning	
Spiritual	

3 She has a set of identifiable resources and demands that influence the status of her mental and physical health.
4 She experiences a variety of stressful life events that affect her health.
5 She may bypass or experience subsequent traumatic life events.

In effect, the model theoretically allows for the possibility that healing may occur with the passage of time; well-being may be an outcome without intervention beyond the use of natural support networks; and intervention may occur at any point.

The fifth component of the model, referenced by the second triangle from the left (see Table 4-3), identifies the interaction of the person and environmental factors with a traumatic event that occurs subsequent to childhood. This component of the model takes into account variables considered in victimization studies such as the nature and severity of the stressor or event; the emotional, cognitive, behavioral, biologic, and interpersonal responses of the victim to the most recent trauma; and ways in which contextual factors or the environment interact with the victim's processing of a trauma to facilitate or impede resolution. (One graphic example of this intersection was depicted in the 1989 movie *The Accused*. This movie portrayed the rejecting and stigmatizing response of a community to the reported gang rape of a young woman on a pool table in Big Dan's Tavern in New Bedford, Massachusetts, in the spring of 1983.) Further, the model accounts for the possibility that in response to the event (bounded by prior SLEs and the passage of time) the direction of nonsupportive and destructive responses of significant others and community can be reversed as happened in the New Bedford case (see Koss & Harvey, 1987).

The sixth component of the model describes pathways (referenced by the direction of arrows, see Figure 4-1) in which the victim's response to a trauma may proceed. It includes consideration of the influence that post-event SLEs contribute to trauma resolution. The pathways depicted reflect, for example, that a victim may, theoretically receive no intervention post-event and evidence well-being; not seek intervention until an intermediate or longer-term point when faced with resolving psychiatric morbidity or accommodation of the trauma (discussed below); and progress from psychiatric morbidity or accommodation to a state of well-being through intervention. The theoretical possibility of resolving a trauma and evidencing well-being without professional intervention, but with the use of one's natural support network, remains to be tested. Finally, this component of the model depicts pathways in which three trauma-specific patterns of response may proceed (Burgess, 1983).

By definition each pattern precludes a state of well-being (without intervention), may proceed to intervention at varying points in time, and resolve in one of three outcomes. These trauma-specific patterns include: 1) a *delayed reaction* in which trauma-specific symptoms are considered to be latent in expression; 2) a *silent reaction* in which the trauma remains unresolved and the psy-

Table 4-3   Interaction of Traumatic Event with Person and Environment

Event ×	Person ×	Environment
Situation variables	Mood disturbance	Social support
Assailant known/not	Anxiety, fear	
Substance use/abuse	Depression	Dyadic response
Weapons	Shame	Family response
Physical injury	Self-esteem	
Confidence/blitz style	Anger	Legal response
Acts performed/demanded	Numbing	Prosecution
Duration of event	Anhedonia	Case precedent
Alone vs. with others		Appeals
	Cognitive	Expert testimony
Single vs. multiple	Attribution	Sentencing of
Marital rape	Mythology	offender
Domestic violence	Interpretation/	
Repeat rape	Meaning/processing	Social action
Exploitation	Self-concept	Community
Sexual harrassment	Dissociative phenomena	Task forces
Elder abuse	Alexithymia	Social policy
Institutional abuse	Biological	Social inequality
Nursing home	Physiologic	
Hospital negligence	Hyperarousal	Health care
Health professional	Somatic disturbances	Direct services
Clergy	Diseases	Research utilization
		Education
Witness	Behavioral	Research
Homicide survivor	Substance abuse	Teaching
Child abuse/death	Suicide attempts	
Gang rape	or completion	
	Avoidance	
Accommodation destruction	Goal oriented	
Sexual harrassment	Coping style	
combined with	Resistance to act,	
disconfirmation	Comply to survive	
syndrome	Prosecute	
Consent competency		
destroyed	Interpersonal	
Sex exchanged to retain	Sexual dysfunction	
job, advance career	Impaired social	
ladder, regain	adjustment (work,	
self-esteem	school, social/leisure)	
via employer-	Dyadic/family	
sanctioned or required	function/dysfunction	
sexualized compliance	Violence against others,	
	identify with offender	
Other Acts		

chological burden is carried in silence by the victim; and, 3) a *compounded reaction* in which the most recent trauma exacerbates pre-event psychiatric, physical, or social difficulties. In the near future these patterned responses may be eliminated in the model, as the accuracy of stage and phase theories of trauma resolution are being challenged (Kilpatrick, Veronen, & Best, 1985).

The seventh component of the model depicts one of three outcomes in response to a traumatic life experience: well-being, accommodation, and psychiatric morbidity (see Table 4-4). The model asserts that, given treatment efficacy, a victim may move from psychiatric morbidity to accommodation and on to well-being.

Psychiatric morbidity is a severe outcome of violence against women in which the victim has integrated unresolved traumatic violence into her "self" and her view of the world (e.g., Mackey, Sereika, Weissfeld & Hacker, 1991b). She shows symptoms consistent with the diagnosis of a mental disorder specified by the *DSM-III-R* (e.g., posttraumatic stress disorder, borderline disorder, major depressive disorder, or sexual dysfunctional disorder). Such individuals may commit suicide. Psychiatric morbidity also includes diagnoses that emerge as a result of the woman's presenting complaint being embedded in a hidden or undisclosed trauma, or because of the clinician's failure to detect and treat a trauma-specific history; for example, conduct disorder, psychoactive substance use disorder, borderline disorder, sexual dysfunctional disorder (Herman, Perry, & van der Kolk, 1989; Mackey, Hacker, Weissfeld, Ambrose, Fisher, & Zobel, 1991a; Morris & Bihan, 1989; Rohsenow, Corbett, & Devine, 1988).

Accommodation represents an intermediate position between psychiatric morbidity and well-being. Accommodation is a state in which the victim has integrated unresolved traumatic violence into her "self" and her view of the world, and her life reflects this integration. However, her level of functioning and adjustment is consistently higher than that observed in victims experiencing psychiatric morbidity (Bass & Davis, 1988; Kilpatrick et al., 1987; Siegel & Romig, 1988; Summit, 1984). Even though the woman or child appears to many to be recovered or adjusted, careful scrutiny of her life will uncover some residual unresolved trauma. For example, the victim evidencing accommodation may be a valued student receiving high grades or honors, an employee who consistently receives maximum merit raises, a valued committee member at church or political campaigns, or a highly esteemed colleague. However, scars of the unresolved trauma remain evident in subtle measures of impairment—delayed or interrupted career achievement, or trauma-induced sexual dysfunction (Mackey et al., 1991a).

Finally, the model also acknowledges that the victim may progress from accommodation to either more severe morbidity, or to well-being. The condition is not static. *Well-being,* the third outcome, represents a state of health and wellness without the trauma-specific symptoms that characterize accommodation or psychiatric morbidity. The model recognizes the possibility of a victim

Table 4-4   Outcomes in Response to Trauma: Psychiatric Morbidity, Accommodation, and Well-Being

Psychiatric Morbidity	
Adult Disorders	
Anxiety	Dissociative
Posttraumatic stress	Multiple personality
Anxiety disorder	Psychogenic amnesia
Social phobia disorder	Depersonalization
Sexual	Schizophrenia
Desire dysfunction	Alexithymia
(hypoactive, aversion)	
Arousal dysfunction	Psychoactive substance use
Orgasmic disorder	Alcohol
Sexual pain	Drugs
(dyspareunia, vaginismus)	Polysubstance
Sleep	Personality
Insomnia	Borderline personality
Hypersomnia	Histrionic personality
Sleep-wake schedule disorder	Avoidant personality
Dream anxiety	Dependent personality
Sleep terror	Eating
Dual diagnosis	Anorexia
PTSD, borderline	Bulemia
PTSD, substance abuse	Mood
Substance abuse, depression	Major depressive disorder
	Bipolar-affective disorder
Child/Adolescent Disorders	
Disruptive Behavior	Anxiety
Attention-deficit hyperactive	Separation anxiety
Conduct disorder	Avoidant disorder
Oppositional defiant disorder	Overanxious disorder
	Posttraumatic stress
Eating	
Anorexia	Elimination
Bulemia	Functional encopresi
	Functional enuresis
Mood	
Major depressive disorder	

Accommodation	
Silent reaction	Sexuality
Unresolved sexual trauma	Promiscuity
	Dissociate during sex
Life disruptions	Sexualize relationships
Delayed and/or interrupted	even though it is
career ladder/achievement	ego-dystonic
Underwork or overachieve	Sterility/infertility

(Table continues on next page)

Table 4-4 Outcomes in Response to Trauma: Psychiatric Morbidity, Accommodation, and Well-Being (Continued)

Accommodation (Continued)	
Life Disruptions (Cont.) Multiple marriages/partners Multiple physical illnesses/ somatic disturbances (migranes, sciatic nerve, low back pain, T.M.J., G.I., G.U. disturbances) Chaotic life-style Therapy/counseling for alternative presenting problems Unresolved grief reaction Marital/partner conflict or dysfunction Adjustment reaction Appearance Deliberate unattractiveness, includes weight problems Compulsive self-mutilation (picking at skin, nail biting, cutting)	Interpersonal Unable to sustain an intimate relationship Difficulty parenting Elective nonparenting Difficulty with authority figures Self-sacrificing, primarily caretaker of others at own "costs"/ expense Revictimization/abuse, symbolic reenactment Feelings Powerlessness Low self-esteem Immobolizing fears Difficulty trusting Anhedonia Alexithymia Impulsive Behaviors Eating Money, credit cards, gambling

Well-Being	
Positive growth outcomes Improved self-concept Self-directed activity Reduced passivity Reduced stereotyped attitudes Positive Values Feminist consciousness raising Appreciation of life A challenge to surpass	Restored Meaning Mastery Self-esteem (higher) Common measures of "adjustment" Physical health Intact marriage/remarriage Employed or student Promotion/merit raise Sexually active Socially active Low psychological distress Satisfaction with perceived social support

achieving well-being by use of natural support networks without professional intervention, and it allows for the possibility of health and well-being even though post-event SLEs may arise. In addition, the model recognizes that with effective treatment, well-being is achievable by a victim experiencing either accommodation or psychiatric morbidity. At this time, however, little research exists to document well-being as a post-event outcome of trauma.

LITERATURE RELATED TO THE MODEL

Processing and Outcomes of Childhood Trauma

The developmental stage of the young victim is generally believed to affect a child's cognitive processing of a traumatic event. At this time there is an insufficient but growing body of research on how a traumatic event, the nature and severity of the stressor, contextual or environmental factors, and the child's developmental level interact to affect outcomes (van der Kolk, 1987). However, a family environment that is abusive or violent—i.e., where there is a predominance of anger, shame, guilt, fear, loneliness, and pain (Bradsaw, 1988; Forward & Buck, 1989; Mellody, Miller, & Miller, 1989)—and traumatic life experiences in childhood are known to impair a child's emotional and cognitive development, and to impair the child's ability to assimilate and process the trauma and subsequent life experiences (Bowlby, 1968, 1973a, 1973b). Studies of traumatized children supporting these results include children who are the victims of physical and sexual abuse, or witnesses to violence and terrorism such as those children who survived the Chowchilla, California, school bus kidnapping in 1976.

A number of authors have noted that there are some common elements in the response of children to traumatic events. These include cognitive and perceptual changes that result in distortions of time, the sequencing and duration of events or acts (Terr, 1983a); a resorting to magical explanations for events beyond their control (Green, 1983); a reliance on rhythmical activities; repetitive play that is devoid of pleasure and expresses unresolved traumatic themes (Green, 1983; Terr, 1981a, 1981b); conscious or unconscious reenactments of the trauma—"you play dead, and I'll pick you up" (Eth & Pynoos, 1985, p. 46; Green, 1983; Terr, 1983c); the formation of premonitions and retrospective presifting (Ayalon, 1983); and pessimism with expectations of a foreshortened life span (Terr, 1983b). Examples of common responses of children to trauma are noted in the following two reports.

In a follow-up study of 26 children between the ages of 5–14 who were kidnapped from the school bus in Chowchilla, California, Terr (1979, 1983a, 1983b, 1983c) found a similarity in the symptoms of these children even though their ages varied. Every child evidenced some degree of posttraumatic stress, symptoms of time distortion, reenactment of the kidnapping, cognitive and perceptual changes, and a heightened sense of vulnerability. Efforts to achieve cognitive mastery were evidenced by a sense of clairvoyance, a belief in omens, and a sense of a foreshortened future. A regression of pre-event developmental accomplishments was noted in all the children. In this sample, none of the children suffered physical harm. A similar posttraumatic pattern has been observed in physically abused children (Green, 1978, 1980, 1983) displaying splitting, denial and projection, hyperarousal and vigilance, and compulsive repetition and reenactment of the trauma in dreams and play activities.

Hartman and Burgess (1986, 1988) report similar findings with sexually abused children. They found that these children attempt to resolve the trauma via information processing (see Chapter 14), however their efforts are impeded as the trauma interferes with their developing ego. Disclosure of the event is particularly distressing to the child because it "requires a breakdown of defensive structures in order to retrieve and disclose the information" (p. 86).

The child responds to the event in a variety of ways: encapsulation of the event, whereby the ongoing abuse is kept silent and maintained active in present memory, and thus interferes with development; and, dissociation from the abuse, defined as "a general process in which the mind fragments psychic integrity in the service of survival" and attention is focused away from the abuse (p. 88). The authors note that dissociation is considered a normal response of self-preservation to highly charged and overwhelming stimuli, and may call forth the mechanism of splitting. When splitting occurs two processes can be observed: ego-fragmentation of "cognitions, self-representation, and body state" (p. 90); and sexual and aggressive drive disharmony where relationships are sexualized, body integrity is confused, and hypersexuality occurs.

Hartman and Burgess (1986) found that the child responds to this trauma with one of five patterns:

1   An *avoidant pattern* in which the child seals off memory of the abuse and may deny it.

2   A *stress pattern* in which self-blame, depression, and self-destructive behaviors emerge.

3   A *symptomatic pattern* in which acute symptoms become chronic.

4   A pattern of *identification with the aggressor* in which the child introjects qualities of the offender and masters anxiety from the trauma by violence against or exploitation of others.

5   A *psychotic pattern* in which the child is unable to distinguish reality and ego boundaries are blurred.

In contrast to authors who emphasize a continuum of responses and common elements in response to trauma by children across all age groups, Eth and Pynoos (1985) stress the importance of clinicians being aware of and designing interventions that are specific to developmental phase-salient differences among children of different ages. In addition to the common responses among children to a trauma, these authors report age-specific responses of children based on the researchers' work with 40 children who witnessed the homicide of a parent. The children were about equally divided across preschool, school-age, and adolescent groups. For example, they urge the clinician not to view a preschool child's silence as an indicator of amnesia or disavowel that the event occurred. They cite the example of a 2-year-old child who witnessed her mother shotgunned to death by her mother's estranged husband. The child did not speak of the event for one year, at which time the child vividly recalled the event in detail with recently acquired language. The authors describe other age-specific responses of these children to a trauma. The following case study illustrates one woman's processing of childhood trauma, including evidence of a silent and compounded reaction to trauma.

The Wake of Trauma: A Case Study Illustration

The following is what "Deb" shared with Dr. Roland Summit (1984) about the impact that "just being touched" had on her life between the ages of 4 and 11. By age 5 she believed suicide to be her only recourse; at age 7 a failed attempt at suicide left her with the additional pain of inadequacy; at age 11, after attempting to hang herself, she was referred for treatment. Summit comments:

> She got treatment, but she didn't share the nature of her humiliation or fear. Instead, the treatment was for her drug abuse, for her suicidal inclinations, her sexual promiscuity, and her tendency to mutilate and cut at herself, which was seen as a terribly manipulative attention-getting gesture . . . it always seemed as if the therapists were bent on dealing with her symptoms and afraid or unwilling to cope or deal with the source . . . (she) went on to graduate school and prepared for a variety of professions. But she never felt authentic, never could get the sense of goodness or reward or adequacy; she always felt bad, always felt estranged from those people who gave her praise and comfort; she thought if they really knew what she was, they would hate her. . . . Listen in this for the behavior of a small child and how a regressed individual would cope with a sense of assault and helplessness. (pp. 143–44)

Reading from Deb's journal entries, which she gave to Dr. Summit to share with others, she tells us:

> I'm crying, I'm hurt. I just can't help it. I just viewed *The Silent Shame* about child sexual abuse. I saw you, Dr. Summit. I felt comfortable, protected, seeing you. I touched the screen and cried to you. You're my friend. I sat there watching with pain, with anger, with nausea, and revulsion.
> "I'm the one who every day of my life is reminded of what happened to me for seven years. I'm the one who became depressed, suicidal, distrustful, gay, insecure, hopeless. I'm the one who became plagued with a wide assortment of psychosomatic disorders. I'm the one who acted out throughout life, who became involved with drug abuse, promiscuity, stealing, physical abuse of others and myself, and I'm the one who is blamed for these very behaviors and disorders that were precipitated by a piece of slime that wanted a perverse sense of control and sexual satisfaction.
> It wasn't my fault people. I really was a good person inside. I could have been a different person, a good person. (p. 145)

Summit then describes journal entries by Deb marking the recovery of repressed memories. She recalled memories of having been penetrated and left bleeding; in later years of sexual intercourse that made her feel worse; about whether life was worth living; and, doubts about whether she could withstand daily assaults to her fragile self-esteem. And he notes how Deb would pass him in the halls at work (he was not her therapist), smile and reassure him she was doing fine, and did not overtly reach out in therapy for help with her pain. Her journal continues:

> God, Deb, what are you afraid of? Me, I guess, Journal, just me. It's sad, Deb, it's very sad, it's always been sad to me to watch the destruction of your soul, you're just going to complete what was done by someone else.
>
> I know that; I'm just not going to struggle anymore. Yes, but sometimes I wonder if you ever knew what you were struggling for and for the times you were struggling to self-destruct, well, that was the destruction.
>
> Are you saying that maybe I didn't give life a good enough chance. Yeah, I guess so, but I don't know any other way to live it, I'm so used to self-destruction. You know, I guess the real me died before the age of four. I'll never know what I could have been, having not been molested. It's changed my whole life, probably changed most of my actions and sentiments.
>
> My parents had their child taken away from them and they didn't even know it. I had my life taken away. Hey, Deb, I'm going to miss you. What are you going to do with me? I'm going to leave you with Dr. Summit. I want him to see what happened to one child who was molested. Maybe he can perform a psychiatric autopsy on me. Maybe it will help others understand the possible long-term effects of molestation.
>
> Are there any regrets? Yeah, I regret I could never accept myself, I regret that. Hey Deb, can we go home now? Yeah, let's go home. (p. 146)

Dr. Summit then describes how Deb tidied up her personal affairs, and brought her journal to his office. She left it with his secretary, went across the hall to the bathroom and "blew her brains out." Before she died she wrote:

> Dr. Summit, I'm sorry to inconvenience you. I died here because this is where I feel the safest. I trust you, Dr. Summit, and you trust Harvard General.
>
> I've left some material for you. Please read it. This is one kid's story about what happened. I'm compulsive about writing things down and so I thought since I did, I wanted you to read it.
>
> Two important things: No. 1, I love life, Dr. Summit, I just didn't like me. No. 2, being gay is not the source of my problem, being molested is. (pp. 145–146)

Dr. Summit brought closure to this tragic account, commenting:

> Those were her last words to us. I think when we decide that sexual abuse is more than a passing trauma, when we decide that therapy has to consist of knowing that trauma intuitively and internally; knowing how it hurts and know that it is worth probing for, worth uncovering, worth saving, worth reparenting, and mobilizing resources we haven't even thought of yet. When we know that no child can achieve absolution and forgiveness from the incredible badness of inviting sexual abuse— because, remember, that's the message we keep reinforcing and which the child reinforces—no child can get absolution from that sin unless we transfer the badness

to the people who do it instead of the people who get it. It doesn't mean we hate the abusers. It does mean we accept and acknowledge and define them as abusive, and the children as helpless and blameless, and then deal with their reasonable symptoms in trying to heal those deep scars that we don't even want to look at. (pp. 146–147)

Research with adult survivors of childhood sexual trauma indicates that the way in which the child processes the event and the patterns that develop in childhood to master trauma-specific anxiety often persist into adulthood, remaining undetected for years. Yet these patterns are expressed within a variety of psychiatric diagnostic categories and life-styles of accommodation (HaLevy, 1988; Herman, Perry, & van der Kolk, 1989; Herman & Schatzow, 1987; Herman, 1986; Hilberman, 1980; Lowery, 1987; Reiker & Carmen, 1986; Siegel & Romig, 1988). Mechanisms that began as a self-protective and survival response in childhood impair health and the ability to function in adulthood. While quantitative and group data are important to understanding the psychological sequelae of violence, let us not ignore what there is yet to learn from qualitative and case study data, nor pursue one method of inquiry to the exclusion of the other.

The Wake of Trauma: Psychiatric Morbidity and Accommodation in Children and Adults

Community and Out-patient Settings   Summit shared Deb's life with us in 1984. Today research data continues to substantiate a positive relationship between childhood physical and sexual abuse and psychiatric morbidity. As early as 1979, Rosenfeld found that among 18 female patients seen for out-patient therapy, 33% had a history of sexual abuse. Ten years later, Herman et al. (1989) tested the hypothesis that childhood trauma is common among patients diagnosed with a borderline personality disorder. In a sample of 55 patients, recruited from ambulatory mental health settings and advertisements, the researchers found significantly more (81%) borderline personality disorder subjects to have histories of such trauma. Physical abuse was the most frequently reported trauma (71%), sexual abuse was next (68%), and these were followed by the witnessing of serious domestic violence (62%). Borderline subjects reported, almost exclusively, trauma in early childhood (ages 0–6 years); more types of trauma; trauma occurring earlier in childhood; and, trauma repeated over a greater length of time.

All three forms of childhood trauma were positively correlated with the degree of borderline pathology. Women reported more physical and sexual abuse; however, there was no significant effect for gender related to witnessing domestic violence. No significant differences were found between comparison groups on symptoms of posttraumatic stress, and no evidence of exaggeration or fabrication in the histories was found. Herman et al. suggest that while no definitive conclusion regarding the etiology of this disorder can be drawn, the findings suggest strong support for the association of childhood abuse as a significant factor in the development of the disorder.

Herman (1986) also found a significant positive association between a history of physical and sexual assault or abuse and psychiatric disorders in an outpatient population (n = 190), with pronounced gender differences. The majority of subjects were single and between 20–30 years of age. Most victims (81%) were female while the majority of males (81%) were identified as offenders, a finding consistent with Carmen et al. (1984). Women with a history of victimization were four times as likely to be diagnosed as having a borderline personality ($p < 0.01$), and twice as likely to be given a diagnosis of substance abuse ($p < 0.05$), as compared to those without a victimization history.

Psychotic illness and/or substance abuse did not distinguish abusive men from nonabusive men. The only diagnosis characteristic of male offenders was antisocial personality; however, since abuse toward others is a major criteria of the disorder, this association was not considered by the author to be very illuminating. Rather, Herman states:

> These negative results area consistent with the views of many social theorists who argue that a great deal of sexual and domestic violence falls within the range of normative social expectations for men and cannot be explained easily by deviance or psychopathology. (p. 48)

Herman and Schatzow (1987) comment on the striking contrast of adult survivors of incest. The authors describe these women as presenting to the external world a highly functional, competent, and successful work life as well as a life characterized by effective parenting or caretaking of others. However, in their internal life and intimate relationships they are "painfully constricted, isolated, or chaotic and self-destructive" (p. 3), with marked deficits in self-care. The authors note that today these women would be diagnosed as experiencing a clinical depression, and, in order of descending frequency, have earned a diagnosis of histrionic, borderline, or avoidant personality disorder.

The long-term damages sustained from childhood sexual abuse are recognized by many, and the itemization of these outcomes reads like an unwanted laundry list of symptoms. These include:

- Repeated victimization, suicide attempts, substance abuse, and negative identity formation as compared to nonvictimized patients (Herman, 1981).
- Adolescent pregnancy and runaway behavior (Densen-Gerber & Benward, 1976; Herman, 1981; Burgess, 1986).
- Prostitution (James & Meyerding, 1977).
- More sexual dysfunction, somatic complaints, interpersonal relationship disturbances, and total symptoms than a comparable patient group (Meiselman, 1978).
- Chronic depression combined with recurrent nightmares, episodic depersonalization, impulsivity, and confusion (Gelinas, 1983).
- An integration of posttraumatic stress disorder into the structure of the victim's personality (Goodwin, 1985).

- A multiple personality disorder (Putnam, 1984).

Silver, Boon, and Stones (1983) found that women were still trying to make sense out of incest 20 years after it had terminated. The authors found that the passage of time did not help these women find meaning in their victimization or decrease their search for meaning about that trauma.

In-patient Settings The association of childhood abuse with adolescent and adult psychiatric morbidity is supported by a number of studies. These studies also note patterns of severe symptoms among these subjects. Carmen et al. (1984) examined the psychiatric inpatient records of 188 adult and adolescent male and female patients for the presence of physical and sexual abuse and its association with psychiatric illness. Physical and/or sexual abuse was present for 43% of the sample, with a higher percentage (53%) reporting physical abuse as compared to sexual abuse (19%). Among female patients, sexual abuse began in childhood and continued through adulthood. Among this sample, the abused patients were more likely to have past histories of suicidal and assaultive behaviors, alcohol abuse by parents, and criminal justice system involvement. The majority (81%) of abused female patients were adult, and the majority of these women (66%) demonstrated patterns of directing their anger passively inward (by being depressed or withdrawn, and feeling worthless and undeserving) or actively inward (by suicidal intent, savage self-hatred, and self-mutilating behaviors) as compared to male patients.

The authors suggest that the differential response of males and females to abuse reflects patterns of sex-role socialization. Further, they note that, although the trauma is expressed differently by gender (inward vs. outward), the psychic trauma is similar and reflects "extraordinary damage to the self, which then becomes the object of the victim's hatred and aggression" coupled with "extreme difficulty with anger and aggression, self-image and trust" (Carmen et al., 1984, p. 36).

Green (1978) found similar results with abused children. For example, Green found that abused children directed aggression inward (by biting, cutting, head banging, burning, and suicide attempts), and instances of self-mutilation and suicide attempts were more likely to occur in abused children than in neglected children or controls. Green concluded that "the abused child's sense of worthlessness, badness, and self-hatred as a consequence of parental assault, rejection, and scapegoating formed the nucleus for subsequent self-destructive behavior" (p. 581).

Finally, based on the assumption that abused patients are more difficult to treat, Mills, Reiker, and Carmen (1983) conducted a separate analysis of the parent project to see if longer hospital stays, a measure used to determine severity, were positively associated with abuse. They report that female victims, victims of sexual abuse, and victims abused by family members experienced longer hospital stays; shorter hospital stays were experienced by male victims, victims of physical abuse, and victims abused by persons outside their family.

Craine, Henson, Colliver, and MacLean (1988) conducted a randomized chart review on 105 adult women hospitalized as inpatients in a state psychiatric facility for evidence of a history of child sexual abuse. The authors found that more than half (51%) of the sample had a history of sexual abuse, and of this number more than half (56%) did not have sexual abuse identified in the course of their treatment. In addition, severity of a sexual abuse history was noted by the finding that two thirds of these subjects met the criteria for a posttraumatic stress disorder.

Among children and teens hospitalized for psychiatric illnesses, record reviews also report a high incidence of sexual and physical abuse. Kohan, Pothier, and Norbeck (1987) found that among 110 children between the ages 4–12 who were admitted to a child psychiatric inpatient unit, nearly half of the girls (48%) had a history of sexual abuse as compared to boys (16%). Emslie and Rosenfeld (1983) found that of 65 hospitalized children and adolescents, 35% of the girls and 8% of the boys reported a history of sexual abuse. In another study, Morris and Bihan (1989) conducted a random review of 110 closed records over a 5-year period among children at an inpatient psychiatric facility. They found that the majority (73%) of the sample displayed prevalent (defined as more than 10) symptoms of sexual abuse. Of the sample, 31% of the children had a history of sexual abuse identified and documented in the record. When controlled for gender, more than half (55) of the girls had a positive history. For 33% of the sample, no history of physical or sexual abuse was identified by the treatment team, but the record reflected a high prevalence of these symptoms. In this study, the only *DSM-III-R* diagnosis found to have a significant positive association with the sexual abuse history was conduct disorder. (This disorder does not specify a sexual abuse history as a diagnostic criteria.) The authors suggest that the antisocial and aggressive behavior associated with this diagnosis reflects the child's identification with the offender, a pattern noted by Hartman and Burgess (1986). However, Morris and Bihan note that the treatment team failed to see this possible association.

THE WAKE OF TRAUMA: SOME CONCLUSIONS ON CHILDHOOD TRAUMA

The studies presented in this chapter suggest that:

1 The female sex is a high-risk indicator for sexual and physical abuse especially among psychiatrically hospitalized female children and adults.

2 Identification of a sexual or physical abuse history for active (vs. closed or discharged) cases is inadequate.

3 Immediate measures need to be taken to implement rigorous protocols to assess for the presence of a sexual or physical abuse history, or history of other traumatic events, among women across the life cycle.

4 Without adequate assessment of sexual and physical abuse, effective treatment of the presenting problem is in jeopardy—the therapist will be treating the symptom and not its source.

5 Little is known about positive growth outcomes post-event, or the mechanisms by which these are achieved, so that health professionals can support and facilitate these client strengths.

At this time there is no *DSM-III-R* diagnosis for incest. It is not surprising, therefore, that adult survivors of abuse and violence are assigned a multitude of diagnoses (e.g., depression, bipolar affective disorder, personality disorder) as are child victims (e.g., attention deficit, conduct disorder, depression, anorexia). Lowery (1987) suggests that treatment for a diagnosis such as depression or hyperactivity may mask the true etiology, lead clinicians to conceptualize and attempt to treat the problem from an inappropriate theoretical approach, result in an unsuccessful outcome, and the patient seen as a failure. Gelinas (1983) concurs with the position that if a "disguised presentation" is the focus of treatment, therapy tends to be relatively unsuccessful, the patient tends to repetitively seek therapy, and the patient lives a life impaired by the abuse. Frederick (1986) suggests that a diagnosis of posttraumatic stress disorder is a more accurate conceptualization and fit with symptom patterns evidenced by sexually abused children.

The ravages of violence on children almost universally evoke the rage of humanity. Echoing this outcry, Conte (1984) suggested that our definition of violence is too narrow, culturally bound, and sexually biased in favor of men. He asserts that prevalent definitions of violence fail to consider the psychological force and violence that men use against women and children. Victimology researchers have documented that every act of child abuse involves coercion and manipulation, force and violence. As long as the perpetrator is regarded as nonviolent, we fail to see the assailant as the child sees the assailant—big and overpowering (Conte, 1984). Straus (1974) notes, in the forward to Gelles' study of physical violence between spouses, that as long as society continues to define the family as nonviolent the net effect is to cause "a perceptual blackout of the family violence going on daily all around us in 'normal' families." Clearly, aggressive steps need to be taken to prevent and treat the wake of trauma sustained by female children and adults.

REFERENCES

Antonovsky, A. (1987). *Unraveling the mystery of health*. San Francisco: Jossey-Bass.
Ayalon, O. (1983). Coping with terrorism. In D. Meichenbaum, & M. Jaremko (Eds.), *Stress reduction and prevention* (pp. 293–340). New York: Plenum Press.
Baillie, V., Norbeck, J., & Barnes, L. (1988). Stress social support, and psychological distress of family caregivers of the elderly. *Nursing Research, 37*, 217–222.
Bass, P., & Davis, L. (1988). *The courage to heal: A guide for women survivors of child sexual abuse*. New York: Harper & Row Publishers.
Bowlby, J. (1969). *Attachment and loss. Vol. 1: Attachment*. New York: Basic Books.
Bowlby, J. (1973a). *Attachment and loss. Vol. 2: Separation*. New York: Basic Books.
Bowlby, J. (1973b). *Separation: Anxiety and anger*. New York: Basic Books.

Bradshaw, J. (1988). *Healing the shame that binds you.* Deerfield Beach, FL: Health Communications, Inc..

Burgess, A. W. (1983). Rape trauma syndrome. *Behavioral Sciences & the Law, 1,* 97–112.

Burgess, A. W. (1986). *Youth at risk: Understanding runaway and exploited youth.* Washington, DC: National Center for Missing and Exploited Children.

Carmen, E. (H.), Reiker, P., & Mills, T. (1984). Victims of violence and psychiatric illness. *American Journal of Psychiatry, 141,* 378–383.

Carmen, E. (H.), Russo, N., & Miller, J. (1981). Inequality and women's mental health: An overview. *American Journal of Psychiatry, 138,* 1319–1330.

Conte, J. (1984). University of Chicago, School of Social Service Administration, Chicago, IL, personal communication.

Craine, L., Henson, C., Colliver, J., & MacLean, D. (1988). Prevalence of a history of sexual abuse among female psychiatric patients in a state hospital system. *Hospital & Community Psychiatry, 39,* 300–304.

Densen-Gerber, J., & Benward, J. (1976). *Incest as a causitive factor in anti-social behavior: An exploratory study.* New York: Odyssey Institute.

Emslie, G., & Rosenfeld, A. (1983). Incest reported by children and adolescents hospitalized for severe psychiatric problems. *American Journal of Psychiatry, 140,* 708–711.

Eth, S., & Pynoos, R., (1985). Developmental perspective on psychic trauma in childhood. In Figley, C. (Ed.), *Trauma and its wake: The study and treatment of posttraumatic stress disorder, Vol. 1* (pp. 36–52). New York: Brunner/Mazel Publishers.

Finkelhor, D. (1979). *Sexually victimized children.* New York: Free Press.

Finkelhor, D., & Browne, A. (1986). Initial and long-term effects: A conceptual framework. In D. Finkelhor (Ed.), *A sourcebook on child sexual abuse* (pp. 180–198). Beverly Hills, CA: Sage Publications.

Foley, T., & Grimes, B. (1987). Nursing intervention in family abuse and violence. In G. Stuart & S. Sundeen (Eds.), *Principles and practice of psychiatric nursing* (pp. 925–971). St. Louis: C. V. Mosby Company.

Forward, S., & Buck, C. (1989). *Toxic parents: Overcoming their hurtful legacy and reclaiming your life.* New York: Bantam Books.

Frederick, C. (1986). Post-traumatic stress disorder and child molestation. *Sexual Medicine, Vol. 4.,* New York: Prager.

Frieze, I., Parsons, J., Johnson, P., Ruble, D., & Zellman, G. (1978). *Women & sex roles: A social psychological perspective.* New York: W. W. Norton.

Gelinas, D. (1983). The persisting negative effects of incest. *Psychiatry, 46,* 312–332.

Goncalves, F. (1990). Child abuse shows up in abusive bosses. *The Ann Arbor News,* (September 18, 1990, Section D1).

Goodwin, J. (1985). Post-traumatic symptoms in incest victims. In R. Pynoos & S. Eth (Eds.), *Post-traumatic syndromes in children* (pp. 155–168). Washington, DC: American Psychiatric Press.

Green, A. (1978). Self-destructive behavior in battered children. *American Journal of Psychiatry, 135,* 579–582.

Green, A. (1980). *Child maltreatment.* New York: Aaronson.

Green, A. (1983). Child abuse: Dimensions of psychological trauma in abused children. *Journal of the American Academy of Child Psychiatry, 22,* 231–237.

HaLevy, L. (1988). Incest: Learning to remember. *Changes*, July–August, 28–29, and 58–60.

Hartman, C. R., & Burgess, A. W. (1986). Child sexual abuse: Generic roots of the victim experience. *Journal of Psychotherapy & the Family, 2*, 83–92.

Hartman, C. R., & Burgess, A. W. (1988). Information processing of trauma: Case application of a model. *Journal of Interpersonal Violence, 3*, 443–457.

Herman, J. L., Perry, C., & van der Kolk, B. (1989). Childhood trauma in borderline personality disorder. *American Journal of Psychiatry, 146*, 490–495.

Herman, J. L., & Schatzow, E. (1987). Recovery and verification of memories of childhood sexual trauma. *Psychoanalytic Psychology, 4*, 1–14.

Herman, J. (1981). *Father-daughter incest*. Cambridge, MA: Harvard Press.

Herman, J. L. (1986). Histories of violence in an outpatient population: An exploratory study. *American Journal of Orthopsychiatry, 56*, 137–141.

Hilberman, E. (1980). Overview: The "wife-beater's wife" reconsidered. *American Journal of Psychiatry, 137*, 1336–1347.

Holmes, T., & Rahe, R. (1967). The social readjustment rating scale. *Journal of Psychosomatic Research, 11*, 213.

Israel, B., & Rounds, K. (1987). Social networks and social support: A synthesis for health educators. *Health Education and Promotion, 2*, 311–351.

James, J., & Meyerding, J. (1977). Early sexual experiences and prostitution. *American Journal of Psychiatry, 134*, 1381–1385.

Kilpatrick, D. G., Saunders, B. J., Veronen, L. J., Best, C. L., & Von, J. M. (1987). Criminal victimization: Lifetime prevalence, reporting to police & psychological impact. *Crime & Delinquency, 33*, 479–489.

Kilpatrick, D. G., Veronen, L. J., & Best, C. L. (1985). Factors predicting psychological distress among rape victims. In C. R. Figley (Ed.), *Trauma and its wake: The study and treatment of post-traumatic stress disorder* (pp. 113–141). New York: Brunner/Mazel.

Kohan, M., Pothier, P., & Norbeck, J. (1987). Hospitalized children with history of sexual abuse: Incidence and care issues. *American Journal of Orthopsychiatry, 57*, 258–264.

Koss, M., & Harvey, M. (1987). Rape as a community issue. In M. Koss & M. Harvey (Eds.), *The rape victim: Clinical and community approaches to treatment*, (pp. 50–71). Lexington, MA: The Stephen Greene Press.

Lowery, M. (1987). Adult survivors of childhood incest. *Journal of Psychosocial Nursing, 25*, 27–31.

Mackey, T., Hacker, S., Weissfeld, L., Ambrose, N., Fisher, M., & Zobel, D. (1991a). Comparative effects of sexual assault on sexual functioning of child sexual abuse survivors & others. *Issues in Mental Health Nursing, 12*, 89–112.

Mackey, T., Sereika, S., Weissfeld, L., & Hacker, S. (in press). Factors associated with long-term depressive symptoms of sexual assault victims. *Archives of Psychiatric Nursing*.

Meiselman, K. (1978). *Incest*. San Francisco: Jossey-Bass.

Mellody, P., Miller, A., & Miller, J. (1989). *Facing codependency*. San Francisco: Harper & Row Publishers.

Miller, A. (1984). *For your own good: Hidden cruelty in child-rearing and the roots of violence*. New York: Farrar, Straus and Giroux.

Miller, A. (1986). *Thou shalt not be aware: Society's betrayal of the child*. New York: Penguin Books.

Mills, T., Reiker, P., & Carmen, E. (H.). (1983). Hospitalization experiences of victims of abuse. *Victimology: An International Journal, 9,* 436–449.

Morris, P., & Bihan, S. (1989). *A retrospective study of the prevalence of children with a history of sexual abuse hospitalized in the psychiatric setting.* Unpublished master's thesis, The University of Michigan School of Nursing, Ann Arbor, MI.

National Institute of Mental Health. (1986). *Women's mental health: Agenda for research.* Washington, DC: U.S. Department of Health and Human Services.

Norbeck, J. (1984). Modification of life event questionnaires for use with female respondents. *Research in Nursing & Health, 7,* 61–71.

Norbeck, J., & Tilden, V. (1983). Life stress, social support, and emotional disequilibrium in complications of pregnancy: A prospective, multivariate study. *Journal of Health & Social Behavior, 24,* 30–46.

Putnam, F. (1984). The psychophysiological investigation of multiple personality disorder. *Psychiatric Clinics of North America, 7,* 31–41.

Reiker, P. P., & Carmen, E. H. (1986). The victim-to-patient process: The disconfirmation and transformation of abuse. *American Journal of Orthopsychiatry, 56,* 360–370.

Rohsenow, D., Corbett, R., & Devine, D. (1988). Molested as children: A hidden contribution to substance abuse. *Journal of Substance Abuse Treatment, 5,* 13–18.

Rosenfeld, A. (1979). Incidence of a history of incest among 18 female psychiatric patients. *American Journal of Psychiatry, 136,* 791–795.

Rutter, P. (1989). *Sex in the forbidden zone: When men in power—therapists, doctors, clergy, teachers & others—betray womens' trust.* Los Angeles: Jeremy P. Tarcher, Inc.

Schechter, S. (1982). Toward an analysis of violence against women in the family. In S. Schechter (Ed.), *Women and male violence: The visions and struggles of the battered women's movement* (pp. 209–240). Boston: South End Press.

Siegel, D., & Romig, C. (1988). Treatment of adult survivors of childhood sexual assault: Imagery within a systemic framework. *American Journal of Family Therapy, 16,* 229–242.

Silver, R. L., Boon, C., & Stones, M. H. (1983). Searching for meaning in misfortune: Making sense of incest. *Journal of Social Issues, 39,* 80–102.

Silver, R. L. & Wortman, C. B. (1980). Coping with undesirable life events. In J. Garber & M. E. P. Seligman (Eds.), *Human Helplessness* (pp. 279–375). New York: Academic Press.

Straus, M. (1974). In Gelles, R. (Ed.). *The violent home: A study of physical aggression between husbands and wives.* Beverly Hills: Sage Publications.

Summit, R. L. (1983). The child sexual abuse accommodation syndrome. *Child Abuse and Neglect, 7,* 177–193.

Summit, R. L. (1984). Caring for the child molestation victims. In *Protecting our children: The fight against molestation, a national symposium* (pp. 139–147). Washington, DC: U.S. Department of Justice.

Taylor, S. (1983). Adjustments to threatening events: A theory of cognitive adaptation. *American Psychologist, 38,* 1161–1173.

Terr, L. (1979). Children of Chowchilla: A study of psychic trauma. *Psychoanalytic Study of the Child, 34,* 547–623.

Terr, L. (1981a). "Forbidden games": Post-traumatic child's play. *Journal of the American Academy of Child Psychiatry, 20,* 741–760.

Terr, L. (1981b). Psychic trauma in children. *American Journal of Psychiatry, 138,* 14–19.

Terr, L. (1983a). Chowchilla revisited: The effects of psychic trauma four years after a school bus kidnapping. *American Journal of Psychiatry, 140,* 1543–1550.

Terr, L. (1983b). Time sense following psychiatric trauma. A clinical study of ten adults and twenty children. *American Journal of Orthopsychiatry, 53,* 244–261.

Terr, L. (1983c). *The aftermath of a kidnapping.* Paper presented at Symposium on Psychological Trauma in Children and Adults: Implications for Diagnosis and Treatment in Psychiatry. Boston, MA (30 November–1 December 1984).

van der Kolk, B. (1987). *Psychological trauma.* Washington, DC: The American Psychiatric Press.

Weitzman, L. J. (1979). Sex-role socialization. In J. Freeman (Ed.), *Women: A feminist perspective* (pp. 153–216). Palo Alto: Mayfield Publishing Co.

Chapter 5

A Review of Nursing Research on Battering

Jacquelyn C. Campbell

In the last few years there has been an emergence of a growing body of nursing research on the battering of women. Nurses' research is being published in both nursing journals and interdisciplinary forums. Woman abuse is an appropriate area for nursing inquiry in light of the significant health problem represented by intimate violence toward women, the holistic responses to violence experienced by those victimized, the potential for further morbidity and mortality when battering escalates, and the effect of woman abuse on children, both born and unborn.

NURSING'S UNIQUE CONTRIBUTION

Nursing research has added a unique perspective to knowledge development in the study of violence against women because of its holistic perspective. The literature in psychology, sociology, and even victimology and women's studies on abused women tends to concentrate on documenting emotional effects and sociological and psychological factors. The nursing research to date has been more concerned with responses to and characteristics of woman abuse rather than focused upon causation. Moreover, nurse researchers have added both physical injury and physical responses to the emotional and behavioral reactions usually studied. This is reflective of nursing's Social Policy Statement (American Nurses Association, 1980) definition and allows an easily comprehensible identification of nursing's unique body of knowledge in this field.

A women's health orientation, either using an overtly feminist framework or at least avoiding the androcentric biases of much early research and some of the continued research in other fields, is also apparent. Nursing studies have avoided the victim blaming and emphasis on pathology characteristic of much other research that has served to encourage a distancing perspective of battered women as a deviant group (Campbell, 1991; Schur, 1980; Wardell, Gillespie, & Leffler, 1983). There also have been connections with the battered woman's movement by most nursing authors in the field and a general avoidance of the controversies surrounding the extent and nature of female violence against male partners. Nursing has concentrated, and rightly so, on the threat that wife abuse poses for women's health rather than obscuring the issue under such labels as "spouse abuse" or "domestic violence."

Nursing research on battering also has approximated a critical theory approach (Allen, 1986) in that the published reports have almost always had an emancipatory component, either in terms of the clinical prescriptions derived for nursing care or in the way the study itself was conducted (e.g., Hoff, 1990). The findings from at least one nursing study (Campbell & Alford, 1989) were used for emancipation through a state legislative change. Nurse researchers almost always provide interventions when they work with battered women, either directly with the women or by providing staff training. They also almost always make clinical suggestions in research reports. These nursing implications often go beyond what has been found in the study, but reflect the nurses' concern and rich clinical background with battered women and the shelter movement that they bring to their research. These additions are not usually deliberately guided by a theoretical or philosophical premise of emancipation. Rather they reflect the clinical grounding characteristic of nursing research and encompass the recognition of these women's need for empowerment, both in the health care system and in their lives.

Nurses who conduct research in this area have worked closely with abused women and have grown to know them well, in contrast to many sociologists in the field. Nursing research generally has grown out of clinical concerns rather than a deductive theoretical testing approach. Thus, our research is, in general, congruent with the calls for an "activist research agenda" being proposed by those who align themselves with the grassroots battered women's movement, feminist theory, and critical theory (Dobash & Dobash, 1988). These researchers and activists want to make sure that the primary agenda for future research on battering is to empower the women and children involved (rather than further blame or pathologize them) and to put the onus of responsibility on the social system to change, rather than the individual women. Nurse researchers' knowledge of and ability to influence the health care system in combination with their women's health orientation and clinical concerns gives them a unique and crucial part in that agenda.

ORGANIZATION OF REVIEW

This review of research will be limited to data-based inquiries related to physical, sexual, or emotional abuse of female partners published in nursing literature or in interdisciplinary journals by authors who identify themselves as nurses. There has not been an extensive search of journals primarily identified with other disciplines. We have been fortunate to see the emergence of a great deal of clinical nursing literature on battered women in the last decade. This body of knowledge will not be reviewed here; however, it can be noted that there is enough original research, theory, and clinical nursing literature currently published that nurses need no longer rely on publications from other disciplines.

The nursing research on battered women could be conceptually divided in a number of ways. For this review the literature will be divided into the following categories: battered women in the health care system, battering during pregnancy, responses of women to battering, homicide of women, and marital rape.

BATTERED WOMEN IN THE HEALTH CARE SYSTEM

Several research efforts have been aimed at identification of battered women in the health care system, both in terms of establishing prevalence in various populations and determining how best to assess for battering. There also have been investigations of attitudes of health care professionals conducted by nursing researchers.

Emergency Departments

Drake (1982), and Goldberg and Tomlanovich (1984), and Grey, along with her better known New Haven hospital colleagues, Evan Stark and Anne Flitcraft (Stark et al., 1981) all elicited data about emergency department visits from battered women. While Drake's study was a small ($N = 12$) retrospective pilot, Goldberg and Tomlanovich surveyed 492 urban emergency room patients while waiting for care, and the New Haven group reviewed 481 emergency room patient charts. All three samples were primarily African-American and Euro-American, ranging in proportion from approximately 50–50 to 70–30. The cumulative data from different methods and different geographic locations were persuasive that battered women were a significant proportion (at least 10–22% and probably as much as 25%) of women in emergency settings, were sustaining significant injuries from beatings, and wanted to receive services specific to abuse from health care professionals. However, only 2–8% were identified as abused on their records, and, when asked, they reported not receiving as much (or as useful) assistance as they wanted.

Stark et al. (1981) documented a significant increase in prescriptions of minor tranquilizers and pain medications for abused women than for other women in emergency rooms, but Goldberg and Tomlanovich (1984) did not, perhaps because they did not control for gender in that analysis. Stark and his colleagues interpreted this finding as evidence of the health care system's perpetuation of abuse, since these medications might hinder the woman's motivations to end an abusive relationship. However, given the increased prevalence of chronic pain in spouse-abuse victims found by Goldberg and Tomlanovich (1984), pain medication may be the appropriate intervention. A useful, as yet unexplored study would be to compare tranquilizer prescriptions (with pain medications separated out) in abused versus non-abused women, controlling for severity of anxiety complaints.

Goldberg and Tomlanovich (1984) found that chronic pain, not trauma, was the most frequent complaint in their sample. The New Haven group (Stark et al., 1981) identified a pattern of proximal rather than distal injuries that has been particularly useful in subsequent identification of abused women in emergency departments and the development of protocols. Drake's (1982) research report gave compelling evidence of the lack of sensitive care from the health care system and the kinds of barriers to care these women encounter. For instance, women discussed being prevented from seeking health care by their male partners. Women were unsure if their partners would be notified if the women went without them.

These three studies in combination have been instrumental in changing the approach of many emergency departments to wife abuse and is the empirical basis of most emergency protocols in use today. One of the early myths, that abused women will hide their battering from health care professionals and/or find questioning about abuse intrusive, was effectively dispelled by this important work.

Tilden and Shepherd (1987) used a time-series quasi experiment to demonstrate a significant increase in nurses' documentation of wife battering after staff training and implementation of an abuse-victim protocol. The findings support the magnitude of emergency department prevalence (at least 16% of women) from review of a total of 992 records. They also support the importance of training nurses to increase emergency record documentation of abuse. However, the increase from 9.72% recorded identification to 22.97%, although significant, was not to an optimal level.

The lack of identification and useful interventions by doctors and nurses was further supported by Brendtro and Bowker (1989). Mary Brendtro used her nursing expertise in the analysis and reporting of the health-related questions of Bowker's sample of 854 women returning a *Women's Day* magazine questionnaire. The least effective formal source of help in that study was the assistance of "health care personnel" to which only 31% of the women gave an effective rating in comparison to 56% (the largest percentage) giving that rating to battered women's shelters. However, it should be noted that the question did not differentiate between physicians' and nurses' attitudes.

Attitude Studies

Attitudes of nurses have been explored by King and Ryan (1989) and are compared with other health care professionals by Shipley and Sylvester (1982) and Rose and Saunders (1986). In the comparisons, both nurses and physicians believed some of the myths about battered women, including that women are somewhat responsible for their victimization. Although the Rose and Saunders (1986) study seemed to indicate that nurses were less victim blaming and more sympathetic than physicians, gender rather than profession was the differentiating factor. However, backgrounds including intensive training (Rose & Saunders, 1986) and increased clinical contact with victims (Shipley & Sylvester, 1982) increased sensitivity in all groups. King and Ryan's (1989) work was also important in documenting the proclivity of clinical nurses to use a paternalistic rather than empowering model of helping with abused women. This work in total suggests that specific training on abuse, including affective domain work, intervention philosophies, and clinical experience is needed in basic and continuing nursing education.

Other Health Care Settings

Although there are rich opportunities to do so, the work in emergency settings has only been extended in nursing research to prenatal settings (described in subsequent section) and one exploration in a primary care setting (Bullock, McFarlane, Bateman, & Miller, 1989). These researchers used record review ($N = 793$) in a Planned Parenthood clinic where all intake forms had recently been expanded to include four questions about violence. An 8.2% prevalence rate was found, indicating both significant intervention opportunity and an important means of assessment for abuse easily implemented in all health care settings. All staffs were trained in the dynamics and assessment of abuse, and the nurses were trained in intervention for those battered. Battered women in the sample were also found to have significantly more recent life changes as well as parenting, legal, and emotional problems.

BATTERING DURING PREGNANCY

The excellent program of research on battering during pregnancy initiated by Anne Helton in conjunction with Elizabeth Anderson and Judith McFarlane and continued by McFarlane and Linda Bullock has established the importance and legitimacy of nursing research in the area of woman abuse. Thanks in great part to that ongoing research, former Surgeon General Koop, the March of Dimes, the Centers for Disease Control (CDC), and the American College of Obstetrics and Gynecology have all identified battering during pregnancy as a serious health care problem. The CDC is currently funding McFarlane and Barbara Parker's major cohort study of the patterns of abuse during pregnancy and associated infant outcomes.

The program of research has established a baseline prevalence of approximately 8% of pregnant women physically abused during the current pregnancy and an additional 15% who were beaten prior to the pregnancy. This makes them highly at risk for further abuse as well as subject to the atmosphere of threat and coercive control that accompanies physical violence (Helton, 1986; Helton, McFarlane, & Anderson, 1987). Important additional findings were that demographic variables, including ethnicity, did not predict abuse during pregnancy, but physical violence before pregnancy did. A balanced sample of 290 African-American, Mexican-American, and Euro-American women was used. In an important postpartum extension of the research, Bullock and Mc-Farlane (1989) found that abuse was significantly associated with low birth weight and corroborated the prevalence and demographic findings of prenatal abuse documented in the earlier work. Other detrimental infant outcomes, such as 9% of the Brendtro and Bowker (1989) sample reporting miscarriages from abuse, have been suggested in retrospective studies but not yet established in cohort designs.

Findings from an independent postpartum sample of 900 poor women in Detroit (Campbell, Poland, Waller, & Ager, in press) using the same questions about abuse as the program of research described above also supported the significant prevalence of abuse during pregnancy. Hillard's (1985) medical study published just prior to Helton (1986) documented a similar prevalence of battering during pregnancy. The Campbell et al. (in press) research added the important additional findings of a decrease in adequate prenatal care and an increase in substance abuse (both illicit drugs and alcohol) associated with physical violence from a male partner as well as the already documented emotional problems.

WOMEN'S RESPONSE TO BATTERING

How women respond to repeated acts of violence in an intimate partner relationship can be conceptually divided into physical, psychological, and behavioral responses. Physical responses, other than the documentation of injury described above, have only been measured in Campbell's (1989) research. In this work battered women (N = 97) were found to have significantly more and more troublesome stress related symptoms than a group of other women (N = 96) who were also having significant problems in an intimate relationship. The sample was recruited from the community using newspaper advertisement and was both economically and ethnically diverse. The presence of physical symptoms was one of the few significant differences between the two groups. The other major difference was that the abused women had thought of or tried significantly *more* solutions to the relationship problems.

Psychological Responses

In terms of emotional responses, the two groups of women in my study were not significantly different on mean levels of depression or self-esteem, but there were proportionately more battered women who were seriously depressed using the Beck Depression Inventory (Campbell, 1989). Both groups were significantly below the norms on the Tennessee Self Concept Scale. Using the same instrument, both Drake (1982) and Ulrich (1989) also found scores in approximately the same range for abused women from shelters. Mahon (1981) documented significantly ($p < .10$) lower scores on ego strength using the Cattell 16PF Questionnaire and significantly ($p < .05$) *increased* self-sufficiency, but her extremely small sample ($N = 11$) limits the usefulness of her findings. Trimpey's (1989) sample of 32 women from a shelter support group showed significantly lowered self-esteem and increased anxiety using other normed instruments. Thus, there is considerable support in nursing research for problems with self-esteem in battered women as well as some indication of anxiety and depression (supported in other discipline research). However, these emotional problems can be viewed as part of a response to the actual or threatened loss of the woman's most important attachment relationship, which can also occur without physical violence.

The nursing research has also suggested that abused women display emotional strength in some areas. This has been further elucidated in qualitative studies by Ulrich (1989) and Landenburger (1989).

Landenburger (1989) used a triangulation design to identify a process of entrapment in and recovery from an abusive relationship. Thirty women from both shelters and the community were interviewed using an ethnographic interview schedule, phenomenology principles, and both domain and comparative analytic strategies. This work helped to illuminate the process that women go through in the course of an abusive relationship and to explain why women respond differently, both to the violence and to people trying to provide help, at different points in time. Landenburger (1989) identified stages of binding, which included aspects of self-blame, covering up the abuse and "shrinking of the self"; disengaging, a period of help seeking; and recovering, wherein the abused woman completes grief work, tries to find meaning in her experience, and works at the pragmatics of survival. Ulrich's (1989) qualitative application of Gilligan's self-in-relationships framework also has been an excellent addition to understanding the extrication process that abused women go through in terms of the disappearance and then reconstruction of self. Both of these studies were of predominantly white women, however, and need to be replicated with culturally diverse samples.

Behavioral Responses

The work of Sara Torres (1987) has provided a needed cultural comparison of some of the responses of women to abuse. She found her sample of 25 Hispanic-American battered women to have experienced similar frequency and severity of violence as 25 Anglo-American women in shelters, but Hispanic-Americans were more tolerant of the abuse. In addition, concerns for the children were more salient (primary for 40% of the women) in the decisions to leave or stay with the father in the Hispanic women, although also important (primary for 20%) for the Anglo women. Lichtenstein (1981) found a similar percentage of a primarily Anglo sample of 30 women citing their children's welfare as a primary reason for staying and/or returning. Importance of cultural considerations are also demonstrated in the Torres (1987) analysis by the tendency of the Hispanic-American women to stay in the relationship longer because of pressure from extended family and/or threats to family members, while Anglo women in both samples were more influenced by lack of resources.

Parker (Parker & Schumacher, 1977) has also provided insights into the process of leaving or remaining in a battering relationship. Parker and Schumacher's work is considered classic in the field of woman abuse. The article is almost always cited by researchers in all disciplines as one of the first controlled wife-abuse investigations. It is also known as the article that coined the term battered wife syndrome to describe a symptom complex occurring when a wife received deliberate, severe, and repeated (more than three times) demonstrable injury from her husband. This early definition was later improved by Walker (1979) and others by making it apply whether or not the couple was married, but was unfortunately expanded to include an assumption of psychological deficits ascribed to all battered women. Parker and Schumacher (1977) were careful to identify a separate group of abused women (violence syndrome averters) who were able to decrease the violence, either by leaving or getting help. These women were more likely to have never observed their mothers beaten by their fathers.

Four separate nursing studies have examined the influence of social support on the behavioral responses to abuse. Both McKenna (1985), using established instruments, and Hoff (1988) with feminist ethnographic methodology, have documented a different picture than commonly assumed for battered women in terms of informal support. Most women in both samples had some family or friends who were supportive and were not isolated (although their batterer often tried to impose isolation). However, Hoff (1990) found her sample's natural network to be insufficient and the formal system unresponsive, while McKenna

(1985) found network support to be significantly related to psychological adaptation by canonical correlation analysis in her sample of 112 women in shelters. Henderson (1989) and Campbell (1986) used qualitative data to examine support provided by shelters. Henderson interviewed eight women to identify four stages of need for support in a shelter:

1 Reassurance, when the women gather information to make sense of the past.
2 Analysis, after which they are able to put the past into perspective.
3 Reciprocity, when the women give back to newly arriving residents, a stage as important to the giver of support as to those receiving.
4 Independence, the period of adjustment accompanied by feelings of self-growth that began in the shelter but was mainly concluded after residence.

The description of these stages generally supported the findings by Landenburger (1989) of her stages of disengagement and recovery.

The themes identified by Campbell (1986) in her analysis of shelter support group meetings provided further documentation of abused women's active participation in mutual affirmation support in the process of recovering, as identified by Henderson (1989) and Landenburger (1989). This study also provided support for women's search for meaning in the abusive experience as also described in the other two studies.

HOMICIDE

One of the influences on women's behavioral response to battering is the realistic fear of homicide (Lichtenstein, 1981). Although not a common area of nursing inquiry, homicide is definitely a significant health problem in terms of mortality. For example, a historical and epidemiological exploration of homicide of women within a feminist framework in Dayton, Ohio, between 1975–1979 was the beginning of Campbell's (1981) work with battered women. The homicide study documented that 57% of those homicides involving adult women were between intimate partners (current or estranged husband and wife or boyfriend and girlfriend). In at least two thirds of the cases, the woman was battered before the homicide. When a woman killed her current or ex-partner, the man was the first to use violence in 80% of the cases. The findings also indicated the reality of women's fears that an abusive husband will kill them if they actually try to leave.

Based on that study and other retrospective work, Campbell (1986) formulated a clinical assessment instrument for helping battered women determine their relative risk of homicide in the relationship. The original instrument development work indicated initial support for internal consistency reliability and concurrent construct validity. Stuart (Stuart & Campbell, 1989) found additional reliability and validity support for the instrument in a small sample (N =

30), plus the indication that an additional item on suicide threats by the male partner should be added. The danger assessment instrument needs considerable work, especially predictive validity assessment, before it can be considered an empirically useful instrument. However, the research completed so far supports clinical relevance.

Foster, Veale, and Fogle (1989) added important information about women who killed their abuser from a very small ($N = 12$) retrospective study of those incarcerated. They reported emotional abuse and isolation as extremely important precipitating factors in the perception of the women involved, but they cited less escalation of violence and sexual abuse as other work has suggested.

SEXUAL ABUSE

Both nursing (Brendtro & Bowker, 1989; Campbell, 1989) and other discipline research (e.g., Russell, 1982) indicates that at least 45% of all battered women are also being sexually assaulted. This sexual assault fits the criminal definitions for rape and is often referred to as marital rape in the literature. However, since these assaults are usually repeated in the context of a battering relationship, the term sexual abuse is more accurate. In the sample described previously (Campbell, 1989), self-esteem and especially body-image scores were significantly lower for those 97 battered women who were also being sexually abused than those subject to physical violence only. Sexual abuse was also correlated with more frequent and severe physical violence in the relationship. In a descriptive analysis of questionnaires from a separate sample of 120 women in shelters, Campbell and Alford (1989) reported women's perceptions of serious physical consequences, including vaginal and anal infections, tearing and chronic pain, from sexual abuse.

SUMMARY

Nurse researchers have investigated many different aspects of woman abuse, and the body of knowledge accumulated is beginning to be impressive. One of the most useful trends is beginning programs of research (e.g., McFarlane, Campbell) and research that builds on prior work by other nursing investigators. Nursing is approaching a point where a knowledge base can be generalized for nursing interventions in multiple settings.

The findings accumulated thus far which can be said to be trustworthy include that at least 8% of women in prenatal and primary care settings are abused by a male partner, and approximately 20% of women in emergency rooms have a history of abuse. Obviously, this prevalence data, coupled with consistent findings of significant health problems, lack of documentation, and abused women's perceptions of poor care by health care professionals, indicates a need for nursing continuing and basic education in all settings. Tilden and

Shepherd (1987) have provided evidence of the effectiveness of an emergency training program, but further studies like theirs are needed in other arenas. Nursing research has also documented a consistent finding of problems with self-esteem in battered women, perhaps especially those also sexually abused. However, in addition to emotional problems, nursing studies have identified significant strengths of battered women, indications of normal processes of grieving and recovering, and cultural and social support influences on responses to battering. These findings, taken cumulatively are beginning to indicate data-based nursing interventions that will in many cases duplicate the clinical suggestions already in the literature. Many of the studies reviewed have very small samples and/or unsophisticated methodologies; however, the findings from those studies in many cases support more advanced research, both inside and outside nursing. Most exciting is the emphasis on strengths, rather than pathology, and the implications for interventions that empower rather than patronize. This kind of inquiry, continuing to build on prior nursing work and expanding in complexity, sophistication, theoretical underpinnings, funding, and recognition, is the future of nursing research on battering.

REFERENCES

Allen, R. B. (1986). Measuring the severity of physical injury among assault and homicide victims. *Journal of Quantitative Criminology, 2.*

American Nurses Association Social Policy Statement (1980). Washington, DC: American Nurses Association.

Brendtro, M., & Bowker, H. L. (1989). Battered women: How can nurses help? *Issues in Mental Health Nursing, 10,* 169–180.

Bullock, L., & McFarlane, J. (1989). Battering/low birthweight connection. *American Journal of Nursing, 89,* 1153–1155.

Bullock, L., McFarlane, J., Bateman, L., & Miller, V. (1989). Characteristics of battered women in a primary care setting. *Nurse Practitioner, 14,* 47–55.

Campbell, J. (1981). Misogyny and homicide of women. *Advances in Nursing Science, 3,* 67–85.

Campbell, J. (1986). Nursing assessment for risk of homicide with battered women. *Advances in Nursing Science, 8,* 36–51.

Campbell, J. (1989). A test of two explanatory models of women's responses to battering. *Nursing Research, 38,* 18–24.

Campbell, J. C. (1989). Women's response to sexual abuse in intimate relationship. *Health Care for Women International, 8,* 335–347.

Campbell, J. C. (1991). Health care system response to family violence. In D. Knudson & J. Miller (Eds.), *Abused and Battered.* New York: Aldine de Gruyter.

Campbell, J. C., & Alford, P. (1989). The effects of marital rape on women's health. *American Journal of Nursing 89,* 946–949.

Campbell, J. C., Poland, M. L., Waller, J. B., & Ager, J. A. (in press). Correlates of battering during pregnancy. *Research in Nursing and Health.*

80 J. C. CAMPBELL

Campbell, J. C., & Sheridan, D. J. (1989). Emergency nursing interventions with battered women. *Journal of Emergency Nursing, 15,* 12–17.

Dobash, R. E., & Dobash, R. (1988). Research as social action: The struggle for battered women. In K. Yllo & M. Bograd (Eds.), *Feminist perspectives on wife abuse* (pp. 51–74). Beverly Hills: Sage.

Drake, V. K. (1982). Battered women; A health care problem in disguise. *Image, 14,* 40–47.

Foster, L. A., Veale, C. M., & Fogle, C. I. (1989). Factors present when battered women kill. *Issues in Mental Health Nursing, 10,* 273–294.

Goldberg, W. G., & Tomlanovich, M. C. (1984). Domestic violence victims in the emergency department. *Journal of the American Medical Association, 251,* 3259–3264.

Helton, A. S. (1986). Battering during pregnancy. *American Journal of Nursing, 86,* 910–913.

Helton, A. S., McFarlane, J., & Anderson, E. T. (1987, October). Battered and pregnant: A prevalence study. *American Journal of Public Health, 77,* 1337–1339.

Henderson, D. A. (1989). Use of social support in a transition house for abused women. *Health Care for Women International, 10,* 61–73.

Hillard, P. J. (1985). Physical abuse in pregnancy. *Obstetrics and Gynecology, 66,* 185–190.

Hoff, L. A. (1988). Collaborative feminist research and the myth of objectivity. In K. Yllo & M. Bograd (Eds.), *Feminist perspectives on wife abuse* (Chapter 13). CA: Sage.

Hoff, L. A. (1990). *Battered women as survivors.* London: Routledge.

King, M. C., & Ryan, J. (1989). Abused women: Dispelling myths and encouraging intervention. *Nurse Practitioner, 14,* 47–58.

Landenburger, K. (1989). A process of entrapment in and recovery from an abusive relationship. *Issues in Mental Health Nursing, 10,* 209–227.

Lichtenstein, V. R. (1981). The battered woman: Guidelines for effective nursing intervention. *Issues in Mental Health Nursing, 3,* 237–250.

Mahon, L. (1981). Common characteristics of abused women. *Issues in Mental Health Nursing, 3,* 137–157.

McKenna, L. S. (1985). Social support systems of battered women. *Dissertation Abstracts International, 47,* 1895A.

Parker, B. Y., & Schumacher, D. N. (1977). The battered wife syndrome and violence in the nuclear family of origin: A controlled pilot study. *American Journal of Public Health, 67,* 760–761.

Rose, K., & Saunders, D. G. (1986). Nurses' and physicians' attitudes about women abuse: The effects of gender and professional role. *Health Care for Women International, 7,* 427–438.

Russell, D. (1982). *Rape in marriage.* New York: MacMillan.

Schur, E. M. (1980). *The politics of deviance.* Englewood Cliffs, NJ: Prentice Hall.

Shipley, S. B., & Sylvester, D. C. (1982). Professionals' attitudes toward violence in close relationships. *Journal of Emergency Nursing, 8,* 88–91.

Stark, E., Flitcraft, A., Zuckerman, D., Grey, A., Robison, J., & Frazier, W. (1981).

Wife abuse in the medical setting (Domestic Violence Monograph Series No. 7). Rockville, MD: National Clearinghouse on Domestic Violence.

Stuart, E. P., & Campbell, J. C. (1989). Assessment of patterns of dangerousness with battered women. *Issues in Mental Health Nursing, 10,* 245-260.

Tilden, V. P., & Shepherd, P. (1987). Increasing the rate of identification of battered women in an emergency department: Use of a nursing protocol. *Research in Nursing & Health, 10,* 209-215.

Torres, S. (1987). Hispanic-American battered women: Why consider cultural differences? *Responses, 10,* 20-21.

Trimpey, M. L. (1989). Self-esteem and anxiety: Key issues in an abused women's support group. *Issues in Mental Health Nursing, 10,* 297-308.

Ulrich, Y. C. (1989). *Formerly abused women: Relationship of self concept to reason for leaving.* Unpublished doctoral dissertation, The University of Texas at Austin.

Walker, L. E. (1979). *The battered woman.* New York: Harper & Row.

Wardell, L., Gillespie, D. L., & Leffler, A. (1983). Science and violence against wives. In R. J. Gelles, G. T. Hotaling, M. A. Straus, & D. Finkelhor (Eds.), *The dark side of families* (pp. 69-84). Beverly Hills, CA: Sage.

Chapter 6

Violence Against Women: Overarching Themes and Implications for Nursing's Research Agenda

Angela Barron McBride

The previous chapters, originally prepared for the 1990 Synthesis Conference on Violence Against Women, sponsored by the Women's Health Research Section of the Midwest Nursing Research Society, collectively move forward the women's mental health research agenda developed in October 1986 by the National Institute of Mental Health (NIMH). Violence against women was one of the five areas identified as a priority research topic by an interdisciplinary panel of experts (Eichler & Parron, 1987). In subsequent papers commissioned to summarize major research findings in these designated areas, Russo (1990) noted how intimate violence is characteristically responded to by the victim and society as a whole with disbelief and denial, processes that actually thwart the pressing need for treatment research on how to mitigate the effects of violence on its victims.

This chapter is dedicated to Dr. Ann Burgess who has been the driving force in nursing's development of a research agenda in this area.

An abbreviated version of this paper was published in Sigma Theta Tau International's newsletter, *Reflections,* soon after the synthesis conference on violence against women took place, in order for this research agenda to be broadly disseminated.

Koss (1990) developed recommendations for future research in this area, which dovetail with the major points made in this edited volume. The intent is to move the research emphasis away from studying perpetrators of violence against women and toward making understanding the experience of victims the major concern. In reviewing the causes and mental health effects of violence against women, Koss suggested the following directions for future research:

1   Focus more on intimate violence, because of its incidence, than criminal violence.
2   Develop accurate statistics regarding violence against women at all ages, especially, minority women.
3   Examine women's responses in the context of their past and continuing exposure to violence.
4   Study coping strategies that mediate traumatic consequences.
5   Develop instrumentation that reflects the complexity of the problem.
6   Formally evaluate existing prevention and treatment efforts.
7   Identify problems that are unique to victimized women.
8   Understand posttraumatic stress disorder as it applies to incest and rape victims.

OVERARCHING THEMES

If there is one overarching theme to the chapters in Part One, it is that nursing's research agenda when considering violence against women should be extensive. It can sustain scores of individual programs of research. This is not a small area of concern to a few nurse scientists, but one with extremely broad implications for knowledge and research in all of the clinical specialities. Violence against women is not a monolithic concept; it includes a range of behaviors from incest, battering, and rape to pornographic and violent media depictions of women, the untoward consequences of domestic law, and demeaning verbal abuse. Violence against women occurs across the life span, and its prevalence even sets the stage for the increasing rape of boys and for abusive practices between men in institutions where the lack of women means some men are forced to play "womanish" roles.

The first chapter of this volume introduced the subject matter with a powerful overview of the incidence of violence against women. Women are recipients of abuse 10–15 times more frequently than men; at least 1 out of every 3 women is likely to have experience with incest, rape, or battering. Most violence is likely to be initiated by a family member or acquaintance rather than by a stranger. To be the target of abuse at the hand of an intimate imposes the added burdens of betrayal, fear of reprisal, and guilt—all of which compound the physical trauma. Women are socialized to believe that they incite abuse or that violence is evidence of their inadequacy. There are a number of myths that continue to support violence against women, e.g., that women want to be raped; that men normally have uncontrollable sex drives; that abuse is not widespread; that men are entitled to express anger or frustration physically. Violence against women is of special concern to nurses because the physical and emotional sequelae fit the diagnostic classification of Post-Traumatic Stress Disorder; the violence can lead to serious injury, even death; and battered women themselves and their children often become abusers.

Lee Ann Hoff provided the anthropological perspective, beginning with a cautionary note about how language deflects from reality if the focus is on spouses when in fact wives are the more likely to be abused, or on family violence when the reality is that individuals act violently. Instead of looking for the *cause* of violence, she advocates being concerned about the sociocultural *context* of violence, since individual acts exist because of socially approved violence and culturally embedded values regarding women, children, and the elderly. Cross-cultural surveys have established the worldwide incidence of wife-beating; however, the societies in which violence is negligible are characterized by the virtual absence of sex-role divisions of labor and by the belief that all people are entitled to respect.

Hoff's emphases on the advantages of ethnographic methods and on the sociocultural construction of meaning drew particular attention to the Catch-22 problems of any battered woman's proving she is homeless "through no fault of her own" when public officials do not regard domestic violence as reason enough for being awarded emergency housing.

Diane K. Kjervik provided the legal perspective, starting off by criticizing the spurious legal premise that victim and abuser are both adults and have equal power to effect change. She urged nurse scientists to do all they can to elucidate battered woman syndrome so that they can effectively act as expert witnesses around the legal questions that are part of the consequences of domestic violence. Any analysis of a woman's response to violence, she argued, should dwell less on personal characteristics than on the social conditions that make for inequities between victim and abuser in a patriarchal society—inequities that persist both when a woman attempts to gain access to the legal system and when she acts in self-defense. The most effective way of stopping domestic violence is to arrest the perpetrator. Our models, therefore, should emphasize oppression more than victimization. This area is best understood in terms of the exercise of power rather than in terms of individual psychology. This recommendation is in keeping with Webster and Ipema's (1986) clinical suggestion that nurses distinguish between oppression and depression because factors shaping the latter (e.g., learned helplessness) emerge as features of women's lives because of socialization rather than genetic predisposition.

Theresa Foley Mackey's analysis provided an integrated model of trauma and its wake that shows the preconditions and variables bearing on the event and the resulting interaction between all aspects of the victim and her environment. In sketching out responses to trauma, Mackey distinguished psychiatric

morbidity (sexual dysfunction, psychic numbing, depression, sleep/eating disorders) from accommodation (underwork/overachievement, multiple
marriages/partners, chaotic life-style) and well-being or resolution (feminist
consciousness raising, mastery, reduced passivity). In the process, she pointed
out that violence against women can be both an acute problem and a chronic
one depending upon the extent of trauma and of intervention. There are an
array of immediate effects/reactions as well as long-term consequences to be
understood. Mackey reminded us that psychobiological theories must frame our
thinking because trauma-induced anxiety can lead to both psychological and
physiological hyperarousal.

Jacquelyn C. Campbell noted that nursing research in this area has been
largely shaped by clinical concerns, particularly the physical responses as well as
the emotional and behavioral reactions that are typically studied by other social
scientists. In emergency rooms, pregnancy services, shelters, and other health
care settings, nurses have demonstrated the usefulness of intake questions that
assess the extent of abuse, and have described stages in the recovery process.
Training programs sensitizing caregivers to the enormity of the problem have
been evaluated for their effectiveness. Nursing research has urged strategies that
encourage empowerment rather than emphasizing pathology. Nurses have played
a key role in identifying battering during pregnancy, a serious problem best predicted by a history of physical violence before pregnancy.

DEVELOPING NURSING'S RESEARCH AGENDA

In developing nursing's research agenda, it is necessary to review some of the
advantages nurses have as a group in this area. Because the profession is largely
peopled by women, nurses can bring both personal investment to this research
on woman abuse and interview sensitivities that are beyond those of most male
investigators. Nursing's longstanding focus on the person-environment fit has
prepared clinicians to look at mind-body problems embedded in a social context. The emphasis on appreciating the lived experience of the clients (Mac-
Pherson, 1983; McBride & McBride, 1981) has made us likely to include
qualitative methods that complement quantitative approaches in the study of an
individual's perspective. Nursing's predisposition is to do research *with*
women, not just *on* women. The interdisciplinary focus of our doctoral programs lends itself to proceeding from models that are truly biopsychosocial in
their nature. The mandate as members of a practice profession, is to be concerned about treatment research. We also have easy access to the clinical settings to which women in crisis go, as well as to opportunities for health teaching. Given all of the issues raised in the previous chapters, nurses should
assume leadership in answering the following major questions, which collectively reflect treatment research as a priority:

1 What is the true incidence of violence against women? Incidence statistics will be greatly improved if nurses make questions in this area part of all intake histories and searching for telltale bruises an essential component of all physical assessment. Every time one asks, "Has anyone ever forced you into sex that you did not wish to participate in?", such experiences generally become less invisible (Campbell & Alford, 1989). Some questions in this general area might become part of nursing's agreed-upon minimum data set.

2 How does one make a differential diagnosis between primary violence against women and relevant secondary responses, for example, depression, chronic pain, psychic numbing, eating disorders, image problems, nightmares, substance abuse, panic attacks, attempted suicide, which are often treated symptomatically without regard to underlying causes?

3 How are we to describe the battered woman syndrome? What is involved in identifying with the aggressor, and how does the process of reciprocal violence or of irresponsible-behavior-begetting-irresponsible-behavior develop?

4 How is posttraumatic stress disorder the same or different for violence against women as opposed to violence affecting men? This question requires some understanding of the storage and recall of traumatic memories, physiologic hyperarousal, and the coping strategies which mediate the extent of symptomatology (Hartman & Burgess, 1988).

5 How does one prevent violence against women? In developing prevention strategies, one would have to confront society's notion that men are entitled to display anger and express frustration ("only being macho"), and to catalogue the characteristics of safe environments. In careful assessment of the risk of homicide with battered women, one can strive to prevent the further escalation of an already difficult situation (Campbell, 1986).

6 How does one sensitize the legal system to the illogic of describing a man as a nonviolent perpetrator because he did not cause any *lasting* physical harm? Related to this issue generally are how economic realities and laws (including marriage and abortion laws) affect the public's views of the perpetrator and the victim.

7 In incest cases, how does one influence the daughter's anger against her mother for not satisfying the father or restraining him, which is often used to limit the accountability of the victimizer (Jacobs, 1990)?

8 How can school nurses effectively make high self-concept and respect for one's body a part of all health education? This question would include confronting prevailing myths about women wanting to be raped and about violence not happening much (Burt, 1980).

9 What kinds of treatments for the delayed and compounded effects of exposure to violence should be developed and evaluated in clinical trials? Special attention should be paid to the development of new strategies that emphasize reempowerment in the move from victim to survivor (Walker, 1989).

10 What can nurses do to prevent or limit violence against women in institutional settings, for example, state hospitals, nursing homes?

11 What is the response of family members and intimates to various

forms of violence against women, and can nurses limit these individuals' negative responses and support their attempts to be helpful (White & Rollins, 1981)?
12 How effective are existing social or legal policies in shaping care? This question means evaluating the codes under which our profession has to act, including the limits of health insurance when policies cover the victim only because of the perpetrator's employment.

In setting priorities among scientific initiatives, one must consider scientific merit, social benefits, and whether an infrastructure exists to support the initiative (Dutton & Crowe, 1988). Violence against women is an area that meets all three criteria for adoption as a major research initiative because enough is already known, as evidenced by the previous chapters, so that the potential for closing major gaps in knowledge exists. Research in this area certainly addresses discernible public need and the development of effective treatment strategies would benefit more than one region or country. The fact that the National Institute of Mental Health (NIMH) has an Antisocial and Violent Behavior branch with funding available for new or established researchers is evidence that resources already exist to support that broad area of research. (It should also be noted that that branch recently hired NIMH's first nurse scientist, Karen Babich, to serve as a Senior Research Staff Fellow.) What remains an issue as to whether nurses will work to answer systematically the questions posed by the chapters in this section is the extent to which violence against women, which has heretofore been relatively invisible as a curriculum topic, is acknowledged by our educational programs as a major area of study—the subject matter of the next section.

REFERENCES

Burt, M. R. (1980). Cultural myths and supports for rape. *Journal of Personality and Social Psychology, 38,* 217–230.

Campbell, J. C. (1986). Nursing assessment for risk of homicide with battered women. *Advances in Nursing Science, 8,* 36–51.

Campbell, J., & Alford, P. (1989). The dark consequences of marital rape. *American Journal of Nursing, 89,* 946–949.

Dutton, J. A., & Crowe, L. (1988). Views: Setting priorities among scientific initiatives. *American Scientist, 76,* 599–603

Eichler, A., & Parron, D. L. (Eds.). (1987). *Women's mental health: Agenda for research.* Rockville, MD: National Institute of Mental Health.

Hartman, C. R., & Burgess, A. W. (1988). Information processing of trauma: Case applications of a model. *Journal of Interpersonal Violence, 3,* 443–457.

Jacobs, J. L. (1990). Reassessing mother blame in incest. *Signs: Journal of Women in Culture and Society, 15,* 500–514.

Koss, M. P. (1990). The women's mental health research agenda. Violence against women. *American Psychologist, 45,* 374–380.

MacPherson, K. I. (1983). Feminist methods: A new paradigm for nursing research. *Advances in Nursing Science, 5,* 17–25.

McBride, A. B., & McBride, W. L. (1982). Theoretical underpinnings for women's health. *Women and Health, 6,* 37–55.

Russo, N. F. (1990). Overview: Forging research priorities for women's mental health. *American Psychologist, 45,* 368–373.

Walker, L. E. (1989). Psychology and violence against women. *American Psychologist, 44,* 695–702.

Webster, D., & Ipema, D. K. (1986). Women and mental health. A model for practice. *Nursing Clinics of North America, 21,* 137–149.

White, P. N., & Rollins, J. C. (1981). Rape: A family crisis. *Family Relations, 30,* 103–109.

Chapter 7

The Research Base
for Treatment
of Sexually Abused Women

Karen S. Babich and Ecford S. Voit, Jr.

- A woman is raped every 45 seconds in the United States.
- One in 3 girls and one in 6 boys will be sexually abused by the age of 18.
- One in every 2 women will become a victim of sexual assault in her lifetime.

These unsettling facts are displayed on the wall of the Violence and Traumatic Stress Research Branch, Division of Applied and Services Research, at the National Institute of Mental Health (NIMH). They are a sobering reminder of the endemic nature of sexual violence toward women and reflect its public health significance. Indeed, as underscored in the Report of the Surgeon General's Workshop on Violence and Public Health (DHHS, 1987), rape is *not* just a sexual act but a crime of violence, "whether it occurs between strangers, acquaintances, or intimates," and violence—by virtue of its pervasiveness and toll of injuries and deaths—cannot meaningfully be viewed as simply a "problem of disparate acts by individual offenders." Moreover, as awareness of its

The opinions expressed in this chapter are those of the authors, and do not necessarily reflect the official position of the National Institute of Mental Health or any other part of the United States Department of Health and Human Services.

91

public health dimensions has grown in recent years the far-reaching consequences of nonfatal interpersonal violence, in terms of morbidity and quality of life (Centers for Disease Control, 1985), has received increasing public and scientific attention. Sexual violence against women, then, places victims at increased risk of severe emotional impairment, and is therefore an essential element of any national program aimed at promoting mental health and preventing mental illness (Russo, 1985).

In her paper on "The Women's Mental Health Research Agenda," Mary Koss (1990) identifies two overlapping forms of interpersonal violence that touch the lives of women. These are criminal violence, which includes such offenses as aggravated assault, homicide, and forcible rape, and intimate violence, which encompasses child abuse, child sexual abuse and incest, courtship violence, date rape, wife beating or battering, marital rape, and elder abuse. Although most forms of intimate violence are also officially sanctioned crimes, this is not always true, Koss observes, and cites the instance of a husband's statutory right in 29 states to physically force his wife to engage in sexual relations. Clearly, then, there are many areas in which women experience interpersonal violence. This chapter, however, will focus on the scope, consequences, and treatment of *sexual* violence toward and victimization of women. In particular, studies will be highlighted that have been supported by the Violence and Traumatic Stress Branch over the past decade that provide a more reliable knowledge base for understanding, treating, and preventing sexual violence.

HISTORICAL OVERVIEW

With public awareness of rape and sexual assault heightened through the women's movement during the early 1970s, the National Center for the Prevention and Control of Rape (NCPCR) was established by Congressional mandate (P.L. 94–63) at NIMH in 1975. Its purpose was to support research on the causes and mental health consequences of rape and sexual assault, the efficacy of treatment for both victims and offenders, and the development and evaluation of sexual assault prevention programs. While these objectives were at some variance with advocates' principal interest in achieving federal funding for rape crisis services, the research supported by the Center nevertheless made important contributions to our knowledge about sexual assault and its mental health impact.

As part of a reorganization at NIMH in 1985, the National Center program was dissolved and its research and technical assistance functions were merged with another program to form the Antisocial and Violent Behavior Branch. This new branch assumed responsibility within NIMH for research on antisocial and violent behavior and its mental health consequences, and on issues of civil and criminal commitment at the boundaries of the legal and mental health systems. Studies of sexual assault, as well as the etiology, course, and correlates of sexually aggressive behavior, continued to be a priority of this branch as part of its research program on interpersonal violence. More recently, in October 1990, the scope of this program was further expanded to encompass studies of the mental health consequences of natural and manmade disasters and other traumatic events. It is now called the Violence and Traumatic Stress Research Branch and studies on the sexual victimization of women are now conceptualized as a component of the program on traumatic stress.

Studies reviewed and highlighted in the remainder of this chapter will be presented in four principal areas or stages of knowledge development. Although these stages overlap somewhat, it is helpful to view each as an essential component for generating knowledge about sexual assault that can ultimately be useful in program planning, policy, and services.

Scope of the Problem This stage is concerned with producing largely descriptive and survey data on the incidence and prevalence of sexual violence and helps to establish its public and mental health significance. As a general rule, a problem's ability to attract the attention of the research, service delivery, and public policy communities is often proportional to the general perception of the number of people who are affected by that problem. Problems that affect many people tend to be taken more seriously than those that affect only a few (Kilpatrick, Saunders, Veronen, Best, & Von, 1987b).

Mental Health Consequences The second stage is designed to provide empirical information on the short- and longer-term reactions and consequences of sexual victimization. Attention here focuses on understanding the type and degree of severity of psychiatric morbidity following an assault, factors that are associated with symptom development (e.g., anxiety, fear, and depression), and factors that seem to foster or otherwise impede recovery.

Treatment Interventions The third stage seeks to determine what treatments are most effective for what types of victims, and at what particular times following a sexual assault. Ideally, treatments provided and evaluated should emanate from our understanding of the psychological maladjustments and emotional needs resulting from the trauma of sexual violence. More often, however, it is the clinical interventions themselves that seem to drive our appreciation of victim response and recovery patterns.

Prevention The fourth and final stage, that of prevention research, focuses on attempts at eliminating the problem altogether (e.g., by offering courses in self-defense) or, more realistically, at alleviating the secondary effects of sexual victimization through education (e.g., of police and emergency room personnel) or provision of counseling services.

Most social and mental health problems, like sexual assault and rape, cannot wait for this orderly sequence of knowledge development to produce effective service programs. Still, research findings are currently available for all stages of the process that can aid in understanding the more global dimensions of the problem and the people affected. Once the contours of the larger problem are appreciated, more targeted studies then become possible on the uniqueness and commonality among subgroups of victims in terms of their particular responses to sexual trauma, treatment interventions, and strategies of prevention.

SCOPE OF THE PROBLEM

Efforts to better understand the true scope and dimensions of sexual assault have been hampered by inconsistent definitions of the problem. Sexual assault is a broad term that includes many forms of unwanted sexual activity, including rape. Some studies have used legal definitions of *rape*, which may or may not include forms of penetration other than penile-vaginal, while others have focused on more generic concepts of *sexual assault* with varying degrees of specificity regarding victimization (e.g., sexual contact, coercion, imposition, etc.). In general, as Ageton (1983) has cautioned, "Research on this topic must employ precise behavioral and physical definitions of the forced sexual behavior of interest." And because there is so much disagreement and ambiguity surrounding the meaning of such phrases as "being raped," "sexually assaulted," or "forced sexually," Koss (1987) suggests that all future studies collect data that will permit determination of whether legally defined forcible rape has occurred.

In addition to this general definitional problem, since official arrest statistics are based only on cases of rape *reported* to police and only a fraction of reported rapes ultimately result in conviction, the true scope of rape has also been greatly underestimated. It is estimated, for example, that only 7–10% of all rape cases are reported to the police (Kilpatrick et al., 1987b). As a consequence, surveys of the general public about crime victimizations they might have experienced, such as the annual National Crime Survey (NCS) conducted by the Bureau of Justice Statistics, Department of Justice, have become the principal basis for estimating the full extent of sexual assault. Yet when viewed from the standpoint of clinical relevance, criminal victimization data are somewhat limited in value (Koss & Harvey, 1970). For example, the NCS adopts a typological approach to rape, that is, a woman is either a rape victim (during the past six months) or she is not. Clearly, finer gradations are necessary. Just as rape is known to have traumatic impacts on victims, slightly lesser degrees of sexual victimization could also have harmful consequences.

For clinical purposes, then, rape can be viewed as the *endpoint* of sexual victimization, inasmuch as other experiences that are less extreme than rape, may nevertheless be harmful, including coercive sexual contacts, sexual harassment, and attempted rape (Koss, 1987). Furthermore, prevalence data, or the cumulative number of people who have been victimized over a period of time, are more appropriate and useful than 6-month incidence data because the aftereffects of sexual assault can remain for a considerable period.

In an effort to obtain more accurate and reliable prevalence data on sexual assault, Koss et al. (1987) conducted a national survey of "hidden rape" among an approximately representative sample (access was denied at several colleges) of 6,158 students (3,187 women and 2,971 men) in 32 colleges across the country. The designation "hidden" was used because subjects had not been judicially identified or recruited through victim assistance case records, which tap only a small fraction of the population of sexually victimized women (as well as sexually aggressive men). A scoring system was used to represent five classes or levels of victimization: nonvictimization, sexual contact (sexual "play" without attempts at penetration following verbal pressure, misuse of authority, threats of physical harm, or actual physical force), sexual coercion (sexual intercourse following verbal pressure or misuse of authority without threat of force or direct physical force), attempted rape, and rape.

The major findings reported from this study were:

- Of the women responding, 54% reported some form of sexual victimization. Unwanted sexual contact was experienced by 14% of the women, sexual coercion by 12%, attempted rape by 12%, and rape by 15%.
- There was 70–86% of lesser forms of victimization, and 57% of the rapes involved dating couples. Rapes, as well as attempted rapes, were also more violent. Violence was experienced by more than half of rape victims (64%) and attempted rape victims (41%) but by fewer than 10% of other victims.
- Rape victims reported higher frequencies of childhood sexual abuse and acts of physical violence in their families. Victims had a younger age of sexual initiation, were somewhat more likely to have experienced family instability as children, and reported greater use of drugs and alcohol than nonvictimized women.
- Of male respondents, 25% reported some form of involvement in sexual aggression. The most frequent was sexual contact for 10% of the men, sexual coercion for 7%, attempted rape for 3%, and rape for 4%.

These data suggested some important differences between women who are sexually victimized and those who are not in terms of their past experiences as well as their current behavior, which in turn suggested the possibility of a vulnerability to sexual victimization that may develop over the course of a woman's history. In a subsequent analysis of 14 risk factors based on these results, Koss et al. (1987) found that:

• Of all the risk factors considered, only those reflecting traumatic experiences (e.g., family violence or childhood sexual abuse) were capable of predicting sexual victimization with an accuracy better than chance. However, the vast majority of sexually victimized women (75–91%) could not be differentiated from nonvictims on these factors.

• A high-risk profile for rape was nevertheless identified among 10% of the women. The chances of being sexually victimized were twice as high (77%) in this group than among those who did not fit this profile (38%).

These results suggest that since a high-risk profile for rape was present among a minority of women (10%), clinical intervention targeted at the reduction of risky behaviors might be warranted among clients who are potential targets of sexual assault. On the other hand, inasmuch as rape victims were no different from nonvictimized women on critical risk factors in the majority of cases, these findings provide clinicians with increased empirical support with which to dispel victims' tendencies to blame themselves or their behavior for an assault.

Two other studies of sexual assault and rape prevalence in a general population sample should be mentioned that were conducted as part of the Durham, North Carolina (Duke University), and Los Angeles, California, Epidemiological Catchment Area (ECA) Project of multisite research on mental illness. Supplemental funds were awarded in 1981 to two of the five research sites for the purpose of including a screening question about sexual assault experiences. (Information was not collected on whether a completed rape had occurred.) Results in the Los Angeles study showed that 13.5% of 2,738 women (55% of whom were Hispanic and 45% where White) had been victims of sexual assault since age 16. In the Durham study, 4.9% of 3,147 women (63% of whom were White and 37% Black) had been sexually assaulted during their lifetime.

NIMH-funded studies, as well as others, have used different screening questions and have operationally defined rape and sexual assault somewhat differently. The studies have used different prevalence periods (e.g., lifetime vs. age 14, 16, 18 and over), and have employed samples from different parts of the county, and it is not yet possible to estimate the lifetime prevalence of rape. However, it is clear that all studies that used the most sound screening questions and that collected information on whether forcible rape occurred, found a lifetime or since-age-14 prevalence rate for rape of at least 20% (e.g., Kilpatrick, Veronen, Saunders, Best, Amick-McMullen, & Paduhovich, 1987; Koss, 1987; Russell, 1982; Wyatt, 1985).

Research Directions

Despite progress in gaining more reliable estimates of the incidence and prevalence of sexual assault, no nationally representative data are available yet. As Koss (1987) points out, collection of these data should ideally be based on a behaviorally specific definition of rape and sexual assault; include questions about lesser degrees of sexual victimization, childhood victimization, and physical assaults; allow separate consideration of legally defined completed and attempted forcible rape to facilitate comparison with other data sources; and include oversamples of special populations and ethnic groups, including especially those at high risk between the ages 16–24. The study should also include a panel design, permitting collection of both prevalence (at first interview) and incidence (second and subsequent interviews) data to allow for examination of mental health impact over time.

MENTAL HEALTH CONSEQUENCES

In addition to providing data on the incidence and prevalence of sexual assault, the ECA data from North Carolina (George & Winfield-Laird, 1986) and Los Angeles (Seigel, Burnam, Stein, Golding, & Sorenson, 1986), coupled with a study in a Charleston, South Carolina (Kilpatrick, Saunders, Veronen, Best, & Von, 1987a), provide important new information on the mental health sequelae that are associated with sexual assault and rape, in contrast to nonsexual crime victimization.

Results from these studies showed a strong link between sexual assault and rape history and the existence of major mental disorders. For example, while victims of crime were more likely (6.4 times) than nonvictims to have or have had major episodes of depression, victims with histories of sexual assault (7.7%) and rape (9.9%) were even more likely to have this diagnosis at the time of the survey. This same pattern of greater psychiatric morbidity for rape victims, sexual assault victims, and crime victims (respectively), as compared with nonvictims, also held true for both suicidal ideation and suicide attempts.

In additional to a higher prevalence of depression and suicidal thoughts and attempts, sexual assault and rape victims were also more likely to meet the diagnostic criteria for agoraphobia, obsessive-compulsive disorder, social phobia, and sexual dysfunction. Kilpatrick et al. (1987a) also found that the experience of rape, threat against life, and physical injury produced an additive effect, so that victims who had been exposed to all three elements were 8.5 times more likely to develop posttraumatic stress disorder (PTSD) than nonvictims. Moreover if PTSD prevalence rates (16.5%) are combined with estimates of lifetime rape (20% equaling 18.3 million women), it is likely that more than 3 million women are currently suffering rape-related PTSD—a figure much higher than that calculated for combat veterans suffering from combat-related PTSD (Burge, 1988).

Risk factor analyses such as these cannot demonstrate causal links between sexual assault or rape and mental illness because the data were not collected prospectively, *following* the assault; however, the strong association found in these studies does suggest either that victimization can produce these disorders or that these disorders might increase victims' vulnerability to attack.

Course of Sexual Assault Trauma Syndrome

Research over the past decade or more has identified a rather consistent pattern of reactions to and recovery from rape:

1 The initial response is marked by a sense of confusion and terror. These feelings dissipate after two to three hours, but are replaced with feelings of depression, exhaustion, and increased restlessness (Burgess & Holmstrom, 1974a, 1974b; Veronen, Kilpatrick, & Resick, 1979).

2 At about two weeks, distressful feelings decrease slightly, but then peak at the third week (Peterson, Olasov, & Foa, 1987).

3 Clinically significant symptoms of fear and depression, as well as problems of self-esteem, social adjustment, and sexual dysfunction, are very marked until the third month postrape when they ease gradually, with dramatic improvement shown by the 18th month (Resick, 1987b).

4 Follow-up studies at three and six years (Kilpatrick & Veronen, 1983; Burgess & Holmstrom, 1978) suggest that chronic problems of fear, social adjustment, depression, and sexual dysfunction remain.

Resick (1987a) found in her longitudinal study that rape and robbery victims both reported higher rates of fear than nonvictims, but that rape victims understandably also experienced more sexual fears than robbery victims. Rape victims reported more avoidance behaviors and thought intrusions of the traumatic events at 6 months postrape, and continued to show symptoms for 18 months. Kilpatrick et al. (1987a) also found that victims of aggravated assault, like rape victims, similarly experienced significantly higher levels of thought intrusion and avoidance behavior than victims of other crimes, but that these reactions were strongest in rape victims.

Preliminary findings from a currently active NIMH grant conducted by Libby Ruch (1990) at the University of Hawaii suggest that an even wider range of symptoms is experienced by rape victims than previous studies have suggested. Using a 32-item instrument she developed to measure immediate response postrape, Ruch has been able to distinguish 10 clusters of assault-specific symptoms that appear to form the conceptual dimensions of the sexual assault trauma: depression, fear/anxiety, cognitive confusion/shock, self-blame/guilt, loss of trust, disclosure anxiety, survival shame, and anger targeted at the assailant, the police, and significant others. Further analyses of these data will focus on the dimensions of longer-term trauma and recovery over time using this wider range of symptoms.

Efforts have also been made in recent years to identify those women who will need more assistance in recovering from rape, as well as to add the knowl-

edge of those factors that seem to mediate the short- and long-term consequences of sexual assault. Table 7-1 summarizes some of the research on variables affecting recovery. In general, the most salient findings to date suggest
that women with previous psychiatric problems or those who have experienced
multiple incidents of sexual assault are at greatest risk for depression or PTSD.
If the perpetrator was believed to be under the influence of drugs or alcohol, or
a physical beating occurred during the rape, victims are less likely to evidence
symptoms of depression. Also, while little research has been done on the impact of the legal system on postrape symptomatology and adjustment, it appears
that women who elect to prosecute their assailant show higher levels of self-
esteem and fewer severe symptoms.

Research Directions

As with information on incidence and prevalence, there is also a need for a
nationally representative study on the mental health impact of rape and sexual
assault. In such a study, cultural diversity and selected high-risk groups (e.g.,
children and adolescents) would need to be properly represented, and standard-
ized assessment instruments would need to be employed. The relationship between sexual assault and PTSD must be examined more systematically. In general, previous studies have found various PTSD symptoms in sexual assault
victims, but have not specifically determined the extent to which victims meet
DSM-III-R, 3rd Edition (American Psychiatric Association, 1987) criteria for
this disorder. In addition, cognitive theories of impact and readjustment must be
tested among actual victims of sexual violence, focusing on the coping strategies or appraisals that mediate, and perhaps moderate, the relationship between
the traumatic experience of assault and symptomatic outcomes (Koss, 1990).

TREATMENT INTERVENTIONS

Most of the early work on rape focused on crisis intervention models of treatment. Based on the rape trauma syndrome as described by Burgess and Holmstrom (1974a), treatment in most rape crisis centers focused on medical complications, crisis counseling (education about rape, active listening, and emotional
support), and group psychotherapy (Koss & Harvey, 1987). Harvey (1985), in
her review of 50 exemplary rape crisis programs, noted that they were more
similar in *purpose* (viz., victim advocacy and social change through broadened
knowledge and awareness) than in the content of the service programs provided. These differences, coupled with an absence of program content descriptions (as well as inadequate and nonuniform assessment methods, nonrandom
assignment of victims to different types of services, and the general omission of
comparison groups), have also made it difficult to evaluate the efficacy of crisis

Table 7-1   Variables Affecting Recovery

Event variables	Effect on recovery	Research study
	Preassault variables	
Demographics	No effect	Kilpatrick & Veronen, 1984
		Kilpatrick et al., 1985
Age & low SES	Depression at 12 mos.	Atkeson et al., 1982
Low SES	> In symptoms 4–6 yrs	Burgess & Holmstrom, 1978
Asian	> Trauma	Ruch & Chandler, 1980
Prior psychiatric diagnosis	> Depression	Frank & Anderson, 1987
Prior victimization	> Trauma scores	Ruch & Leon, 1983
Multiple incidents	< Social adjustment	Frank & Anderson, 1987
Severity of prior	> PTSD symptoms	Resick, 1986
victimization		
Misjudgment in	> Fear and depression	Frank & Stewart, 1984
cognitive appraisal		
	Assault Variables	
Perpetrator known	No change in long-term	Kilpatrick, Veronen,
	mental health	et al., 1987
	Less likely to seek	Stewart et al., 1987
	treatment	
Seriously injured	> Rate of PTSD	Kilpatrick, Saunders
Use of a weapon	No long-term change	et al., 1987
Perceived death/	PTSD	
injury		
Physical beating	Decrease in depression	Frank & Stewart, 1983
and belief assailant		
was drunk or on drugs		
	Post-assault variables	
Chose to prosecute	> Self-esteem	Cluss et al., 1983
		Sales et al., 1984

intervention. The problem is further compounded by the symptomatic improvement shown by a majority of victims within three months postrape, regardless of whether professional help was provided (Ellis, 1983). Thus, without wait-list control subjects, it has been difficult to know whether any improvement toward recovery is the result of crisis services or simply the passage of time.

Three empirical studies conducted to evaluate the efficacy of psychotherapy for rape victims all reported improvement in symptom reduction (Cryer & Beutler, 1980; Perl, Westin, & Peterson, 1985; Becker & Skinner, 1983). However, a lack of both control subjects as well as clear criteria for their inclusion or exclusion rendered their findings inconclusive. Foa, Rothbaum, and Steketee (1987) argue that the need for inclusion criteria (to constitute a diagnostically homogeneous sample) really amounts to specifying the impairment, problems, or symptoms caused by the rape trauma. The target of treatment is not the rape victim but rather the specific impairment caused by the rape trauma (e.g., agoraphobia or sexual dysfunction).

Cognitive-behavioral treatment studies have concentrated primarily on rape-related symptoms of fear, anxiety, and accompanying avoidance patterns, social and sexual dysfunctions, and depression (Foa et al., 1987). Both systematic desensitization and cognitive behavior therapy have been used alone and together, as well as in tandem with other treatment modalities. The aim of systematic desensitization is to decrease the anxiety associated with situations or objects that are not realistically dangerous through use of imaginal exposure with relaxation (Wolff, 1977). Cognitive behavioral therapy procedures include self-monitoring activities, graded-task assignments, and identification and modification of maladaptive cognitions (Beck, 1972).

Tested individually, both systematic desensitization (Turner, 1979; Frank & Stewart, 1983) and cognitive behavioral treatment (Frank & Steward, 1984) have shown significant outcomes based on ratings of improved social adjustment and decreased fear, anxiety, and depression. When these treatments were compared using two different rape populations, viz., those who sought treatment immediately and those who delayed seeking treatment until several months postassault (Frank et al., unpublished manuscript), analyses showed no effect differences between types of therapy or for time elapsed since the assault. It is important to note that the delayed-treatment group that served as a quasi-control was initially more symptomatic than immediate-treatment seekers, but responded equally well to the therapeutic components of the treatment. In their review of treatment strategies, Holmes and St. Lawrence (1983) suggest that the active ingredients for effective treatment are to provide rape victims with specific coping mechanisms and alternative responses to anxiety.

Using a composite model, Kilpatrick, Veronen, and Resick (1982) designed a treatment program called Stress Inoculation Training (SIT) for rape victims who had marked symptoms three months postassault. Their 20-hour program included training in coping skills, relaxation and breathing, communication skills through role-playing, and thought-stopping, as well as a form of cognitive therapy for correction of irrational thoughts. An empirical evaluation of the SIT model (Veronen & Kilpatrick, 1982) showed it to be effective in improving rape related fear, anxiety, phobic anxiety, tension, and depression. In a related case study, Kilpatrick and Amick (1985) reported successful treatment using a shortened 8-hour version of SIT. That report provides an excellent example of a thorough assessment procedure with measurements of physiological, cognitive, and behavioral variables.

In a more ambitious treatment evaluation, Resick et al. (in press) compared six 2-hour sessions of three types of therapy: stress inoculation, assertion training, and supportive psychotherapy with a psychoeducation component. A naturally occurring wait-list group was used as the control. Analyses of the data indicated that all three treatments were highly effective in reducing symptoms and no improvements were found in the wait-list control group. At the 6-month follow-up, rape-related fear measures remained improved, but symptoms of depression, low self-esteem, and social fears returned. Substituting exposure treatment (Foa & Kozak, 1985) for assertion training, Foa et al. (1987) are currently conducting a similar study, but with 3-month post-assault victims who meet diagnostic criteria for PTSD. Preliminary analysis suggests that improvement on core PTSD symptoms is evident only after completion of the full program, whereas other symptoms seem to diminish at midpoint in treatment.

Research Directions

Treatment studies will continue to focus on isolating the active ingredients in effectively treating the symptoms of the rape trauma syndrome. It is likely that more attention will be given to identifying and treating the faulty cognitive processing component that is evident in PTSD. In these and other studies, research designs will be expected to correct earlier methodological shortcomings by developing clear inclusion and exclusion criteria for subjects (wait-list control groups and diagnostically homogeneous samples); including random assignment to treatment conditions; and providing detailed descriptions of treatment for replication (requiring treatment manuals in most cases).

PREVENTION RESEARCH

Sexual assault has the distinction of being both a crime involving the legal system and an act that has mental health consequences for the victim. The prevention models used have focused either on crime control (legal sanctions as a deterrent) or on a public health approach.

The public health approach for primary prevention is designed to either alter environmental conditions that perpetuate the stressor agent (e.g., draining the swamp) or strengthen the vulnerable host population (e.g., inoculations). Burt (1983), in her effort to develop a typology of rape crisis centers, noted that centers with a feminist philosophy were more likely to stress primary prevention than rape avoidance; empowerment, choice, and growth for victims than symptom reduction; and to support various community consciousness raising and mobilization activities (e.g., rape awareness week).

Efforts to educate the public about the prevalence and mental health consequences of sexual assault, as well as about related rape myths, pornography, and sexual exploitation in advertising, are all part of trying to "drain the swamp." By changing the environment that either actively or passively gives support to perpetrators, it is hoped that reporting of assault and the indictments of rapists will increase, and that—as the ultimate goal—violence against women and children will be eradicated. If public awareness of the widespread prevalence of sexual assault is used as the measure, then there is reason to believe that some of these prevention efforts have been moderately successful. If, however, attitude change, sexual exploitation, and violence against women in the media are the standard, then the "swamp remains full."

The second prevention strategy has focused on strengthening the vulnerable hose through such efforts as teaching rape self-defense, and educating women about rape with the hope of decreasing the guilt and low self-esteem induced by self-blame. In an investigation by Furby and Fischhoff (1987), 24 studies were examined that had sought to determine the consequences of different strategies used by women. These researchers assessed each strategy in relation to outcome—whether a rape and/or physical injury occurred. In particular, they wanted to know the effectiveness of one kind of self-defense strategy versus another so that women would have information to make educated defense choices. Furby and Fischhoff concluded:

> With respect to rape per se, a moderately consistent overall pattern emerged: Nonforceful strategies, such as pleading and moral appeals, were associated with a slightly lower likelihood of avoiding rape. By contrast, more forceful strategies, such as screaming and physical resistance, were associated with a somewhat higher chance of rape avoidance. Similar patterns were observed whether or not a gun was present and whether or not the assailant was an acquaintance. With respect to physical injury other than rape, the evidence suggests that physical injury is positively associated with more forceful strategies. However, the several studies that have examined temporal order of events in assaults suggest that the direction of causation may be from injury to strategy use rather than vice versa, that is, women who are being injured appear to react with more forceful strategies. (p. 2, Appendix B)

These researchers caution, however, that the outcome really depends on the interaction between three variables: the situation in which the attempted rape occurs, the characteristics of the rapist, and personological variables of the intended victim. More detailed descriptions of strategies and decision-making in response to options available are presented in articles by Furby, Fischhoff, and Morgan (1989, 1990). This information, as well as the monograph, *Rape and Older Women: A Guide to Prevention and Protection* (Davis & Brody, 1981), are of particular import to nurses working with community populations.

RESEARCH ON SEX OFFENDERS

Although more is known about victims of rape than about rapists, research undertaken over the past decade has included the development of typologies of sexually aggressive men (Knight, 1988), the development and refinement of

psychophysiological measures of sexual arousal (Laws, 1988), and the testing
and refinement of various treatment approaches (Marques, 1989). A review of
the body of literature available on profiles of rapists, as well as potentially
significant studies on interactive elements that might be predictive of sexual
aggression (Malamuth, 1989), is beyond the scope of this chapter. However,
since preventing rape really means eliminating the agent (rapist), brief mention
will be made of several of the more salient findings.

From a prevention standpoint, some of the more interesting data suggests
that sexual aggression starts early and becomes progressively more serious.
Using a sample of volunteers from the community who were guaranteed treatment and nonreporting, Abel, Mittelman, and Becker (1984) found that:

- Of 240 youths under age 18, each reported an average of 6.75 sexual
assault victims as a youth compared to 380 victims, on average, as an adult, or
an increase of more than 55 times as many victims.
- Of rapists, more than 50% were involved in child molestation, more
than 11% were sadists, 29% were exhibitionists, and 20% were voyeurs. Since
sex offenders are often involved in a number of different types of paraphilias
(sexual deviations), interviews and assessments should obviously include questions about activities other than presenting behaviors.
- Forty-two percent of the paraphiliacs had deviant arousal by age 15 or
younger, and 57% by the age of 19. Same-sex pedophilia had the earliest onset.

Abel et al. (1984, p. 6) conclude:

Since these are crimes that begin at a very early stage, we have to develop a system
that allows us to access these adolescents earlier, because most of these people
develop arousal patterns far anterior to their actually committing the crime. . . . If
we are able to stop child molestation and rape, we should treat such young people
before the deviant behavior becomes reinforced and habitual.

RESEARCH DIRECTIONS

A host of questions about sex offenders, such as parenting, emotional and
sexual development, thought patterns, social relationships, etc., is discussed in
a compendium of articles entitled *Adolescent Sex Offenders: Issues in Research
and Treatment* (Otey & Ryan, 1985), available from NIMH. As this monograph
makes clear, better understanding of the factors involved in creating sexual
aggression will continue to be the focus of future research. In addition, researchers will continue to assess the contributions of biological factors and of
pharmacological agents that alter the behavior, and to study the role of cogni-
tion in the initiation and perpetuation of paraphilia. It is also likely that more
attention will be given to determining the most effective methods for dissemi-

nating to health professionals, educators, and the public significant research findings in the area of prevention and treatment for victims and sex offenders. In *Women's Mental Health Research Agenda: Violence Against Women*, Koss (1990) captures many of the same concerns that are presented in this chapter. The goals that Koss (1990), Russo (1990), and McBride (1990) identify for this agenda will likely guide research on sexual assault for the foreseeable future.

RESOURCES

Research Funding

National Institute of Mental Health (NIMH)
Violence and Traumatic Stress Branch
Division of Applied and Services Research
5600 Fishers Lane, Room 18–105, Rockville, MD 20857
(301) 443-3728

Throughout this chapter, the research supported by NIMH has been highlighted. As mentioned earlier, the Violence and Traumatic Stress Research Branch is the major source of funding within NIMH for research on sexual assault. Although studies that focused on incidence and prevalence, identification of risk factors, mental health consequences, treatment strategies, and prevention have been the thrust of this chapter, grants dealing with child abuse (sexual and physical), domestic violence (battering), and sexual aggression are also part of the Branch's grant portfolio.

Figure 7-1 depicts funding trends for research on sexual assault for the past decade. The high rate of funding for rape research during the period 1984–1987 probably is related to grants transferred to the Branch by the National Center for the Prevention and Control of Rape when they were merged in 1985. Child sexual abuse research peaked in 1986 as did research on violence in the family (see Figure 7-2). Research grants on sexual offenders have remained quite stable over the past decade.

In Figure 7-2, it is interesting to note that while the number of rape-related research grants is lower in recent years, there is a corresponding increase in funding of research related to spouse abuse, which partly reflects the heightened attention given to this subject by the media during this period. The research focus is on understanding the interface between situational and interpersonal dynamics (Malamuth, 1989). However, it is important to note that all aspects of sexual assault (scope, risk factors, treatment, and prevention) as noted under Research Directions in each section, still have important questions

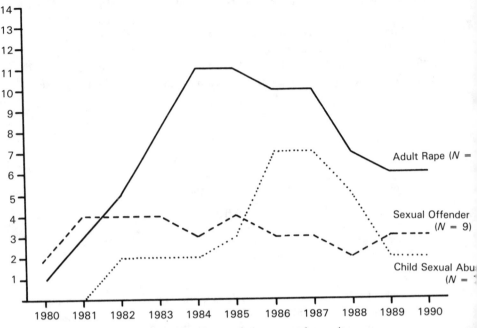

Figure 7-1   NIMH branch funding for research on sexual assault.

that need addressing. More information on research opportunities and abstracts of currently funded grants are available by contacting the Branch office.

Research training   Despite the generally recognized need for sound research data on the incidence, prevalence, mental health consequence, and effective treatment of sexual assault, a shortage exists of researchers who have the research and clinical expertise necessary to conduct clinically relevant studies in this area. Skilled researchers often lack exposure to samples of sexual assault victims while those with exposure often lack adequate research training and expertise. Research on sexual assault, for example, that is not based on a thorough understanding of the mental health problems of sexual assault victims runs the risk of being theoretically interesting but clinically sterile.

In an effort to address this need, Dean Kilpatrick and his colleagues at the Medical University of South Carolina (MUSC) were awarded a research training grant from NIMH several years ago, which was the first program in the area of sexual assault. This 5-year program is being conducted at the Crime Victims Research and Treatment Center, a division of the Department of Psychiatry and Behavioral Sciences at MUSC. The program is actively involved in both mental health services for sexual assault victims and their families as well as a broad spectrum of sexual assault research. Two predoctoral and three postdoctoral trainees each year are exposed to a variety of research strategies to facilitate clinically relevant investigations of sexual assault topics.

National Institute of Justice (NIJ)
633 Indiana Avenue, N.W., Washington, DC 20531
(202) 724-2942

NIJ, a multifaceted program, announces research priorities annually and awards grants primarily on the basis of peer reviews. While the amount of support and duration of grants are usually limited, the priority areas of NIJ have become more general in recent years and permit opportunities for investigator-initiated projects. A primary interest is in research with immediate applicability to the criminal justice system, e.g., domestic violence and police responses, sexual victimization and the effects of criminal justice processing, and classification of sex offenders for handling by the justice system.

Centers for Disease Control (CDC)
Division of Injury Epidemiology and Control

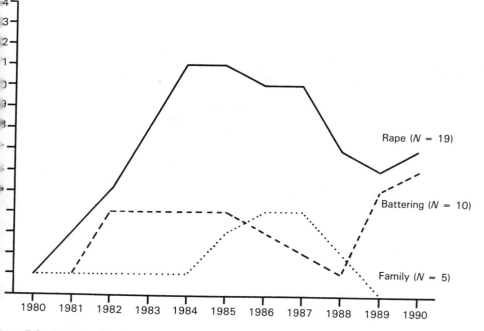

3ure 7-2 NIMH funding for research on adult rape, spouse abuse, and family violence.

1600 Clifton Road, N.E., Atlanta, GA 30333
(404) 639-3291

The Intentional Injuries Section of the Division of Injury Epidemiology and Control primarily conducts intramural (in-house) epidemiological research on interpersonal violence, using aggregate state and county data. Some extramural grants are also available that focus on understanding interpersonal violence in terms of its social contexts, physical injury outcomes, and opportunities for primary prevention.

National Center on Child Abuse and Neglect (NCCAN)
330 C Street, N.W., Washington, DC 20201
(202) 245-0586

This is the leading federal agency responsible for child abuse and neglect, with a multifaceted program that includes a national clearinghouse, technical assistance and grants to states, training and related assistance for family violence, and demonstration and research grants.

National Center for Nursing Research (NCNR)
Division of Health Promotion and Disease Prevention
Research Building 31, 5B-03
9000 Rockville Pike, Bethesda, MD 20892
(301) 496-8230

Limited funding is available for research on sexual assault (with the NCNR). The topic must show clear relevance for nursing. More recently funded grants have examined a combination of factors, such as battering during pregnancy and low birth weight.

National Institute on Drug Abuse (NIDA)
5600 Fishers Lane, Room 10-42, Rockville, MD 20857
(301) 443-6480

For grants submitted to NIDA, one of the primary variables must be related to drug (ab)use. An example of a study fitting NIDA requirements would be one related to the incidence of sexual violence toward homeless drug-abusing women.

National Victims Resource Directory
Box 6000, Rockville, MD 20850
1-800-627-6872

Demonstration grants   For the most current list of agencies that support program research on new models of treatment use the National Victims Resource Directory. This directory summarizes the services provided by a range of agencies and indicates their involvement in information and referral, victim assistance, legal services, advocacy, counseling, crisis intervention, public education, tracking victim-related legislation, conducting research, providing legislative advocacy and testimony, training programs and technical assistance, and conference sponsorship.

Clinical resources Throughout this chapter, primary consideration has been given to providing nurses with ideas through research findings and references that can be translated into practice. Listed are additional helpful and informative publications that are available from NIMH upon request:

NRC–12 *Setting Up a Rape Treatment Center*
ADM 85–1382 *The Sexual Victimization of Adolescents*
ADM 85–1396 *Adolescent Sex Offenders: Issues in Research and Treatment*
ADM 85–1409 *The Evaluation and Management of Rape and Sexual Abuse: A Physician's Guide*
ADM 87–1504 *Treating Family Violence in a Pediatric Hospital: A Program of Training, Research, and Services*

To obtain a courtesy copy of these publications write to:

Public Inquiries Branch
Office of Scientific Information
National Institute of Mental Health
Room 15C-05, 5600 Fishers Lane
Rockville, MD 20857

REFERENCES

Abel, G., Mittelman, M., & Becker, J. (1984). *Sexual offenders: Results of assessment and recommendations for treatment.* (Unpublished manuscript available from New York State Psychiatric Institute, Sexual Behavior Clinic.)
Ageton, S. S. (1983). *Sexual assault among adolescents.* Lexington, MA: Lexington Books, D. C. Heath.
American Psychiatric Association. (1987). *Diagnostic and statistical manual of mental disorders—Revised.* 3rd Edition. Washington, DC: Author.
Atkeson, B. M., Calhoun, K. S., Resick, P. A., & Ellis, E. M. (1982). Victims of rape: Repeated assessment of depressive symptoms. *Journal of Consulting and Clinical Psychology, 50,* 96–102.
Beck, A. T. (1972). *Depression: Causes and treatment.* Philadelphia: University of Pennsylvania Press.
Becker, J. V., & Skinner, L. J. (1983). Assessment and treatment of rape-related sexual dysfunctions. *The Clinical Psychologist, 36,* 102–105.
Burge, S. K. (1988). Post-traumatic stress disorder in victims of rape. *Journal of Traumatic Stress, 1,* 193–210.
Burgess, A. W., & Holmstrom, L. L. (1974a). The rape trauma syndrome. *American Journal of Psychiatry, 131,* 981–986.

Burgess, A. W., & Holmstrom, L. L. (1974b). *Rape: Victims of crisis.* Bowie, MD: R. J. Brady Company.

Burgess, A. W., & Holmstrom, L. L. (1978). Recovery from rape and prior life stress. *Research in Nursing and Health, 1,* 165–174.

Burt, M. R. (1983). *Assessing the impact of rape victim support programs.* (Final report, NIMH Grant No. R18 MH34835). Rockville, MD.

Centers for Disease Control, DHHS (1985, December 13). *Morbidity and Mortality Weekly Report, 34*(49), 738–741.

Cluss, P. A., Boughton, J., Frank, L. E., Stewart, B. D., & West, D. (1983). The rape victims: Psychological correlates of participation in the legal process. *Criminal Justice and Behavior, 10,* 342–357.

Cryer, L., & Beutler, L. (1980). Group therapy: An alternative treatment approach for rape victims. *Journal of Sex and Marital Therapy, 6,* 40–46.

Davis, L. J., & Brody, E. M. (1981). *Rape and older women: A guide to prevention and protection.* (DHHS Publication No. (ADM)81–734). Rockville, MD.

Department of Health and Human Services. (1987). *Surgeon General's workshop on violence and public health report.* Washington, DC: U.S. Government Printing Office.

Ellis, E. M. (1983). A review of empirical rape research: Victim reaction and response to treatment. *Clinical Psychology Review, 3,* 473–490.

Foa, E. B., & Kozak, M. J. (1985). Emotional processing of fear: Exposure to corrective information. *Psychological Bulletin, 99,* 20–35.

Foa, E. B., Rothbaum, B. O., Steketee, G. S. (1987). *Treatment of rape victims.* Paper presented at the NIMH State of the Art in Sexual Assault Research, Charleston, SC.

Frank, E., & Anderson, B. P. (1987). Psychiatric disorders in rape victims: Past history and current symptomatology. *Comprehensive Psychiatry, 28,* 77–82.

Frank, E., Anderson, B., Stewart, B. D., Dancer, C., Hughes, C., & West, D. (1986). *Efficacy of cognitive behavior therapy and systematic desensitization in the treatment of rape trauma.* Unpublished manuscript.

Frank, E., & Stewart, B. D. (1983). Treatment of depressed rape victims: An approach to stress-induced symptomatology. In P. J. Clayton & J. E. Barrett (Eds.), *Treatment of depression: Old controversies and new approaches.* New York: Raven Press.

Frank, E., & Stewart, B. D. (1984). Depressive symptoms in rape victims. *Journal of Affective Disorders, 1,* 269–277.

Furby, L., & Fischhoff, B. (1987). *Rape self-defense strategies: A review of their effectiveness.* (Final report, NIMH Grant No. MH 40481). Rockville, MD.

Furby, L., Fischhoff, B., & Morgan, M. (1989). Judged effectiveness of common rape prevention and self-defense strategies. *Journal of Interpersonal Violence, 4,* 44–64.

Furby, L., Fischhoff, B., & Morgan, M. (1990). Preventing rape: How people perceive the options. I: Assault prevention. *Victimology, 15,* 93–97.

George, L. K., & Winfield-Laird, I. (1986). *Sexual assault: Prevalence and mental health consequence.* (Final report, Duke University Epidemiological Catchment Area Program.) Rockville, MD: National Institute of Mental Health.

Harvey, M. R. (1985). *Exemplary rape crisis programs: A cross-site analysis and case studies.* Rockville, MD: DHHS Publication No. (ADM) 85–1423.

Holmes, M. R., & St. Lawrence, J. S. (1983). Treatment of rape-induced trauma: Proposed behavioral conceptualization and review of the literature. *Clinical Psychology Review, 3,* 417–433.

Kilpatrick, D. G., & Amick, A. E. (1985). Rape trauma. In M. Hersen & C. G. Last (Eds.), *Behavior therapy casebook.* New York: Springer.

Kilpatrick, D. G., Saunders, B. E., Veronen, L. J., Best, C. L., & Von, J. M. (1987). Criminal victimization: Lifetime prevalence, reporting to police, and psychological impact. *Crime and Delinquency, 33,* 479–489.

Kilpatrick, D. G., & Veronen, L. J. (1983, December). *The aftermath of rape: A three-year follow-up.* Paper presented at the World Congress of Behavior Therapy, Association for the Advancement of Behavior Therapy, Washington, DC.

Kilpatrick, D. G., & Veronen, L. J. (1984). *Treatment of fear and anxiety in victims of rape.* (Final report of NIMH Grant No. MH29602). Rockville, MD.

Kilpatrick, D. G., Veronen, L. J., & Best, C. L. (1985). Factors predicting psychological distress among rape victims. In C. R. Figley (Ed.), *Trauma and its wake.* New York: Brunner, Mazel.

Kilpatrick, D. G., Veronen, L. J., & Resick, P. A. (1982). Psychological sequelae to rape: Assessment and treatment strategies. In D. M. Dolays and R. L. Meredith (Eds.), *Behavioral medicine: Assessment and treatment strategies.* New York: Plenum Press.

Kilpatrick, D. G., Veronen, L. J., Saunders, B. E., Best, C. L., Amick-McMullen, A., & Paduhovich, J. (1987). *The psychological impact of crime: A study of randomly surveyed crime victims.* (Final report for the National Institute of Justice, Grant No. 84–1J–CX–0039). Washington, DC.

Knight, R. A. (1988). *Classification of rapists: Implementation and validation.* (NIMH Grant No. MH32309.) Washington, DC.

Koss, M. P. (1987). *Rape incidence and prevalence: A review and assessment of the data.* Paper presented at the NIMH-sponsored workshop, State of the Art in Sexual Assault Research, Charleston, SC.

Koss, M. P. (1990). The women's mental health research agenda: Violence against women. *American Psychologist, 45,* 374–380.

Koss, M. P., Gidycz, C. A., & Wisniewski, N. (1987). The scope of rape: Incidence and prevalence of sexual aggression and victimization in a national sample of higher education students. *Journal of Consulting and Clinical Psychology, 55,* 162–170.

Koss, M. P., & Harvey, M. R. (1970). *The rape victim: Clinical and community approaches to treatment.* Lexington, MA: The Stephen Greene Press.

Laws, D. R. (1988). *Prevention of relapse in sex offenders.* (NIMH Grant No. MH42035).

Malamuth, N. M. (1989). *Predicting men's antisocial behavior against women.* (NIMH Grant No. MH45058).

Marques, J. (1989). *Sex offender treatment.* (NIMH Grant No. R19-46391). Rockville, MD.

McBride, A. B. (1990). Mental health effects of women's multiple roles. *American Psychologist, 45,* 381–384.

Otey, E., & Ryan, G. (1985). *Adolescent sex offenders: Issues in research and treatment.* NIMH publication: (ADM) 85–1396.

Perl, M., Westin, A. B., & Peterson, L. C. (1985). The female rape survivor: Time-limited group therapy with female-male co-therapists. *Journal of Psychosomatic Obstetrics and Gynecology, 4,* 197–205.

Peterson, D. L., Olasov, B., & Foa, E. B. (1987, July). *Response patterns in sexual assault survivors.* Paper presented at the Third World Congress on Victimology, San Francisco, CA.

Resick, P. A. (1986). *Reaction of female and male victims of rape or robbery.* (Final report of NIMH Grant No. MH 37296). Rockville, MD.

Resick, P. A. (1987a). *Reactions of female and male victims of rape or robbery.* (Final report, NIJ Grant No. 85–IJ–CX–0042). Rockville, MD.

Resick, P. A. (1987b, September). *The impact of rape on psychological functioning.* Paper presented at The State of the Art Workshop on Sexual Assault, Charleston, SC.

Resick, P. A., Jordan, C. G., Girelli, S. A., Hutler, C. K., & Marhoefer-Dvorak, S. (1988). A comparative outcome study of behavioral group therapy for sexual assault victims. *Behavior Therapy.*

Ruch, L. O. (1990). Annual progress report. (NIMH Grant No. MH 40329). Rockville, MD.

Ruch, L. O., Chandler, S. M., & Harter, R. A. (1980). Life change and rape impact. *Journal of Health and Social Behavior, 21,* 248–260.

Ruch, L. O., & Leon, J. J. (1983). Sexual assault trauma and trauma change. *Women and Health, 8,* 5–21.

Russell, D. E. H. (1982). The prevalence and incidence of forcible rape and attempted rape of females. *Victimology, 7,* 81–93.

Russo, N. F. (1985). *A women's mental health agenda.* Paper presented at the American Psychological Association, Washington, DC.

Russo, N. F. (1990). Overview: Forging research priorities for women's mental health. *American Psychologist, 45,* 368–373.

Sales, E., Baum, M., & Shore, B. (1984). Victim readjustment following assault. *Journal of Social Issues, 40,* 117–136.

Siegel, J. M., Burnam, M. A., Stein, J. A., Golding, J. M., & Sorenson, S. B. (1986). *Sexual assault and psychiatric disorder: A preliminary investigation.* Final report to the National Institute of Mental Health. Rockville, MD.

Stekette, G., & Foa, E. B. (1987). Rape victims: Post-traumatic stress responses and their treatment: A review of the literature. *Journal of Anxiety Disorders, 1,* 69–86.

Stewart, B. D., Hughes, C., Frank, E., Anderson, B., Kendall, K., & West, D. (1987). Profiles of immediate and delayed treatment seekers. *The Journal of Nervous and Mental Disease, 175,* 90–94.

Turner, S. M. (1979). Systematic desensitization of fears and anxiety in rape victims. Paper presented at the Association for the Advancement of Behavior Therapy. San Francisco, CA.

Veronen, L. J., & Kilpatrick, D. G. (1982, November). *Stress inoculation training for victims of rape: Efficacy and differential findings.* Paper presented at the symposium on Sexual Violence and Harassment at the 16th Annual Convention of the Association for Advancement of Behavior Therapy, Los Angeles.

Veronen, L. J., Kilpatrick, D. G., & Resick, P. A. (1979). Treatment of fear and anxiety in rape victims: Implications for the criminal justice system. In W. H. Parsonage (Ed.), *Perspectives on victimology,* (pp. 148-158). Beverly Hills, CA: Sage.

Wolff, R. (1977). Systematic desensitization and negative practice to alter the after effects of a rape attempt. *Journal of Behavior Therapy and Experimental Psychiatry, 8,* 423-425.

Wyatt, G. E. (1985). The sexual abuse of Afro-American and White American women in childhood. *Child Abuse & Neglect, 9,* 507-519.

Part Two

Implications
for Nursing Education

Chapter 8

Incorporating Violence Against Women Content Into the Undergraduate Curriculum

Rita B. Kerr

Violence against women received increasing attention during the 1980s as society became more intensely aware of women's issues in general. At the same time, nurses began to observe that increasing numbers of women were entering the health care system as a result of being abused. As statistics continued to mount and the scope of the problem became more evident, it became increasingly clear to the nursing faculty at Capital University that nurses providing primary patient care needed to learn to recognize the signs and symptoms of abuse not only to provide nursing care to women who were abused but also to make referrals to appropriate agencies for ongoing care. Hence, the faculty began to look for clinical sites where students could learn to assess and treat women of all ages who had experienced abuse.

The purposes of this chapter are to describe how content about violence against women was incorporated into the undergraduate nursing curriculum at

This chapter is dedicated to women of all ages in Ohio who have been abused and to the nursing students who are learning to provide care for them. May all of you be resilient as you move toward satisfying, productive lives.

Capital University. Discussion will include placement in the curriculum, course objectives and assignments, class content, clinical placements, faculty and agency responsibilities, and possible alternative curriculum plans. It is important to note before discussion begins, however, that content about violence against women can be addressed in numerous ways in an undergraduate nursing curriculum. How content is included in the curriculum about to be described is but one of many alternatives.

BACKGROUND

Capital University is a 150-year-old private Lutheran liberal arts institution. The university serves more than 3,000 traditional and adult-degree students each year in its six undergraduate and five graduate programs. The baccalaureate program in nursing, now 40 years old, currently serves approximately 350 traditional and adult-degree students. Generally, nursing students are White, middle class, and come from all areas of Ohio and surrounding states. Traditional students range in age from 18–24. Adult degree students, all of whom are registered nurses, range in age from 25–65.

Educational innovation within Capital University's School of Nursing has been an ongoing process throughout its existence. One of the innovations, initiated in 1982 by Professors Deborah Hoy and Janice Ryan, was the inclusion of class content and clinical experience related to violence against women in the Psychosocial Nursing course. The initial objective was to assist nursing students to recognize violence against women as a social problem reaching crisis proportions. In order to accomplish this goal, they expanded students' clinical experience in psychosocial nursing beyond the traditional inpatient psychiatric setting. Initially, they chose two clinical placements including CHOICES for Victims of Domestic Violence, a safe house for women and their children, and the Central Ohio Adolescent Center, a state operated inpatient facility for emotionally disturbed teens, the majority of whom had been physically, emotionally, and/or sexually abused either in their own families or in foster care settings. The Central Ohio Adolescent Center has since been closed.

In 1984, two years later, the governor of Ohio convened a 30-member statewide task force of Ohio residents whose mandate was to reduce and eradicate family violence. The task force was considered to possess special skills, education, and experience regarding family violence (Wells, 1984). Members included physicians, attorneys, judges, battered women's shelter directors, police officers, prosecutors, social service providers, child abuse specialists, advocates for the elderly, rape crisis counselors, mental health personnel, and clergy (Wells, 1984). It is interesting to note that no professional nurses were identified as participants.

The task force sought to change laws, norms, and institutional policies that failed to protect Ohio residents, improve existing services and establish needed services for victims of violence, and institute a comprehensive network of state-wide prevention programs focused on all forms of family violence (Wells, 1984). One of the initial recommendations of this committee was to begin a statewide public information campaign that would create an awareness of family violence and the right of residents not to be victims (Wells, 1984). The task force also recommended that the Adult Protective Services Law be amended to require professional service providers, including nurses, to report adult abuse, neglect, and/or exploitation (Wells, 1984). In general, the 17 recommendations stated in the committee's 1984 report (Wells, 1984), and the 32 recommendations stated in the committee's 1985 report (Wells, 1985) launched the state's commitment to eradicating family violence. Although the task force's emphasis was on family violence, violence against women of all ages remained a prominent theme.

COURSE OBJECTIVES

With the publication of the task force's two initial reports and the recommendation that nurses were expected to report abuse, the faculty has maintained its commitment to include content about violence against women in the undergraduate nursing curriculum. The general aim has been to increase students' awareness of the multiple signs of violence within families, and when violence was recognized, to assist adolescent and adult women to obtain protection and ongoing assistance. The specific curriculum objectives were developed so that students would:

1 Become aware that violence exists within families. For some undergraduate nursing students, the fact that all families do not function in a loving, caring style is a difficult dose of reality shock. Presenting reality and overcoming denial are important tasks for students to achieve.

2 Become aware that females of all ages, ethnic, racial, and socioeconomic backgrounds are subject to abuse. Some students believe that violence within families exists only outside of their White Anglo-American middle-class backgrounds. Students' denial is a powerful force to be confronted by faculty.

3 Differentiate between family and nonfamily inflicted abuse. Students discuss rape and date rape when they are oriented to campus life as freshmen. Faculty reinforce caution and safety. Faculty differentiate abuse by a stranger from abuse by a family member because they believe the dynamics of family versus nonfamily inflicted violence are different. Also faculty discuss precise definitions of terms. For example, media tend to use the term *incest* indiscriminately, often using the term to describe a nonfamily member, such as a mother's boyfriend, who hurts a child in the child's own home.

4 Recognize the physical and emotional signs of violence in adolescent and adult women. Students are taught the physical symptoms and emotional

behaviors associated with abuse and the interviewing skills necessary to assess for suspected abuse.

5 Understand the dynamics of abuse. Students are taught the cyclic nature of abuse within families and the difficulties inherent in modifying family behavior patterns or the behavior patterns of even one family member.

6 Identify personality characteristics of abusive men. The focus is on the man's abusive behaviors as learned, the possibility that he was abused as a child, and how his feelings of powerlessness, low self-esteem, anger, rage, and aggressiveness are acted out in family relationships.

7 Identify personality characteristics of abused adolescents and adults. The focus is on abused females' willingness to tolerate abuse as behavior learned in their families of origin as well as females' patterns of helplessness, hopelessness, powerlessness, and perceptions of "normality" about male-female relationships.

8 Define primary, secondary, and tertiary prevention of violence against women. Students recognize primary prevention as occurring before violence happens; secondary prevention as intervening with women at risk or in the early stages of abuse; and tertiary prevention as the rehabilitation of abused women.

9 Relate knowledge of violence to the nursing process.

Assessment—students learn the interviewing skills necessary to assess the presence of abuse in the lives of adolescents and adults.

Planning—students learn about the community resources available to assist abused family members and the abuser to obtain further protection and ongoing assistance. Short-term crisis intervention is differentiated from desired long-term outcomes.

Primary prevention—students observe family interactions and teach classes to adolescents and adults about physical and sexual safety.

Secondary prevention—students participate in crisis intervention, refer abused women and the abuser to existing community agencies, and assist adolescents and adults to find alternative living arrangements. Also, students participate in and co-lead groups for adolescents and women who have been abused. Topics have included self-esteem, personal appearance, protection and safety, parenting, and child care.

Evaluation—students evaluate the results of education, crisis intervention, and referral based on client and agency goals.

10 Identify how society views violence against women, what social programs are available for assistance, what needs remain, and what societal barriers continue to exist against resolving abuse. Students become aware of the disruption and dissolution of families when children, adolescents, and adults are abused. They also become aware that there is minimal help for abused women beyond crisis intervention. Tertiary prevention in terms of physical, emotional, and social rehabilitation; assistance with further education, employment, and housing; and help with child care are virtually nonexistent in many areas of our country. Societal barriers include difficulties in recognizing cases of abuse; health care providers' use of denial, unwillingness to get involved, and reluctance to separate family members; and the cycle that leads to the abused becoming abusers.

PLACEMENT OF THE COURSE IN THE CURRICULUM

Nursing students spend their freshman year taking courses in the physical and social sciences and the humanities. Violence against women is addressed primarily in two nursing courses, a Human Growth and Development course taught during the sophomore year and a Psychosocial Nursing course taught during either the second semester of the junior year or the first semester of the senior year.

The goal within the human development course is to assist students to learn how to recognize the signs of violence within families and to become sensitive to the needs of women who are abused. Teaching methods include both lecture content and discussion. Lecture content about abuse is framed in terms of family functioning and dynamics. Small group discussions, on the one hand, allow students the opportunity to explore the myths that emphasize the happy, functional American family as well as the dynamics of why it might be threatening for some members of the helping professions to either recognize abuse or intervene in abusive situations.

Recently, students who have been abused either during childhood or by a spouse have elected to share their experiences during small group discussions, sometimes as a way of asking for personal help, at other times as a way of sharing information about the help they have received. The goal of the course has never been to expose the personal problems of students, but students have often felt free because of the open nature of the discussions to ask for help, share their past histories, or pursue the help of an individual faculty member privately. The effect of students' disclosures has been to make both faculty and students aware of the reality and intensity of the problems of abuse within their own midst as well as to dispel the myths that abuse occurs only in ethnic, racial, and economic groups other than their own. Faculty sometimes find it necessary to do crisis intervention and further referral for some students who have been abused as well as deal with other students' need to be rescuers. Also, students become aware that women who have been abused often try to become rescuers by joining the helping professions, including nursing.

Clinical goals for intervening in abusive situations are not taught at the sophomore level. However, if a student or faculty member recognizes signs of abuse in the adult medical areas where sophomore students have their clinical experiences, a student would be asked to accompany an instructor, who does the initial assessment and beginning interventions. The student observes how questions about abuse are asked and how women respond to open and direct questioning. She is then asked to share this clinical experience with her classmates in a postclinical discussion group.

The goal of the second course, a clinical course in Psychosocial Nursing, is to extend students' knowledge and clinical skills about family violence to a greater depth. Two hours of lecture/discussion content include the cyclic nature of abuse as learned behavior within the family context; personality characteristics of the abuser and the abused; physical and psychosocial symptoms of abuse; primary, secondary, and tertiary prevention of abuse; the helplessness and powerlessness felt by both the abused and the abuser; legal and ethical issues involved in recognizing and reporting abuse; related nursing process; and a film titled, *Battered Wives, Shattered Lives,* narrated by Ed Asner (see Appendix).

CLINICAL SITES

Classroom content taught in Psychosocial Nursing is enhanced through a wide variety of clinical experiences. All students spend 8 hours a week in an acute adult inpatient psychiatric setting where it would be usual to encounter several patients who had experienced physical, sexual, and/or emotional abuse either as young girls or adolescents in their families of origin or as adults in their nuclear families. In this acute psychiatric setting students observe both the immediate and long lasting repercussions of abuse including diagnosed psychopathology. With both instructor and staff help, students learn to begin to use interviewing skills to assess for the presence of abuse, formulate nursing diagnoses, and develop a plan of care. In summary, students have their first formal opportunity to assess for abuse and provide nursing care to women who have been abused.

Also, as part of the clinical experience, students choose an additional 4 hours a week in one of three adjunctive outpatient settings where violence against adolescents and women is confronted. One agency they may select is called CHOICES, a safe house for abused women and their children. Students interact with the residents and their children on a one-to-one basis, observe and eventually lead a group session, and work with the residents on finding employment, housing, and financial resources. Students selecting this agency get a vivid picture of the intergenerational effects of abuse on adults and children as they observe some of the mothers displace the abuse they have received onto their children. Students are also confronted with the limits within which the social system works. They see many of the women choose to go back to their abuser because they cannot overcome the multiple barriers to starting a new life. In a society that offers them little emotional or financial support, women may not believe they deserve better. Understanding the concept of self-esteem takes on new meaning in this setting.

A second agency students may choose for clinical experience is Huckleberry House, a local safe house and crisis intervention center for teens who have run away from home. Students selecting this agency interact with the young residents, ages 11–17, on a one-to-one basis, attend and eventually lead a group session, listen to crisis phone calls, and observe individual and family sessions. Students hear stories of physical, emotional, and sexual abuse and observe how the young people often displace their aggressions onto each other. Students become aware of how other social services, such as the local children's protective agency, become involved in the adolescents' lives, how the adolescents' education suffers, and how the staff attempts to reunite families. Students also learn the nature of the relationship between chemical abuse and physical/sexual abuse as they begin to recognize behaviors associated with the misuse of illegal chemicals, both by the adolescents and their families.

A third adjunctive area where students confront the effects of violence is Talbot Hall, a family-centered inpatient and outpatient chemical abuse treatment program. This program offers adolescents and their families long-term therapy groups lasting for several weeks rather than the crisis intervention format of CHOICES and Huckleberry House. As a result, students experience how the staff and families attempt to resolve issues related to both chemical abuse and physical violence during the course of ongoing treatment. Students attend group sessions for parents and teens and eventually have the opportunity to plan and co-lead a group. Again, stories of physical, emotional, and sexual abuse abound, all of which are compounded by the misuse of alcohol and illegal drugs. Students become painfully aware of how difficult it is for families, or even one member of a family, to modify their abusive behaviors.

As stated previously, students select one of the three agencies for their adjunctive clinical experience. Remarkably, there have been minimal problems with students adequately spreading themselves out among the agencies; and even more remarkably, students at each agency tend to be pleased with their selection and believe they have made a better choice than their peers.

Since the adjunctive agencies at best have had previous experience only with graduate students, most often in social work, faculty members spend much time and effort planning for students' clinical experiences with a designated staff member from each agency. Faculty discuss the background of the students, previous coursework that contributes to students' preparation for the experience, and the general goals of the Psychosocial Nursing course. However, the specific focus is on the goal faculty hope undergraduate students will attain during their experience at the agency: understanding family violence and its aftermath.

Since students are spread out among three adjunctive agencies and have their clinical experiences at various times of the week, a staff member designated by the agency works with the students on an ongoing basis. However, nursing instructors remain on call, visit the agencies at intervals, and are available to both agency staff and students for consultation. Faculty stress to agency staff that they are *not* responsible for handling student problems beyond letting a faculty member know that a problem exists. Faculty members remain responsible for student discipline and behavior. In general, problems have been minimal.

TEACHING METHODS

Agency staff provide students with materials that explain the goals, policies, and procedures of the agency. Agency staff also orient students to the agency and direct their ongoing experiences, including their participation with clients and families, access to written records and crisis line calls, group participation and co-leadership, and student evaluations.

Faculty members select reading materials and/or video materials that prepare students for their specific experiences. For example, students electing to go to CHOICES are asked to preview the videotape, *Battered Wives* (Learning Corporation of America, 1979), and read two book chapters, one on crisis intervention from their psychiatric nursing text (Janosik & Davies, 1989) and the second, "Shall We Dance," from *Women Who Love Too Much* (Norwood, 1986). Students selecting Huckleberry House are asked to view two videotapes, *Child Abuse* (Films for the Humanities and Sciences, 1987) and *No Easy Answers—Junior and Senior High School,* from the series, *Child Sexual Abuse: What Your Child Should Know* (Hirch, 1983). Students attending the Family Outpatient program are asked to view *Children of Alcoholics* (Films for the Humanities and Sciences, 1988) and *Cruel Spirits: Alcohol and Violence* (Siedor, Byerly, & Byerly, 1989). Students are asked to summarize each videotape they view in their journal. The Appendix lists and describes several videotapes about violence against women purchased by Capital University's Instructional Media Center.

Because students have their clinical experiences at only one of the three adjunctive clinical settings, they are expected to share their varied clinical experiences with each other during clinical discussion conferences. Hence, all students hear about a far wider variety of clinical experiences than any one student would be able to achieve in a single clinical course. Also, it is in these informal discussion settings that faculty encourage students to relate classroom content and nursing process to their clinical work as well as to process their own thoughts and feelings about what they have observed and participated in. Again for some students, this is a shocking dose of reality, while for others, it is reliving parts of their past lives.

As students continue to intervene with adolescents and women who were abused, they begin to get a sense of their own competence in approaching very frightening nursing situations. When discussions become intense or reports of exchanges with clients feel confusing, students are often asked to use role playing to examine the complexity of an interaction. A strength of the program as it currently exists is that each faculty member has her own nursing practice background with clients who have been abused and is able to contribute her own clinical experience to reinforce both theory and practice.

Students are asked to write journal entries for each clinical experience. Their entries include both their subjective and objective clinical experiences and provide yet another means for course faculty to assist students to learn from their clinical experiences. Journal entries are never graded or used for student evaluations. Journals simply become additional means of student-faculty communication.

Students are also asked to complete a community visit as part of the course requirements. This assignment provides yet another opportunity for students to elect to learn about treatment for physical abuse. Students may choose to visit a rape crisis center, an emergency room where women who have been sexually abused are treated, or any number of outpatient agencies within the metropolitan area of Columbus or their hometown.

Students complete this assignment independently. They develop their own rationale for selecting the agency and make their own contact and arrangements for the visit. Although faculty do assist students on deciding what agency to visit, they do not provide students with a list of agencies to visit or act as liaisons with the agencies the students select.

Students prepare for their visit by writing summaries of three professional journal or text readings of their own choosing related to the treatment program of the agency they selected, by summarizing a theory or conceptual framework that provides a basis for the kind of treatment they will be seeing, and by formulating questions to ask while they are in the setting. Experiences at the agency may include a tour of the facilities, observations of a staff meeting, interactions with staff members and clients, observations of groups or crisis calls, or a combination of the above. Students then write a summary of the visit after it is completed and include a copy of the thank you note they sent to the agency staff member with whom they interacted. Again, students are asked to share their experiences during the visit with their classmates during clinical conferences.

IMPACT ON STUDENT LEARNING

Assessing whether or not curriculum goals have been met is done through objective testing, clinical observation, and students' own evaluations, assessment measures similar to those used in other areas of the curriculum. Students are aware that their behaviors and personal evaluations impact on whether the experience will remain available for their classmates. What faculty find gratifying, however, are the success stories that students share about their work with abused teens and adults. A few examples include:

A student worked intensively with a 22-year-old mother of two children who was ambivalent about returning to her husband who had repeatedly physically abused her. The student assisted the young woman to obtain child support, find a satisfactory apartment, use a support group for women who had been in similar situations, and start looking for a job. The young mother perceived alternative options for living her life, a renewed sense of her own competence, and, most especially, a sense of hope that life could be different.

In another example, a student successfully assisted an adolescent to stop her aggressive behavior toward her peers while she was living at Huckleberry House. The student developed a relationship with the teen and, through the relationship, modeled alternate ways of handling anger. The teen, in turn, began to develop a friendship with a peer at the home. This new relationship, though tenuous at times, helped to handle the young girl's loneliness and needs for acceptance and self-esteem.

A story related by Professor Janice Ryan exemplifies the results of a student's clinical intervention in a different clinical setting a few months after she had completed the Psychosocial Nursing course. The student related that the medical staff on a maternity unit suspected that a new mother had been physically abused. The physician ordered an x-ray to confirm his suspicions about the abrasions on her chest. The student simply asked the woman if her husband or someone else in her life was hurting her. The woman immediately replied that her husband repeatedly kicked her in the ribs when he was angry. The hospital staff was impressed with the student's ability to obtain the information.

Results of these adjunctive experiences are also seen through the ongoing experiences that students write about in their clinical journals. The following paragraph is an example from a student's first visit to Huckleberry House:

> The sign on the front of the house, "safe place," really stands up to its meaning. I felt very comfortable and safe in this house in regards to the neighborhood around. This home really does a lot more than I expected. I didn't realize the paper work and process each individual has to go through if they choose to stay. The crisis counselors are those individuals that talk to these teenagers and work out a plan of treatment. I was amazed how much the staff coordinates each person's plan with other staff members. Keeping a log is such a great idea to find out the atmosphere and what is going on in the house from previous shifts. I am really looking forward to talking with these teens. This clinical setting is much more relaxed, and I feel I can relate to these teens because of my age. I am really anxious to find out these individual's problems and help them to sort out ways to get over the stressors in their lives.

The student's next clinical journal entry demonstrated her reaction to her first experience with a young person at the house.

> The young person named P was 14 years old. He appeared a well groomed and well dressed person. His hair was cut and styled nicely. . . . P was rather intelligent and told us his GPA was 3.96. . . . He was excited about starting school but had to miss today because he had a social work consult. I was surprised to find out P's reasons for being here. He was molested when he was younger and has sexual tendencies towards young men . . . sexual incidents with males at church (and) problems in school noticed by teachers. . . . This perfect young boy with such an all-American look and pleasant attitude had so many problems. I just don't understand how

young people of this age can get "so screwed up." I realize he was molested at such a young age which may have resulted in his actions at the present time.

Another student expressed her initial fears as written in the first paragraph. The second and third paragraphs indicate later experiences:

. . . I am a little nervous about working (at Huckleberry House), mainly because of my inexperience in working with adolescents in general. . . . I also don't have any experience with abuse victims, whether it be physical, sexual, or substance. . . . I guess this is another challenging learning experience.

. . . Later in the afternoon, I went into the living room area where there was one girl who arrived today. She kept starting to talk, revealing little bits about herself, then she'd leave. She was friendly and was smiling, and appeared to want to talk but wouldn't sit still long enough to do so.

It's still hard for me to believe that a girl of her young age could have already been through so much in her life. Sort of makes my papers a little less of a hurdle.

Another student commented about her own background:

. . . Coming from B., we do not see as much violence, drugs, gang, etc. as other schools. . . . I cannot imagine being raped, molested, being into drugs, etc. . . . I am scared to start working at Huck House because I've never done anything like this before. . . .

. . . They were disturbing. Most of the young people who come there had been molested or abused at home. I cannot understand how anybody could do such a thing. It ruins these kids' lives—Why can they not think about this! These kids go and do the same thing to others, they do not know any other way. The whole subject is very disturbing to me. It turns out that the young person I was with this afternoon had been molested by her father and by a 15-year-old boy at a group home. . . . I was with this young person all afternoon, and she was such a great kid. . . .

These students' words best demonstrate both their fears and anticipations as well as their beginning sensitivity and desire for confidence and competency. The faculty hopes that these experiences will limit students' denial of suspected abuse when they see it professionally as well as provide them with the skills they need to approach children and adults they suspect are abused as both concerned citizens and competent clinicians.

ALTERNATE CURRICULUM PLACEMENTS

Although Capital University's nursing curriculum addresses violence against women in Human Development and Psychosocial Nursing courses, there are many other alternatives for teaching content about violence against women in an undergraduate nursing curriculum. Health Assessment, Medical-Surgical, Community, and Nursing of Children courses can include content about case finding, history taking, and the interviewing and technical skills necessary to assess for the presence of physical, emotional, and sexual abuse. Community settings, including visits to outpatient clinics and clients' homes, provide excellent arenas for students to assess for the presence of abusive relationships, provide nursing care, and make referrals to appropriate social agencies. Tertiary prevention, that is, providing care for severely abused women, can be addressed through clinical placements in emergency rooms and inpatient settings serving both children and adults. Nonfamily violence such as rape and date rape can be addressed in Medical-Surgical, Maternal-Child Health, and Women's Health Classes.

The list of clinical facilities is endless. Violence against women can be observed in almost any clinical setting in which undergraduate nursing students are placed. Experience with violence demands only the knowledge, commitment, and creativity of faculty.

SUMMARY

Because baccalaureate-educated nurses are often the first health care professionals to recognize abuse and care for abused women of all ages, it is imperative that nursing students at the undergraduate level learn both the dynamics of abuse and intervention strategies. Incorporating violence against women into class content and clinical experience is neither difficult nor time consuming. Before looking for new clinical facilities, faculty need only be aware of how they can assist students to recognize signs of violence in facilities where students currently practice clinically. The greatest impediment to teaching about violence against women is not the lack of available clinical experiences but our own denial that women are abused and our lack of knowledge about its recognition and intervention.

REFERENCES

Films for the Humanities and Sciences. (Producer). (1987). *Child abuse* [Videotape]. Princeton, NJ: Films for the Humanities and Sciences.

Films for the Humanities and Sciences. (Producer). (1988). *Children of alcoholics* [Videotape]. Princeton, NJ: Multimedia, Inc.

Goldemberg, R. (Producer), & Davis, M. (Director). (1986). *The burning bed* [Videotape]. Coronet Productions, Inc.

Hirch, M. (Producer), & Denny, P. (Director). (1983). *Parents* [Videotape]. Part I of, *Child sexual abuse: What your child should know* [Series]. Bloomington, IN: Indiana University A/V Center.

Hirch, M. (Producer & Director). (1983). *Kindergarten through third grade & fourth through seventh grade* [Videotape]. Part II of, *Child sexual abuse: What your child should know* [Series]. Bloomington, IN: Indiana University A/V Center.

Hirch, M. (Producer). (1983). *No easy answers—junior and senior high school* [Videotape]. Part III of, *Child sexual abuse: What your child should know* [Series]. Bloomington, IN: Indiana University A/V Center.

Janosik, E., & Davies, J. (1989). *Psychiatric mental health nursing.* 2nd Edition. Boston, MA: Jones and Bartlett.

Learning Corporation of America. (Producer), McDonald, R., & Graddock, J. (1979). *Battered wives* [Videotape]. Henry Jaffe Enterprises, Inc.

Norwood, R. (1986). *Women who love too much.* New York: Pocket Books.

Selinger, J. (Producer), & Chisholm, W. (Director). (1985). *Battered wives, shattered lives* [Videotape]. New Jersey: New Jersey Network.

Siedor, C. (Producer). (1986). *Someone you know: Acquaintance rape* [Videotape]. Atlanta, GA: Coronet/MTI, Dystar Television, Inc.

Siedor, C., & Byerly, S. (Producers), & Byerly, S. (Editor). (1989). *Cruel spirits: Alcohol and violence* [Videotape]. Atlanta, GA: Coronet/MTI, Dystar Television, Inc.

Wells, L. (Ed.) (1984, December). *Family violence.* Interim report to the Governor. Ohio: Task Force on Family Violence.

Wells, L. (Ed.) (1985, December). *Family violence.* Second interim report to the Governor. Ohio: Task Force on Family Violence.

APPENDIX

Selected Videotapes Related to Violence Against Women

Battered Wives (Learning Corporation of America, McDonald, & Graddock, 1979)

  45 minutes   VIDEO VHS

This is a shortened version of the feature film *Battered.* The film focuses on two situations of family violence. In the first episode, the wife is the target of her impatient husband. In the second episode, the wife is the target of her alcoholic husband.

Battered Wives, Shattered Lives (Selinger & Chisholm, 1985)

  56 minutes   VIDEO VHS

This is a documentary about the scope of wife abuse in the United States narrated by Ed Asner.

The Burning Bed (Goldemberg & Davis, 1986)

  136 minutes   VIDEO VHS

This film is based on a true story about a woman who kills her husband after enduring several years of physical abuse from him. After being charged with murder, she is found not guilty by reason of temporary insanity.

Child Abuse (Films for the Humanities and Sciences, 1987)

  19 minutes   VIDEO VHS

This film deals with the subject of physically and sexually abused children. Issues addressed include the common characteristics of abusers, the behaviors, symptoms, and effects of abuse on physically abused children, the use of anatomically correct dolls to help children recreate what has happened to them, and questions to be addressed when selecting a day care center.

Children of Alcoholics (Films for the Humanities and Sciences, 1988)
    28 minutes   VIDEO VHS
    This film is a specially adapted Phil Donahue program in which Suzanne Somers and members of her immediate family tell their bitter story of growing up in an alcoholic and abusive family. They discuss the legacy of alcoholism including the deep emotional scars inherited by the next generation.

Child Sexual Abuse: What Your Child Should Know (Hirch & Denny, 1983)
    Series   VIDEO VHS
    This series of three videotapes about what children should know about sexual abuse addresses three different audiences: parents, school-aged children, and adolescents.

Parents (Hirch & Denny, 1983)   90 minutes
    This videotape focuses on the sexual abuse of children including its meaning, victims, perpetrators, and methods of prevention.

Kindergarten Through Third Grade and Fourth Through Seventh Grade (Hirch, 1983)   60 minutes
    Story telling and "what if" games are used to help younger children to understand the difference between good and bad touching. In the second part of the tape, older children discuss sex-role stereotypes, communication with parents, and problems with babysitters.

No Easy Answers—Junior and Senior High School (Hirsh, 1983)   60 minutes
    Teenagers discuss the uncomfortable and often dangerous situations acted out by the Minneapolis Illusion Theater Company.

Cruel Spirits: Alcohol and Violence (Siedor, Byerly, & Byerly, 1989)
    32 minutes   VIDEO VHS
    Collin Siedor and several medical experts provide compelling evidence linking alcohol abuse to rape, child abuse, battering, and numerous other violent crimes.

Someone You Know: Acquaintance Rape (Siedor, 1986)
    30 minutes   VIDEO VHS
    This film looks at acquaintance rape and examines its prevention, underlying causes and effects, and aid for the victims.

Chapter 9

Violence Against Women as Content in Graduate Education in Women's Health

Susan M. Cohen and Diane Wind Wardell

INTRODUCTION

Graduate education, whether it be in women's health care, perinatal nursing, or maternal/child health, must address the issue of violence against women. To provide comprehensive care to women means including assessment of violence and abuse as a standard component. The nurse preparing for advanced practice by obtaining a graduate degree must be able to assess and intervene with clients who are survivors of battering, sexual assault, and verbal violence.

In this chapter, three methods of integrating content and clinical experiences will be discussed. The examples range from integrating content concerning violence against women in the clinical course sequence, to an elective in victimology that includes experiences outside the classroom, to a subspecialty program that is designed to prepare a sexual assault nurse examiner. All of the

The authors would like to acknowledge the assistance of Joyce Dains, Dr.P.H., R.N., University of Texas Health Science Center at Houston, Christine A. Grant, Ph.D., R.N., and Ann W. Burgess, D.N.Sc., R.N., University of Pennsylvania.

methods described have been used in graduate education programs. The outlines are derived from programs at the University of Texas Health Science Center at Houston and the University of Pennsylvania.

Violence against women may take the form of physical, sexual, and verbal attacks occurring within interpersonal relationships or in situations involving strangers. In addition, violence against women encompasses a broad range of societal aggression or misogyny such as use of women as sexual objects in the advertising media. The chapters in the preceding section provide conclusive evidence of the high prevalence of woman abuse.

To ensure a comprehensive knowledge base, course content in violence against women must include battering as well as sexual assault. Battering in relationships can encompass many dimensions of physical and psychological abuse. Physical abuse involves various assaults to the body with the batterer's hand and/or feet, objects and weapons, or by rape (Walker, 1979). Such abuse may directly result in the death of a woman or the death of the male partner as a result of the woman's attempts at self-defense (Campbell, 1981). Psychological abuse includes verbal abuse that attacks the woman's self-worth by indicating that she is undesirable, unable to satisfy her partner's sexual needs, lazy, or unable to live without him. Also, included are threats of violence toward her, her children, others, or toward the abuser if she threatens to leave.

Violence against women has been used to exert power and control. Although battering and sexual assault are illegal, the inconsistent application of legal consequences for men who use violence has resulted in an atmosphere of leniency toward the batterers. Often the environment has been one in which the rape survivor was "on trial" rather than the perpetrator. Additionally, tolerance of abuse has been demonstrated by the hesitancy of enforcement officials to interfere with domestic disputes by entering homes or arresting spouses.

Enforcement officials are not the only professionals who are lax in their ability to assist battered women. In Bowker and Maurer's (1987) study of 1,000 battered women, the medical profession, including both physicians and nurses, was ranked last by battered women in its effectiveness in providing assistance when compared to police, social services, lawyers, clergy, shelters, women's groups, and district attorneys. In a study of 290 randomly selected pregnant women, none of the 24 women who had been battered were accurately assessed by a health care provider for the presence of an abusive relationship or provided with community resources (Helton, McFarlane, & Anderson, 1987). According to Campbell (1984), battered women usually do not admit to an abusive relationship and may become isolated and withdrawn from their support systems. Frequently they do not know where to turn for assistance nor do they see health professionals as being able to help (Snodgrass, 1986). Inclusion of content specific to the issues of battering and sexual assault in graduate curricula will improve nursing interventions and thereby, change the perceptions of survivors.

GENERAL GOALS OF CONTENT ON VIOLENCE AGAINST WOMEN IN GRADUATE NURSING CURRICULUM

If nurses are to be recognized as sources of assistance for survivors, at least two things must be accomplished. First, it is imperative that nurses increase their assessment for abuse in order to identify potentially harmful situations. Second, nurses need to make themselves more available to survivors of abuse as sources for advocacy. The nurse is often the first health care worker the victim encounters when entering the health care system either via the hospital or the outpatient setting (Mahon, 1981). Accurate assessment of abuse must occur in order to identify women who are in abusive relationships. The nurse's role is to promote life and health including protection of the abused woman from injury and from inflicting injury on her partner or children. An adequate knowledge base will buttress sensitive assessment and expand ability to intervene.

The ultimate goal in obtaining information about abuse and battering is to apply this knowledge to prevent the violence against women. Many abused women are found to be in an early stage of moral development, which is manifested by powerlessness and dependence on others for survival. Therefore, it is possible that relationships without violence increase the possibility that women will have the opportunity to develop to their fullest potential without fear (Belenky, Clinchy, Goldberger, & Tarule, 1986).

Nursing that aims to empower women utilizes a holistic and humanistic approach. The process of caring for abused and battered women involves communication, nurturing, and knowledgeable activities reflecting empathy, support, compassion, protection, and education (Leininger, 1981; King, 1981). The overall positive effect of nursing care is beneficial for both the client and the nurse through the fostering of healing and growth. The following curricular examples provide profiles for moving content on abuse and survival into graduate programs that focus on women and their health.

SELECTED GRADUATE EDUCATION MODELS THAT INCORPORATE VIOLENCE AGAINST WOMEN

Integrated Curriculum Approach

The Women's Health Care program at The University of Texas Health Science Center at Houston School of Nursing is a 1-year program with three sequential courses in Women's Health Care, two to three role courses depending on the role chosen (clinical specialist, administrator, educator, and nurse practitioner) and support courses. The Women's Health Care courses progress from the presentation of a feminist perspective on women across the life span, normal obstetric and gynecologic experiences, to high-risk conditions that are gynecologic and high-risk obstetrics in the second course, to a broad based issues and policy focus in the final course.

The students enter this program with a wide range of experiences in either inpatient obstetrics, outpatient care, or occasionally from other clinical areas such as emergency care and critical care. Each student develops personal objectives. Clinical exposure is based on the student's role selection, experience, and goals.

Objectives Related to Woman Abuse in the Integrated Approach

1 Recognize the broad range of abuse that women experience.
2 Develop an awareness of the signs of violence toward women.
3 Perform assessments for violence in relationships in clinical settings.
4 Identify individual strengths, personal and community support systems, and other referral sources for women who are survivors of violence.
5 Implement a plan of care for women who experience or have experienced violence.
6 Promote the prevention of violence against women.

Content and Assignments

The didactic content on violence against women is incorporated throughout the Women's Health Care curriculum. The initial introduction begins with a discussion on developmental theories. Traditional male developmental theories are contrasted to those researched and presented by women. *Women's Ways of Knowing* (1986) by Belenky, Clinchy, Goldberger, and Tarule and Carol Gilligan's *In a Different Voice* (1982) are discussed at length. Belenky et al. is emphasized because the authors address the issue of battered women in their developmental stages. A discussion of female sexuality is also provided to explore the issues and values associated with being a woman. The sexuality seminar utilizes a variety of experimental learning techniques such as guided imagery and massage. Questionnaires that address values concerning sexuality are also used.

Later in the first course the students are shown a video that includes various scenes of domestic violence. The objective of this experience is to evaluate the characters using such directives as moral development, symbols, and interactions.

Additionally in the first course, assessment for violence in the antenatal period and for any woman seeking health care is addressed. The signs of domestic violence, interviewing techniques, and referral data are provided to the students.

Clinical activities include direct interviewing of clients, no matter what the clinical focus of the student, in a variety of settings. Since abuse may have detrimental effects in pregnancy, assessment for violence is stressed in that setting. Violence affects all classes of women; therefore, the students are not limited by a clinical placement of a particular socioeconomic class where clients are more representative.

In the second course, the high-risk client is addressed. The clinical content of the course varies based on the student's interests and focus. A requirement for this course includes a clinical project. Some students have elected as their project to institute battering assessments of the hospitalized woman in their institutions. They have utilized existing forms on the assessment of domestic violence available from the March of Dimes, developed their own, or modified forms.

Students frequently identify, as a primary impediment to the project, administrative concerns that this is not a problem in the clientele of the institution. Therefore, education of the administrative body has also occurred in order to guarantee the success of the program. Other clinical projects proposed by the students can be encouraged that address the issues of violence against women such as determining local referral sources, educating the public and professionals, and staff in-services, to name just a few.

The third Women's Health course has one of its concentrated seminars provided by the students on the issue of women as victims. The material in this seminar includes such topics as domestic violence, date and stranger rape, and sexual harassment in the workplace. Additional seminars on advertising are image of women, research on women and the emphasis on male illnesses and subjects, and the association between women and poverty. All seek to address the issues of society's promoting women as victims. The clinical experiences during this course are selected by the students. Options include working with battered women in a shelter, and spending time at a women's center that is instrumental in organizing programs on rape, incest, hot lines, and shelters.

This sequence of courses is designed to provide graduate students with the knowledge needed to intervene in woman abuse. Nurses need to educate battered women about leaving the battering situation; identify women at risk; make referrals to social service agencies; manage health needs; and help prevent violence. To effectively relate to survivors of abuse, nurses must gain knowledge about the multifaceted problem of battered women by learning the influence of physical, sexual, and verbal abuse on behavior. This knowledge will facilitate insight into ways in which nurses and other health care workers can identify abused women and assist them in meeting their health needs. Nurses also need to promote effective strategies that will prevent abuse.

Victimology Course as an Elective

The Victimology course offered at the University of Pennsylvania School of Nursing is a one-semester elective course, open to both senior undergraduate and graduate students. The course explores the range of experiences from the perspectives of the victim, the offender, the family, and society. Crimes used in the course for examination include robbery, burglary, assault and battery, rape, domestic violence, arson, child molestation, and homicide. The response patterns of the survivor are explained in depth.

Objectives

1 Recognize social attitudes and perceptions about violence against women.
2 Identify the psychological, physical, social, and legal aspects of violence against women.
3 Recognize the motivational intent of the offender of sexually-aggressive crimes.
4 Analyze institutional response patterns to survivors of violence.

Content   A topic outline of the Victimology course is presented in Table 9-1. The content for this particular course has a stronger emphasis on rape, but much of the material is readily applicable to battering.

Assignments   Students have observational experiences at emergency departments, police stations, and in courtrooms. Interviews with violence survivors are done using a guided questionnaire. Written assignments include a weekly crime journal, the survivor interview, and a victim-awareness teaching project. A final paper evaluating survivor and institutional responses to violence serves to synthesize the material.

Sexual Assault Examiner Specialization

An additional option available for the student interested in violence against women and, in particular, in the area of sexual abuse, is a program for certification as a sexual assault nurse examiner. The need for an individual educated to care for the sexual assault survivor during the initial crisis phase is recognized by both survivors and health care providers. The program at the University of Texas Health Science Center is taught as a postgraduate course under the auspices of the Division of Educational Outreach. The program could be offered as a subspecialty in either the final clinical course of a women's health nurse practitioner graduate program or as a semester length postgraduate course of study.

The course is composed of both didactic and clinical experiences. The curriculum content requires a multidisciplinary faculty that should include nurse practitioners, law enforcement officers, attorneys, social workers, and survivors. The program prepares the nurse to be the primary care provider for survivors of sexual violence in the emergency center. Referral is made to a physician for any additional care needed for trauma that the woman experienced. Students are taught such vital information as how to conduct an interview that has legal substance, collect evidence, and testify in court.

Table 9-1 Topic Outline of Elective Victimology Course

Attitudes and social perceptions of survivors	Child sexual assault and exploitation
Myths about rape survivors	Incest
Myths about child sexual abuse	Sex rings
Myths about offenders	Pornography
Dynamics of victimization and aggression	Prevention and education
Crime classification	Dealing with dangerous human situations
Offender motivation	
Victim response	Fight vs. flight
Rape (adult and elderly)	Criminal profiling
Targeting victims	Crime scene analysis
Style of attack	Character profiling
Rape trauma syndrome	Youth at risk
Recovery from rape	Runaways
Adolescent assaults	Prostitution
Acquaintance rape	Institutional responses to crime victims
Adolescent sex offender	Hospital
	Police
	Court

Objectives

1 Examine the historical perspective of sexual assault and the current situation at the local level.

2 List the types of evidence that must be collected currently for sexual assault evaluation.

3 Demonstrate the correct methods of evidence collection and handling to preserve the chain of evidence.

4 Demonstrate a sexual assault examination.

5 Present physical findings in an organized, concise manner verbally and in writing.

6 Demonstrate appropriate collection of medical history and documentation of same for later use as evidence in court.

7 Using standard protocols for care, discuss guidelines for treatment and physician consultation.

8 Discuss alterations in approach and examination when the sexual assault survivor is a child.

9 Identify the sexual assault trauma syndrome and discuss variables of behavior and feelings exhibited at each stage.

10 Discuss consultation and follow-up options available for the sexual assault survivor.

11 Utilize appropriate components of crisis intervention that are appropriate for interventions with the sexual assault survivor.

12 Discuss the current social service network for sexual assault survivor and state how to refer the survivor to this network.

13 Identify methods of preparing the court to include preparation for possible testimony as a witness and pretrial preparations with the District Attorney.

14 Identify attitude and role expectations as an expert witness.

15 Discuss medical, legal, and law enforcement aspects of sexual assault data collection and processing of evidence.

16 Discuss the role of the professional nurse in the examination of the sexual assault survivor.

Content A topical outline of the content that is included in the preparation of nurses with a subspecialty as a sexual assault examiner is presented in Table 9-2. Much of this can also be transferred to care of a battered woman.

Assignments During role-play situations, the student simulates the sexual assault examination. After proficiency has been demonstrated in simulations, the student spends a minimum of 16 hours in a precepted emergency department clinical rotation. After completing the course of study, the student receives continued supervision via a clinical log of cases managed by the student and evaluated by the faculty. The log provides information on the student's progress in data collection, handling of evidence, case management, and case outcome. Faculty review all cases with the student during the period of supervision.

SUMMARY

Three examples of content concerning abuse and battering have been presented. The models offer only a small range of the possibilities for curricular organization to address this content at the graduate level. A vital aspect of the health care of women provided by nurses in advanced practice, is the empowerment of all women. At a minimum level, nurses must be able to assess women for

Table 9-2 Topical Outline of Content for Subspecialty in Sexual Assault Examiner

Historical perspective	Role of law enforcement
Current status	Role of forensics
Legal Aspects	Basic science of evidence
Anatomy and physiology	Chain of evidence
Adult	Medical/legal follow-up criteria
Child	Handling of children
Triage	Sexual Assault Trauma Syndrome
Role of hospital	Crisis intervention
Rape protocol	Support services
Sexual assault examination	Postassault intervention
History	Courtroom performance
Physical examination	
Collection of evidence	
Documentation	
Prophylactic treatments	
Counseling for AIDS testing	

battering and abuse. The requirements for masters degree-prepared nurses must include the ability to intervene with survivors. The range of interventions encompass referral to community resources and health care providers sensitive to the needs of survivors of battering and sexual abuse. Furthermore, educational avenues must be provided to instruct graduate students in the subspecialty of sexual assault and abuse. In many hospitals, the least experienced individual (e.g., the intern or first-year resident) is the one called to examine a sexual assault survivor.

One of the ways to provide better health care to survivors is to have nurses educated to both the needs of a survivor and the legal complexities of sexual assault evidence gathering. As nursing researchers continue to add to the understanding of the psychosocial bases of abuse and battering, the content will be integrated into undergraduate programs. When the assimilation occurs, the role of the nurse in advanced practice will have the opportunity to become more specific to the care of survivors of violence against women.

REFERENCES

Belenky, M., Clinchy, B., Goldberger, N., & Tarule, J. (1986). *Women's ways of knowing: The development of self, voice, and mind.* New York: Basic Books.

Bowker, L., & Maurer, L. (1987). The medical treatment of battered wives. *Women & Health, 12,* 25–45.

Campbell, J. (1981). Misogyny and homicide of women. *Advances in Nursing Science, 3,* 67–85.

Campbell, J. (1984). Abuse of female partners. In J. Campbell & J. Humphreys (Eds.), *Nursing care of victims of family violence* (pp. 74–118). Reston, VA: Reston Publishing Co.

Gilligan, C. (1982). *In a different voice: Psychological theory and women's development.* Cambridge: Harvard University Press.

Helton, A., McFarlane, J., & Anderson, E. (1987). Battered and pregnant: A prevalence study. *American Journal of Public Health, 77,* 1337–1339.

King, I. (1981). *A theory for nursing: Systems, concepts, process.* New York: Wiley.

Leininger, M. (1981). *Caring—an essential human need.* New Jersey: Charles B. Slack, Inc.

Mahon, L. (1981). Common characteristics of abused women. *Issues in Mental Health Nursing, 3,* 137–157.

Snodgrass, F. (1986). Where do women turn? *American Journal of Nursing, 86,* 912.

Walker, L. (1979). *The battered woman.* New York: Harper Colophon Books.

Walker, L. (1984). Battered women, psychology and public policy. *American Psychologist, 39,* 1178–1182.

Part Three

Implications
for Nursing Practice

Chapter 10

Woman Abuse and Practice Implications Within an International Context

Phyllis Noerager Stern

You have to die standing, never kneeling. We might have a history of kneeling but we have to die standing. This is something that is under everyone's skin. When you begin to speak with others you discover that it's our dignity that is most important. That's the challenge, the motor that will push us to search for other things.

Monica Ortubia, in Lehmann (1990)

If we look at violence against women from a global perspective, we can see that while the properties within contexts may change, what remains constant is the comparative physical strength of men over women, the social status of women that serves to place them in inferior, powerless positions and thus in jeopardy, and the cultural belief system of a society that condones or allows the behavior. Major categories of violence can be constructed as overt and covert. Under an overt rubric are grouped familiar acts such as battering, rape, and murder. Covert violence includes accepted practices such as female circumcision, allowing more work for women and more food for men (McLean, 1987), unethical medical research, and technological childbirth. These are practices in which the intent is not to do violence, but to follow the normal prescribed order of the society—that is, to do what is right. The themes identified by the authors in this volume can be seen to carry over to a world view. In section one, Campbell (1990), Hoff (1990), Kjervik (1990), Mackey (1990), McBride (1990), and Sampselle, Bernhard, Kerr, Opie, Perley, and Pitzer (1990) suggest strategies for nursing research that apply to the world scene.

INTERNATIONAL CONFERENCES

While there is little published research outside of the developed world devoted to violence against women, a number of conferences have been held that address the international perspective of the problem (Reichert, in press). The international problem of "troubled families" was first addressed in 1975 at the United Nation's World Conference of the International Women's Year in Mexico City. The United Nations (UN) focused its 1980 conference, "Equality, Development and Peace," on victims of family violence. The UN urged member nations to develop centers for treatment, shelter, and counseling. The First Feminist Latin American Encounter was held in Bogota, Colombia, in November 1981. The assembly declared November 25th of that year, the first International Day to End Violence Against Women. In 1985, the World Health Assembly passed a resolution stating the concern of members over the increase in family violence and its impact on women and children. And again in 1985, at the World Conference of the United Nations in Nairobi, a resolution regarding family violence was passed stating that, "Gender specific violence is increasing and governments must affirm the dignity of women as a priority action." The focus of the 1986 meeting of the UN Commission on the Status of Women was to understand the effects of family violence on women.

SCOPE

A popular myth persists that violence against women is more common in industrialized societies. However, as Gelles and Cornell (1983) state, it is incorrect to assume that countries other than the United States have little or no family violence just because there are no scholarly or journalistic discussions of violence in those cultures.

Because we have little research literature to draw from, we must rely on that which does exist, and upon anecdotal material. Therefore, estimations of the scope of the problem of violence against women remain inprecise, but we know it exists. These chilling facts come from the MATCH publication, *Linking Women's Global Struggles to End Violence* (1990):

• More than 90 million African women and girls are victims of female circumcision or other forms of genital mutilation (World Health Organization report).

• Six out of 10 Tanzanian women have experienced physical abuse from their partners (Violence against women in Dar-es-Salaam: A case study of three districts; Tanzania Media Women's Association, 1989).

• 50% of married women are regularly battered by their partners in Bangkok, Thailand (Worldwatch Institute report).

• An estimated 1,000 women are burned alive each year in dowry-related incidents in the state of Gujarat, India (Ahmedabad Women's Action Group Report).

• 78,000 female fetuses were aborted after sex determination tests between 1978–1982 (a study of a Bombay clinic).

• In Mexico, a woman is raped every 9 minutes (Doble Jornada, November 1987).

• In the United States, a woman is beaten every 15 seconds (U.S. Department of Justice).

• One in 10 Canadian women will be abused or battered by her husband or partner (Wife Battering in Canada, Canadian Advisory Council on the Status of Women, 1980).

• Eight out of 10 Aboriginal women in Canada will be beaten by their partner (*Breaking Free: A Proposal for Change to Aboriginal Family Violence,* The Ontario Native Women's Association, p. 9).

SOCIETAL PERSPECTIVE

In most of the world, women hold positions of lesser power than those of men in terms of their ability to earn money, make political decisions, and ability to inherit. Joyceen Boyle (1985) reports that in a Guatamalian colonia, "Women grow up taking care of men, waiting on their needs and occasionally submitting to ill treatment, callousness, and neglect with stoic patience and resignation" (p. 79). She tells us that the male role is most commonly dominant. He expresses this dominance through, "wife abuse, excessive drinking, and occasionally failure to provide money for household expense" (p. 79). Uma Devi Das, Coordinator of the Nursing Education Unit at Tibhuvan University of Katmandu, Nepal wrote to me on February 13, 1990, that "[information on the social status of women and the girl child] will give you a good idea of the treatment of and attitudes toward women in Nepal." Singh (1989) writes of that girl child in Nepal:

Gender bias against the girl child begins from the moment of her birth, and continues in one form or another throughout her life. She is discriminated against in all spheres of life and is denied the opportunity to develop and realize her potential. (p. 49)

Unlike a male child, a female child has no legal right to family property. The law is silent even on her maintenance right in her natal home. This has made the female child a non-entity with the resultant adverse effect on her socioeconomic status. (p. 47)

In an unpublished report of March 8, 1990, Florence Mubichi (1990) of the Methodist Hospital in Maua, Kenya, wrote that societal laws predispose women to violence:

1 Women are regarded to be the property of a clan and therefore belong to the husband.

2 It is the community's expectation that a woman should carry all the burdens and be responsible for both nuclear and extended family without questioning.

3 Sick or well, the woman is expected to nurse and wait on other members of the family, e.g., must cook, wash, cultivate, etc.

4 If there is shortage of commodities, a woman will do without a share and divide it between the man and children even if she is the family's breadwinner.

5 If there are shortfalls within the family's expectations, it is the woman that is blamed for it and if there is success, the man receives credit for it whether involved or not.

6 It is up to the woman to plan the family, whether she is able or not, e.g., she uses methods of contraception. If not, she undertakes the burden of childbearing without much spacing.

7 The woman must have "no voice" against her husband's decisions whether right or wrong. Many women's illnesses are psychological leading to physical problems, and hence they are regarded to be weaklings.

The institution of bridewealth, or money a man must pay a woman's father to gain a bride, erodes the status of women in the family, according to Heise (1989). In some areas of the world, particularly Africa, the bride price tends to inflate to the point that the man is left with the impression that he is *buying* a wife (Barry, 1984). According to Molokomme (1986), in Botswana only men who have met the obligation of *bogadi* (bridewealth) are allowed to chastise their wives.

CULTURAL BELIEFS

As Hoff (1990) suggests, cultural belief systems have an impact on the incidence of violence against women. And if we compare the practices of other cultures in order to judge our own, we can better understand foreign belief/action systems.

A common form of wife abuse is dowry murder or bride burning. Dowry murders are generally disguised as accident or suicide. "A frequent scam is to set the woman alight with kerosene and then claim she died in a kitchen accident—hence the term *bride burning*" (Heise, 1989). Placed within a cultural context, we can see that Hindu beliefs in the importance of the dowry mean that each girl child is a liability—she represents money going out of the family. Dowry money and gifts are recorded, and in the case of divorce, must be returned to the family of the bride. Seeing with Hindu eyes, it is easier to understand why daughters-in-law are murdered rather than being allowed to divorce (Rooshabh Varaiya, personal communication April 15, 1990). If we compare these practices with our own, it must be admitted that killing off a wealthy spouse for inheritance money is not unheard of in the developed world. Singh (1989) tells us that it is not surprising that "Nepal has the second highest index of son preference in the world" when according to the Hindu religion:

> A son and not a daughter is considered necessary to carry out the after-death rituals . . . sons (who inherit parental property) and not daughters are normally responsible for the upkeep of their aged parents. (p. 48)

In India, *suttee,* the practice of the woman throwing herself on her husband's funeral pyre, was outlawed by the English in 1829. It was most common in the Deli region of Uttar Pradsh (north country), which lies near the Kybar Pass. Persians and Mongols would stream through the pass with regularity and rape and pillage. A widow, left without protection might lose not only her property but her virtue. It was clear that her only choice was to die with her husband.

By comparison, in North America we still view the loss of virtue as a disgrace. While we do not encourage rape victims to commit suicide, neither do we print their names in the newspapers because the publicity might destroy their reputation.

Within a cultural/religious framework, female circumcision can be viewed as a procedure intended to give a young woman the best advantage of marriageability (Hezekiah & Wafula, 1989). ". . . uncircumcised women are considered to be unclean and promiscuous. Their chances of marrying are non-existent" (*Linking Women's Struggles to End Violence,* p. 25). The custom of circumcision persists even in countries where it has been outlawed, because according to local lore, especially of older women, it is the way to make the girl presentable (Pauline Peter Mella, personal communication, March 1982).

> Not surprisingly, there are strongholds of support, even among the educated for the continuation of this operation. As late as June 1988, Muslim religious scholars attending an international conference in Somalia argued that milder forms of circumcision should be maintained to temper female sexuality. (Heise, 1989)

By comparison again, the culturally-based practice of female circumcision is analogous to the persistence of male circumcision in the United States, where male infants are circed for cultural/religious reasons, for social status (so he'll look the same as the other boys or his father), and to ward off the folklore hex of forced adult circumcision (Harris, 1986).

OVERT VIOLENCE

Easily identified acts of violence likely happen in all countries. In Kenya women are regularly beaten by their husbands in order to maintain discipline. In a Guatemalian colonia, Boyle (1985) found that 64% of the households in her sample ($N = 134$) "reported a family member (always male) who frequently drank excessively, becoming abusive or threatening with his spouse" (p. 79). In Nicaragua, half the women who reported being beaten by their partners "suffered abuse for more than a year before laying charges" (Ameen, 1990, p. 6). In the Philippines, rape by members of the Filipino military is escalating (Marrs, 1990).

COVERT VIOLENCE

More subtle forms of violence occur within the context of cultural sanction. Less food and more work for women is clearly appropriate when men are seen as more important, more blessed (most gods are male), and the ones who protect women from rape assault and battery by other men. Subtle violence against women can be found in most birth rooms in the civilized world, and increasingly in developing countries as technology distorts the birth process. In his book *The Birth Machine,* Wagner (1990) tells us of a series of World Health Organization consensus conferences held around the world with the expressed purpose of striking a balance between technology and natural biology. As Wagner explains, "scientific evaluation of birth technology has come as an afterthought, not a prerequisite for its application" (p. 17).

Culturally sanctioned violence can appear in the form of medical research. A startling example comes from New Zealand, where women were involved in experimental treatment of cervical cancer in Auckland's National Women's Hospital (Chick & Pybus, 1988). Herbert Green, associate professor at the hospital since 1982, wanted to study the natural history of the disease. Over a period of 20 years, an experimental group of women with positive biopsy were left untreated. The women knew they were involved in a study, but they were never informed of the nature of the experiment. Sandra Coney, a journalist, and Phillida Bunkle, a lecturer in women's studies, found out about the work and blew the whistle on Green when they published an article (Coney & Bunkle, 1986) and Coney wrote a book about Green's experiments (Coney, 1988). A national inquiry was initiated, but not before "of the 25 untreated women, 23 (90%) developed invasive carcinoma" (Stern, 1990). As Chick and Pybus tell us, "Such a procedure could only have evolved from a perspective in which the woman was viewed as a vehicle for a pathological process, rather than as a person" (p. 127).

CONTEXT OF NURSING RESEARCH

The authors of the chapters in the first section of this book discuss the importance of the choice of research method, the relevance of research on violence against women to nursing practice, the need for legal sanctions, the search for a theoretical framework, and the importance of considering these variables in adapting a theoretical framework. Mackey also suggests that a mind-body model is essential.

First, Hoff suggests that anthropological methods are appropriate in the study of women and violence. An understanding of cultural beliefs is necessary to see practices from the perpetrator's point of view before we can develop appropriate interventions. Second, social perspectives play a major role in women and violence. That fact, coupled with Mackey's search for explanatory models, suggests that qualitative-sociological methods such as grounded theory, where a conceptual framework is informed by data rather than theories devised by "great men," might be an appropriate method. Third, another useful method is phenomonology. The lived experience of North American victims of violence may have been investigated, but I know of no like studies involving women from around the globe. Fourth, action research would be appropriate to evaluate those practice models we develop.

Kjervik points out that research on the law involving violence against women is relatively sparse, and that new models of law for the protection of abused women are sorely needed. This dirth of law research on women and violence is reflected worldwide.

Campbell makes the case for research that empowers women rather than examining them—research that allows women to be partners in research.

IMPLICATIONS FOR GLOBAL PRACTICE

While research on violence against women worldwide is sparse, action has begun. As Amelia Mangay-Maglacas (1988) stresses, to be effective, nursing interventions need to be combined with the efforts of other disciplines, and must be aimed at empowering the target population. While nurses bring a valuable point of view to intervention they can be most effective if they observe the lessons taught by those groups who have gone before them, such as the World Health Organization and government sponsored and religious organizations.

One such group is MATCH, a Canadian based international center, that aims to link women's global struggles to end violence. MATCH (not an acronym) is supported by matching funds from the Canadian International Development Agency (CIDA) and private donations. Established in 1975, the center does its work by encouraging women to form groups for political action, and by supporting already established groups. These conglomerates in turn are con-

sulted on which activities of MATCH would be most helpful. Nandipha Ngcobo
(1990) reports:

> When MATCH decided to conduct a series of workshops, a number of themes,
> ranging from women and agriculture or the environment to violence against
> women, were suggested to our Third World and Canadian partners, the response
> was overwhelming—the issue would be violence. (p. 3)

MATCH has recently developed a resource kit for those who wish to work
to end violence. The kit includes, "a collection of materials examining the
global dimensions of violence, international statistics on violence, women's
personal accounts, profiles of groups around the world strategizing to end violence, poetry and art: women's cultural expression, a short list of recent readings and audio-visual materials, and a bumper sticker, *Real Men Don't Abuse
Women*" (MATCH flyer). In *Linking Women's Global Struggles to End Violence* (Resource Kit, 1990), which comes with the kit, are hopeful examples of
women banding together to ward off abuse: The Inter-African Committee on
Traditional Practices Affecting the Health of Women and Children reports, "We
have . . . launched a programme in ten African countries which will work with
traditional midwives—who also perform the circumcisions—to teach them about
the harmful effects of genital mutilation" (p. 24). In Brazil, women organized
into action groups, campaigned for and won a women's police station, Delega-
cia da Mulher, established in 1985. In South Africa, a democratic, nonracist
rape crisis center was established in 1976. In Dar-es-Salaam, the Tanzania
Media Women's Association fights violence against women in that country
(MATCH report). On another front, in a think-tank report for the Canadian
Advisory Council on the Status of Women, MacLeod (1989) suggests:

> The federal government should undertake a major media advertising campaign to
> send out a clear message that the underlying root causes of family violence are
> linked to the "ethic of domination" that has long been accepted in our society as
> the basis for order. The "right" to use violence, if necessary, to maintain that
> domination is based on our belief that it is morally right to do so for the sake of
> preserving order. (p. 39)

CONCLUSION

In the opening chapter of E. L. Doctorow's novel *Billy Bathgate,* a scene
unfolds of sickening violence involving man against man. When negotiations
fail, men consistently settle scores through violent behavior. It is reasonable
then to expect that man's behavior toward woman should be of a gentler sort.
We have to believe that it is eminently reasonable or we are lost. Nursing
research and practice against violence worldwide will find its way in conjunction with other professionals, lay workers, and women of the country. This
effort must be undertaken in partnership with the target group—women—and

must lead to the empowerment of the women themselves. Most importantly, research or practice must follow pioneers in the field, and lend nursing's special perspective, which is always rooted in practice.

REFERENCES

Ameen, F. (1990). Breaking our bondage—ending violence against women. *Match News,* Jan/Feb/Mar, *6–7,* 1. (Available from MATCH International Centre, 1102–200 Elgin Street, Ottawa, Ontario K2P 1L5, Canada).

Barry, K. (1984). The network defines its issues: Theory, evidence and analysis of female sexual slavery. In K. Barry, C. Bunch, & S. Castley (Eds.), *International feminism: Networking against female sexual slavery* (pp. 32–48). New York: International Women's Tribune Centre.

Boyle, J. S. (1985). Ideology and illness experiences of women in Guatemala. *Health Care for Women International, 6,* 73–86.

Campbell, J. C. (1990, April). *Violence against women: Review of nursing research on battering.* Paper presented to the Women's Health Research Section of the Midwest Nursing Research Society Synthesis Conference, Indianapolis, IN.

Chick, N. P., & Pybus, M. W. (1988). Policy reform and women's health in New Zealand. *Health Care for Women International, 9,* 125–139.

Coney, S. (1988). *The unfortunate experiment.* New Zealand: Penguin.

Coney, S., & Bunkle, P. (1986). *Metro,* 47–65. (New Zealand).

Doctorow, E. L. (1989). *Billy Bathgate.* New York: Harper & Row.

Gelles, R. J., & Cornell, C. P. (Eds.). (1983). *International perspectives on family violence.* Lexington, KY: D.C. Heath.

Harris, C. C. (1986). The cultural decision-making model: Focus—circumcision. In P. N. Stern (Ed.), *Women health and culture* (pp. 25–43). New York: Hemisphere.

Heise, L. (1989). International dimensions of violence against women. *Response, 12,* 3–11.

Hezekiah, J., & Wafula, F. (1989). Major health problems of women in a Kenyan village. *Health Care for Women International, 10,* 15–25.

Hoff, L. A. (1990, April). *Anthropological perspective—wife battering.* Paper presented to the Women's Health Research Section of the Midwest Nursing Research Society Synthesis Conference, Indianapolis, IN.

Kjervik, D. K. (1990, April). *Legal analysis of domestic violence against women.* Paper presented to the Women's Health Research Section of the Midwest Nursing Research Society Synthesis Conference, Indianapolis, IN.

Krassen-Maxwell, E. Modeling life: The dynamic relationship between elder modelers and their protegees. *Dissertation Abstracts International, 39,* 7531A.

Lehmann, C. (1990). *Bread and roses: Women living in poverty and popular feminist education in Santiago, Chile.* Unpublished Master's thesis, University of Toronto.

Mackey, T. F. (1990, April). *Violence against women: A psychological analysis of trauma and its wake.* Paper presented to the Women's Health Research Section of the Midwest Nursing Research Society Synthesis Conference, Indianapolis, IN.

MacLeod, L. (1989). *Preventing wife battering: Towards a new understanding.* Think-tank report of Canadian Advisory Council on the Status of Women.

Mangay-Maglacas, A. (1988). Health for all: Nursing's role. *Nursing Outlook, 36,* 66–71.

Marrs, C. (1990). Group profiles. *Match News,* Jan/Feb/Mar, 5–6. (Available from MATCH International Centre, 1102–200 Elgin Street, Ottawa, Ontario, K2P 1L5, Canada.)

MATCH International Centre. (1990). *Linking women's global struggles to end violence.* Ottawa: Match International Centre.

McBride, A. B. (1990, April). *Violence against women: Overarching themes and implications for nursing's research agenda.* Paper presented to the Women's Health Research Section of the Midwest Nursing Research Society Synthesis Conference, Indianapolis, IN.

McLean, E. (1987). World agricultural policy and its effects on women's health. *Health Care for Women International, 8,* 231–237.

Molokomme, A. (1986). Botswana: Women and customary law. In M. Schuler (Ed.), *Empowerment and the law.* Washington, DC: OEF International.

Mubichi, F. (1990). *Violence Against Women in the Cultural Context of Kenya.* Unpublished report.

Ngcobo, N. (1990). Violence against women. *Match News,* Jan/Feb/Mar, 3–4. (Available from MATCH International Centre).

Resource Kit. (1990). Ottawa: MATCH International Centre.

Reichert, E. (1991). International conferences on violence against women. *Health Care for Women International, 12*(4).

Sampselle, C., Bernhard, L., Kerr, R., Opie, N., Perley, M. J., & Pitzer, M. (1990, April). *Introduction to conference on violence against women: Implications for the mental health research agenda and clinical practice.* Paper presented to the Women's Health Research Section of the Midwest Nursing Research Society Synthesis Conference, Indianapolis, IN.

Singh, S. L. (1989, September). *Overview of the girl child in Nepal. Report on the national seminar on the girl child.* Nepal.

Stern, P. N. (1990). Horror story. *Health Care for Women International,* 11, v–vii. (Editorial).

UNICEF. (1987). Part four the situation of women. *Children and women of Nepal: A situational analysis.*

Wagner, M. G. (1990). *The birth machine.* (Unpublished manuscript).

Chapter 11

Ethnicity and Woman Abuse in the United States

Evelyn L. Barbee

INTRODUCTION

"You Black bitch, I'll beat the shit out of you!" Those were the words that began my nightmarish experience with a violent encounter on the streets of New York City. Usually a chapter like this begins with an overview of the problem and definition of terms. However, as I thought about my task it occurred to me that a more appropriate way to introduce the subject of ethnicity and woman abuse was to share an experience, that I, as an African-American woman, had with abuse. I chose to share this experience for two reasons. First, I believe that the experience demonstrates the type of abuse to which African-American and other women of color are subjected. Second, the experience is also illustrative of Euro-American attitudes about violence that are directed toward women of color.

When I was a master's student in nursing education at Teachers College, Columbia University, I had an apartment in Greenwich Village. It was a beautiful spring day and a friend called and suggested that I take a break from writing my master's project to meet her for lunch. We decided to meet at the Chock

The author acknowledges Audre Lorde who encouraged her to put her experience in print.

Full O'Nuts restaurant because it was next door to her supermarket job and around the corner from my house. At the appointed time I grabbed my sunglasses, keys, and change purse and ran downstairs to meet her. On the way to the restaurant, I noticed two young White males soliciting food for Biafra outside the supermarket. My friend was late; it was a sunny day, so I decided to wait for her outside. Sixth Avenue is a very busy Greenwich Village street, so I stepped into a doorway in order to change from regular glasses to sunglasses.

While I was changing glasses, a Black male came by and demanded that I give him some money. His clothing was filthy, and he smelled. His eyes were glazed and bloodshot. Perhaps I was irritated because my friend was late. I know that I was tired of strangers asking me for money. So I said, "Do I look like a bank to you?" That is when he snarled, "You Black bitch, I'll beat the shit out of you!" and moved toward me. My first thought was: "He's serious! I've got to get out of this doorway. He can kill me in here." As I moved out of the doorway, I had several thoughts. The first one was of Kitty Genovese, a 28-year-old Euro-American woman who was stabbed to death in a middle-class neighborhood in Queens, New York, in 1964. None of the 38 witnesses to her stabbing called the police until after she was dead (Rosenthal, 1964). And now, here I was a Black woman being assaulted by a Black man on a busy street full of White pedestrians. I knew that I was on my own.

Lest one think that I was exaggerating, let me share another experience. This took place the previous summer on the same street. On this occasion I witnessed an argument between a Black woman and her Black male partner. Across the street, laughing and talking, stood four White New York City police officers. When the couple's argument deteriorated from verbal disagreements to threats of bodily harm, I crossed the street and approached the police officers. I asked if they believed that the police had a role in the prevention of crime. They replied, "Yes." Then I asked why they were ignoring the increasing volatile situation with the couple across the street. I wrote down their badge numbers and said that if the man harmed the woman then at least I had the badge numbers of the police officers who witnessed the crime. Two of them proceeded to go across the street. Given that the police would only intervene in an altercation between an African-American couple when threatened, I felt that I had good reason to believe that the citizenry would offer little or no help to me.

My second thought was that I had to keep this man from hitting me. I recalled the boxing lessons my brothers had given me when I first started working on psychiatric units. So there we were in the middle of Sixth Avenue, people walking by, this stranger throwing hard punches at me, and me circling and blocking them. His inability to hit me had two results. He became more angry and my arms felt like they were going to fall off. Realizing that I could not block any more of his punches, I ran into Chock Full O'Nuts. He tried to come in after me but was unable because I held the door. While I was holding the door, five or six White men came up to enter the restaurant. They became irritated with me and moved away when they saw what was happening.

I looked for a weapon. A quick glance ascertained what I thought before I ran inside: I could not defend myself with sugar packets. So, I let go of the door and he flew backwards. More enraged, he charged toward me. I remember thinking, "What ignominy. I'm going to die in Chock Full O'Nuts!" Fortunately, I was saved by an elderly White woman with a cane. She approached him and said: "If you think you're a man because you can hit a woman, then hit me." The White men who were waiting outside the door suddenly mobilized, and my assaulter ran across the street. She turned to me and said: "You don't know him, do you, dear." I said, "No." She then said, "I didn't think so." I thanked her profusely and walked next door to the supermarket. The two young White men soliciting food for Biafra outside of the supermarket asked me to "Remember the people of Biafra and buy an extra can to donate." I asked them how could they have the nerve to ask me to donate anything to them when they stood there and watched while this man tried to kill me. Their response, "We thought you knew him." I said: "Why? Because we're both Black?"

I recount this story for several reasons. First, it is a concrete example of the factors that affect the risk of violence to ethnic women of color in this country. These factors, racism and sexism, are important aspects that need to be dealt with whenever the subject is violence and African-American women in the United States. Second, my situation is an example of how deeply ingrained racist and sexist attitudes are in this society. Although I was rescued from bodily harm, it is ironic that both action and nonaction were based upon individual perceptions of whether I "knew" my assailant. Quite obviously, for the bulk of people who chose not to respond to my dilemma, I must have known this man because we were both Black and he was attacking me.

In a sense their perceptions more accurately reflect the nature of violence against women because it is usually committed by someone the woman knows. At the same time, there is tacit approval of the violence because she "knows" him. Fortunately for me, a physically vulnerable person, an elderly White woman who walked with a cane, came to my defense because she decided that I did not know my attacker. Later I wondered what would have happened if I had known him and what gave anyone the right to assume it is all right for a woman to be attacked by a man that she knows. Obviously, it was not all right for him to attack my rescuer. Simply put, in this White patriarchal, racist society, it was all right for him (a Black man) to hit me (a Black woman) but wrong for him to strike her (an older White woman). As hate crimes of violence escalate against people because of their race, ethnicity, sexual orientation, gender, or religion, the history of and structural conditions that contribute to violence against "the other" in this society receive less attention. Yet the fact remains that violence against people of color, particularly women, is a historical reality.

ETHNICITY, CULTURE, AND VIOLENCE

Although there are numerous definitions of ethnicity, this chapter uses a social science definition of ethnic group. This definition of ethnicity refers to a cultural orientation or participation that is shared by a large group of people. Included in this cultural orientation are common customs and traditions. The above definition allows us to recognize African-Americans as an ethnic and cultural rather than a racial group. The definition further enables us to recognize the common cultural orientation of Latinas in a way that the term Hispanic does not.

Culture and Violence

A common theory that has been used to explain violence cross-culturally is the "culture of violence." The culture of violence theory is based upon cultural patterning theory (Levinson, 1989). Cultural patterning theory, in turn, incorporates aspects of social learning theory to explain how people learn certain cultural values. The cultural patterning theory suggests that through socialization, either as a member of a violent family or as a member of a violent society, people learn that the use of violence is an appropriate means of achieving goals. In terms of families, socialization into violence underlies research that suggests that victims of child abuse are more likely to become child abusers than nonvictims of child abuse. As applied to families, the culture of violence theory has been challenged by Cazenave and Straus (1979), and Hampton (1987a) who points out that structural/social (poverty, unemployment) and situational (chemical dependency) conditions, rather than cultural values, may influence family violence. Furthermore, recent research on Latinos in California suggests that despite their poverty and deprivation, they do not demonstrate the traits usually found in the violent underclass (Winkler, 1990).

At the societal level, the cultural pattern model underlies those studies that use the cultural spillover hypothesis (Levinson, 1989). The cultural spillover hypothesis points to a positive correlation between a society's endorsement of the use of physical force to meet certain social ends (e.g., crime control, political hegemony) and generalization of force to other areas of social life (e.g., rape, family violence) (Baron & Straus, 1983, cited in Levinson, 1989). Unfortunately discussions of cultural patterning tend to neglect the influence of social structural conditions on violence. Social structure refers to the relationships between individuals and groups within a society. Social structure is maintained because it is governed by laws, rules, norms, and practices. Two structural conditions that are seldom acknowledged in regard to ethnicity and violence in this country are the patriarchy and racism. As a major structural component of this society, the patriarchy has been used to condone violence against women of color.

Although the traditions and customs of ethnic groups of color sometimes come into conflict with those of Euro-American values, for ethnic women of color the importance of the patriarchy is usually revealed in situations of violence. Across the country there are examples of men using culture, custom, and tradition as excuses for perpetrating violence against women. For example, Findlen (1990) reported two cases of violence against Asian women. In the first case, an Asian man in New York City was sentenced to five years probation for bludgeoning his wife to death. In the second a Hmong man was acquitted of kidnapping, sexual assault, and menacing after abducting a 16-year-old girl. The use of an anthropologist in one case and a cultural defense in both cases simply serves to maintain the status quo of the patriarchy because in both cases the men were viewed as following patriarchal customs.

Racism and Image

Violence toward women of color in this country cannot be fully understood without some understanding of the impact of racism and sexism on attitudes toward women of color and violence. The racist and sexist attitudes toward women of color are best found in the images that are developed by White men. The following discussion of racism and image specifically refers to African-American women; however, the process of devaluation is applicable to Latinas, Native American, and Asian women.

Although, woman abuse cuts across racial, ethnic, social, and economic boundaries, the situation of African-American women in this patriarchal society is particularly unique. As Christensen (1988, p. 191) pointed out "No other woman has suffered physical and mental abuse, degradation, and exploitation on North American shores comparable to that experienced by the Black female." The devaluation of African-American women began with the sexual exploitation of these women during slavery and continues today. Many of the historical incidents of sexual abuse of African-American women during and after slavery are discussed in Lerner (1973, Ch. 1, 3). Today as in the past, the treatment of African-American women is based on a racist and sexist ideology.

In pointing out that race, class, and gender oppression depend on powerful ideological justification for their existence, Collins (1990) identifies four externally defined, controlling images that are applied to African-American women. These images are mammy, the faithful, obedient domestic servant; matriarch, the overly aggressive, emasculating, strong, independent, unfeminine woman; the welfare mother, a breeder who produces children for the state to support; and the Jezebel, a sexually aggressive woman. Although each of these images contributes to society's and consequently nursing's view of abused African-American women, this chapter will only deal with the latter three.

The promiscuous stereotype of African-American women serves several functions. Historically and currently, the sexually promiscuous stereotype is used to contrast African-American women with the "virtuous" White women.

Furthermore, the sexually promiscuous stereotype was used by White men as a reason for sexually abusing African-American women (Hooks, 1981). The view of African-American women as sexually promiscuous is also promoted by the scientific literature. Wyatt, Peters, and Guthrie (1988, p. 290) commented that dated research on African-American women's sexuality is used to "place some of the more controversial aspects of the sexual behavior of white women in perspective." The use of research findings in this way underscores Collins' (1990) point that one purpose of defining African-American women as outsiders is that these women can serve as the point from which other groups define their normality.

Further "evidence" of African-American women's "promiscuous" behavior is found in the research on age of coitus. Wyatt et al. (1988) note most sexuality research concludes that African-American women begin coitus at a younger age than Euro-American women. However, using a multiethnic sample of 248 women between 18 and 36 years of age, Wyatt (1989) found that ethnicity was not significantly associated with the strongest predictors of first intercourse. For both groups, the predictors for an older age at first coitus were stronger parental than peer influence during adolescence, and being in love and ready for sex (Wyatt, 1989).

In addition to being portrayed as sexually promiscuous, another predominant image of African-American women is that of matriarch. As Collins (1990) points out, viewing African-American women as matriarchal allows the dominant group in this society to blame these women for the success or failure of their children. Another effect of this image is that it allows "helping" professionals to not recognize when African-American women need assistance. (Whenever I have pointed out to Euro-American nurses that their unquestioned acceptance of African-American women as strong and independent, allows them to ignore that African-American women have feelings, the response has been silence.)

The problem that arises when the White patriarchal image of African-American women as matriarch is accepted without question is well documented by publications like Shahrazad Ali's *Blackman's Guide to Understanding the Blackwoman*. This undocumented polemic blamed the problems of African-Americans on the ethnic group's women. Moreover, it recommended the beating of African-American women (Ali, 1990, p. 169). Unfortunately, the book received the type of publicity usually reserved for a major work. Although negatively reviewed, the publication of such reviews in *Newsweek* (Wilson, 1990) and several other major magazines and newspapers imparted a credibility the book did not deserve.

Equally damaging is the welfare mother image. This is essentially an updated version of the slavery created breeder image (Collins, 1990). As Collins notes, the breeder image allowed slave owners and others to depict African-American women as being more suitable for bearing children than White women. As a result slave owners felt they were justified in interfering with the reproductive rights of enslaved women. Today, welfare mothers are viewed as being too lazy to work and content to sit around and collect their checks. This current objectification of African-American women as welfare mothers serves to label as unnecessary and dangerous to the values of the country the fertility of women who are not Euro-American and middle class (Collins, 1990). The net result of these externally produced, controlling images is that African-American women's bodies are viewed as expendable (Hooks, 1990).

THE ABUSE OF AFRICAN-AMERICAN WOMEN

Homicide

Of all forms of interpersonal violence, homicide has some of the most devastating effects. Homicide is the leading cause of death in African-American women between 15–34 years of age. African-American women have a 1 in 104 chance of being a homicide victim. African-American women are more likely to be killed by their husband/partner during the course of a verbal argument (Bell, 1990). Using 1976–1979 data from the Federal Bureau of Investigation–Uniform Crime Reporting Program (FBI–UCR), Jason, Strauss, and Tyler (1983) found that African-Americans were more involved in acquaintance homicide incidents than stranger incidents.

Wife Abuse

Unlike the homicide statistics of African-American women, the statistics on wife abuse are contradictory. For example, Straus, Gelles, and Steinmetz (1980) in their study of family violence in 2,143 African-American, White, Jewish, and other both spouse present families, found that a greater percentage of African-American wives were abused than any other group. Wife abuse was nearly 400% more common in African-American than White families. On the other hand, Coley and Beckett (1988), in a review of battered women research that included African-American women, suggest that likelihood of greater spousal wife abuse of African-American and other minority women is a myth. In terms of social class, Cazenave and Straus (1979) indicated that wife abuse was less common among middle income African-Americans than middle income Euro-Americans. They also reported two cultural findings that lessened African-American wife abuse: embeddedness in a network of family and friends and the presence of nonnuclear family members in the home.

Sexual Abuse and Assault

In commenting upon the link between the rape of African-American women and the White patriarchy, Carby (1987) noted:

> Rape has always involved patriarchal notions of women being, at best, not entirely unwilling accomplices, if not outwardly inviting a sexual attack. The links between Black women and illicit sexuality consolidated during the antebellum years had powerful ideological consequences for the next 150 years. (p. 39)

An estimated 1 out of 10 sexual assaults is reported to the police. A low report rate combined with the poor police, public, and media response to sexual crimes against women of color make it very difficult to assess the incidence of sexual assault in African-American communities. The recent differential media circuses that surrounded the Tawana Brawley and the "Central Park Jogger" may only serve to decrease African-American women's sexual assault reports.

In November 1987, Tawana Brawley, a 15-year-old African-American girl, reported that she had been kidnapped, held captive for 4 days, and assaulted by six white men. She was found dazed, semi-conscious, and smeared with feces and semen in a trash bag. The words "KKK" and "nigger" were written on her body (Gillespie, 1988). After a series of investigations, a New York grand jury concluded that she had fabricated her report of kidnap and sexual abuse ("Evidence points," 1988). Her name and photograph were printed by newspapers and seen on television.

On April 19, 1989, a 28-year-old Euro-American female investment banker was beaten, sodomized, and raped while jogging in New York City's Central Park ("Youth rape," 1989). Eventually six African-American and Latino boys were indicted and sentenced for this heinous crime. Both the savagery of the attack and the social class of the victim made the crime national news, yet the jogger's name was not revealed by the *New York Times* (Mosedale, 1989; Harrison, 1989).

These two victims were treated very differently by the media. One, the "Central Park jogger," was treated with respect and dignity. The other, a minor, was treated like a criminal.

Child Abuse

Statistics from 1984 demonstrate that of 100,000 substantiated cases of child sexual abuse, 78% involved a girl (Wyatt & Powell, 1988). Frequently reported long-term effects of child sexual abuse "are self-destructive behavior, anxiety, feelings of isolation and stigma, poor self-esteem, difficulty in trusting others, a tendency toward revictimization, substance abuse, sexual maladjustment and psychological problems" (Wyatt & Powell, 1988, pp. 13–14).

Ethnic differences have been found among African-American, Latinos, and White abused children in regard to age of victim, family income, type and severity of abuse, and perpetrator (Hampton, 1987b). In terms of physical abuse, African-American victims who suffered more serious injuries were in the 6–12 age group, resided in urban areas, and had mothers who had not completed high school. Girls had higher rates of physical, sexual, and emotional abuse than boys (Hampton, 1987b). Russell, Schurman, and Trocki (1988) in a comparison study of African-American and White incest victims found that African-American women victims were more likely to report being extremely upset by the abuse and suffered from greater long-term effects. The African-American women also reported that their abuse was at the very severe level (i.e., involving oral, anal, or vaginal intercourse; that the abuse was more likely to be accompanied by force; that their perpetrators were more likely to be middle-aged; and that they were more likely to be abused by their uncles [Russell et al., 1988]).

THE NURSING PROCESS WITH ABUSED AFRICAN-AMERICAN WOMEN

Assessment

The assessment data that are gathered by the nurse in the area of abused African-American women is largely dependent upon where the nurse encounters the women. It has been found that African-American women are more likely to use medical facilities than they are shelters, law enforcement, or human service personnel (Minnesota Department of Corrections, 1982).

Regardless of where the woman is encountered, there are certain general principles that all nurses need to heed. First, the nurse needs to have a strong awareness of how much she/he believes in the myths, beliefs, and stereotypes that surround African-American women. Although most nurses deny holding deleterious beliefs, as members of this society most nurses are prone to the myths and behaviors that contribute to the oppression of African-American women (Christensen, 1988). The consequences of a nurse holding stereotypical beliefs while trying to assist an abused woman of color can be disastrous. For example, in the case of African-American women, if the nurse believes that they are strong matriarchal figures, there may be less sensitivity to the human fragility of the client. On the other hand, the same belief may lead to the inference that the woman did something to "deserve" the abuse. If of the same ethnicity but different social class from the client, the nurse needs to be aware of when and whether these social class differences prejudice data collection.

Most of nursing literature does not deal with woman abuse and ethnicity, therefore, the nurse needs to become familiar with literature that does deal with these subjects. White (1989) contains several chapters that explore African-American women's experiences with and responses to abuse. Two publications that specifically discuss woman abuse among the two largest ethnic groups of color in this country are White (1985) and Zambrano (1985). *Chain, Chain, Change* (White, 1985) is specifically written for abused African-American women. *Mejor Sola Que Mal Accompanada: For the Latina in an Abusive Relationship* (Zambrano, 1985) is a guide for Latinas who are in abusive relationships. Both books use culturally relevant language and situations. Although written for laypersons, these books are valuable references for professionals.

Euro-American nurses also need to become knowledgeable about the different approaches that are being advocated for those who work with African-American clients. One approach that is gaining increased acceptance among African-American professionals is the Afrocentric perspective. *Afrocentrism* is a sociocultural perspective approach advocated by African-American researchers, scholars, and professionals who are concerned with positively influencing the lives of African-American people. Consequently, these researchers argue that the appropriate theoretical approach used with African-American people is one that is based upon their background and experiences. Essentially, those who are concerned with the problems of African-American violence argue that taking on the Euro-American value system with its emphasis on individual autonomy, materialism, and segmentation of all aspects of reality has been detrimental for a people whose cultural roots place importance on the interrelatedness and interdependence of all things (Bell, 1986; Myers, 1987, 1988, 1990).

Ashbury, (1987) uses the Afrocentric perspective to examine specific factors that influence battered African-American women seeking help. The special factors that influence this are:

1   the number of domestic shelters available in African-American communities
2   the amount and nature of the friend and family support system
3   the level of social isolation African-American women may feel in a shelter that is dominated by Euro-Americans
4   reluctance to expose an African-American man as a batterer because of his more vulnerable position in the larger society
5   reluctance to seek help if she has internalized common media stereotypes of African-American women
6   given the lack of African-American men available, she has concern about endangering her relationship.

Since there is a strong association between violence and other forms of abuse, if possible, data on previous abuse should be gathered. Given the importance of family and friends, the strengths of these networks should be assessed. Nurses should understand that African-American women are socialized to *not* share their concerns and problems outside of the family/friend network. The African-American phrase for telling strangers your problems is "Putting your business in the streets." Often this reluctance to discuss family and personal problems is misinterpreted as strength. For example, professional counselors, Bingham and Guinyard (1982) reported most of the African-American women, including the battered ones, that they saw in their practice "seemed to be strong and able to handle their problems" (Bingham & Guinyard, 1982, cited in Coley & Beckett 1988, p. 268). It would appear that Bingham and Guinyard endorse the matriarchal image of African-American women.

Intervention

Often nurses assume because they are not working with abused women that the problem of woman abuse is not their concern. At other times nurses are unsure how to handle a problem that touches so many women. The type of assistance the nurse can offer is dependent upon where the victim of woman abuse is encountered, the type of abuse, and the level at which the nurse chooses to intervene. In terms of African-American woman abuse, there are four levels of intervention: structural, organizational, institutional, and individual.

Interventions at the structural level require that the nurse begin to understand the consequences of the Euro-American patriarchy upon which this society is based. An ongoing assessment of personal attitudes, beliefs, and stereotypes about African-American women will assist the nurse in understanding the role that racism plays in supporting the abuse. Other structural level interventions include becoming familiar with and supporting local, state, and national legislation that deals with woman abuse. Organizational level interventions include supporting women's organizations that focus on the problem of woman abuse and assessing the position of district, state, and national nurses organizations toward it. At the educational level, nursing curricula content in terms of amount and types of material on abuse and African-American women should be monitored.

At the individual level, the appropriate basic intervention strategies that are used for victims of violence should be engaged. Also, some intervention strategies may be more culturally appropriate for African-American women. Culturally appropriate interventions at the individual level should be based upon the recognition that African-American women have been socialized not to talk about their problems; do not usually seek mental health services for their problems; are aware of the poor treatment given to African-American women by law enforcement, media, and health professionals; may be reluctant to prosecute the involved man; and typically value the importance of family and friend networks.

African-American women do not usually seek mental health services; therefore, establishing rapport is especially critical if the nurse decides that mental health referral is necessary. If the nurse has abused African-American women as mental health clients a major role may be to assist the women in making the private public. Regardless of setting, the nurse should assist the women in overcoming their distrust of law enforcement officers and encourage the women to press charges against the male perpetrator. Given the importance of family and friend networks to African-American women, the nurse should endeavor to include concerned family/friends in interventions (e.g., shelter). If the woman is in a shelter, it may be because of weak or nonexistent family/ friend networks. In this case, the intervention would be to assist the women in strengthening or developing networks.

Since most African-American women are more likely to be killed by their husband/partner during the course of a verbal argument, the potential for violence in the home needs to be reduced. Homicide prevention strategies should emphasize exploring alternative means of dispute resolution. In these instances, the nurse needs to work with the woman and her husband/partner or refer them to the appropriate agency.

SUMMARY

This paper explored some of the social and cultural factors that affect the risk of violence for women of color in general and African-American women in particular. Unfortunately, most of the nursing literature does not deal with African-American women in any capacity. Although they may deny it, as members of this society, nurses are just as influenced by the White male stereotypes and negative images of African-American women as any other group. Four levels of intervention strategies and examples of intervention are discussed.

In addition, an approach advocated by African-American professionals, the Afrocentric approach, was explored. Until there are enough African-American nurses to use the Afrocentric approach, Euro-American nurses need to engage in ongoing assessment of how their own attitudes, beliefs, and stereotypes influence their treatment of abused African-American women. However, unless the White patriarchy's externally generated images of these women and the wholesale acceptance of these images by Euro-Americans and some African-Americans changes, violence against African-American women will continue to be supported.

REFERENCES

Ali, S. (1990). Blackman's guide to understanding the blackwoman. Philadelphia: Civilized Publications.

Ashbury, J. (1987). African American women in violent relationships: An exploration of cultural differences. In R. L. Hapton (Ed.), Violence in the Black family (pp. 89–105). Lexington, MA: D.C. Heath.

Baron, L., & Straus, M. A. (1983). Legitimate violence and rape: A test of the cultural spillover theory. Unpublished paper, Family Research Laboratory, University of New Hampshire.

Bell, C. (1986). Impaired Black health professionals: Vulnerablities and treatment approaches. *Journal of the National Medical Association, 78,* 1139–1141.
Bell, C. (1990). Black on Black homicide: The implications for Black community mental health. In D. S. Ruiz, (Ed.), *Handbook of mental health and mental disorder
among Black Americans* (pp. 191–207). New York: Greenwood Press.
Bingham, R. P. & Guinyard, J. (1982, March). *Counseling Black women: Recognizing
social scripts.* Paper presented at the annual meeting of the Southeastern Psycho-
logical Association, Atlanta, GA.
Carby, H. (1987). *Reconstructing womanhood: The emergence of the Afro-American
woman novelist.* New York: Oxford University Press.
Cazenave, N. A., & Straus, M. A. (1979). Race, class network embeddedness and
family violence: A search for potent support systems. *Journal of Comparative
Family Studies, 10,* 281–300.
Christensen, C. P. (1988). Issues in sex therapy with ethnic and racial minority women.
Woman & Therapy, 7, 187–205.
Coley, S. M. & Beckett, J. O. (1988). Black battered women: A review of the empirical
literature. *Journal of Counseling and Development, 66,* 266–70.
Collins, P. H. (1990). *Black feminist thought: Knowledge, consciousness and the politics
of empowerment.* Boston: Unwin Hyman.
Evidence points to deceit by Brawley. (1988, September 27). *New York Times,* pp. A1,
B4–5.
Findlen, B. (1990, September/October). Culture: A refuge for murder. *Ms: The World
of Women,* p. 46.
Gillespie, M. (1988, April). A crime of race *and* sex. *Ms. Magazine,* vol. 16, p. 18.
Hampton, R. (1987a). (Ed.). Family violence and homicides in the Black community:
Are they linked? *Violence in the Black family* (pp. 135–156). Lexington, MA: D.C.
Heath.
Hampton, R. (1987b). (Ed.). Violence against Black children: Current knowledge and
future research needs. *Violence in the Black family* (pp. 3–20). Lexington, MA:
D.C. Heath.
Harrison, B. G. (1989). The jogger: Running for her life. *Madamoiselle,* Vol. 95,
August, p. 122.
Hooks, B. (1981). *Ain't I a woman: Black women and feminism.* Boston: South End
Press.
Hooks, B. (1990, April). *Representing Blackness: The culture marketplace (fashion,
film, and television).* Paper presented at the University of Wisconsin-Madison.
Jason, J., Strauss, L. T., & Tyler, C. W. (1983). A comparison of primary and second-
ary homicides in the United States. *American Journal of Epidemiology, 117,* 309–
319.
Lerner, G. (1973). (Ed.). *Black women in White America: A documentary history.* New
York: Vintage Books.
Levinson, D. (1989). *Family violence in a cross-cultural perspective.* Newbury Park,
CA: Sage Publications.
Minnesota Department of Corrections Program for Battered Women. (1982). *Data Sum-
mary Report.* St. Paul, MN.
Mosedale, L. (1989). The Central Park rape: Has it made us angry? Scared? or Smart?
Glamour, vol. 87, pp. 212–213, 274–275.

Myers, L. J. (1987). The deep structure of culture: Relevance of traditional culture in contemporary life. *Journal of Black Studies, 18,* 72–75.

Myers, L. J. (1988). *Understanding an Afrocentric world view: Introduction to an optimal psychology.* Dubuque, IA: Kendall/Hunt.

Myers, L. J. (1990). Understanding family violence: An Afrocentric analysis based upon optimal theory. In D. S. Ruiz (Ed.), *Handbook of mental health and mental disorder among Black Americans* (pp. 183–189). New York: Greenwood Press.

Rosenthal, A. M. (1964). *Thirty-eight witnesses.* New York: McGraw-Hill.

Russell, D. E. H., Schurman, R. A., & Trocki, K. (1988). The long-term effects of incestuous abuse: A comparison of Afro-American and White victims. In E. Wyatt & G. J. Powell (Eds.), *Lasting effects of child sexual abuse* (pp. 119–134). Newbury Park, CA: Sage Publications.

Straus, M. A., Gelles, R. J., & Steinmetz, S. K. (1980). *Behind closed doors: Violence in American families.* New York: Doubleday.

White, E. (1985). *Chain, chain, change: For Black women dealing with physical and emotional abuse.* Seattle: The Seal Press.

White, E. (1989). (Ed.), *The Black women's health book: Speaking for ourselves.* Seattle: The Seal Press.

Wilson, L. (1990, September 3). This is understanding? *Newsweek,* p. 77.

Winkler, K. J. (1990). Researcher's examination of California's poor Latino population prompts debate over the traditional definitions of underclass. *Chronicle of Higher Education, 6,* A5, A8.

Wolff, Craig. (1989, April 21). Youths rape and beat Central Park jogger. *New York Times,* p. B1.

Wyatt, G. E., & Powell, G. J. (1988). (Eds.), Identifying the lasting effects of child sexual abuse. *Lasting effects of child sexual abuse* (pp. 11–17). Newbury Park, CA: Sage Publications.

Wyatt, G. E., Peters, S. D., & Guthrie, D. (1988). Kinsey revisited, Part II: Comparisons of the sexual socialization and sexual behavior of Black women over 33 years. *Archives of Sexual Behavior, 17,* 289–332.

Wyatt, G. E. (1989). Reexamining factors predicting Afro-American and White women's age at first coitus. *Archives of Sexual Behavior, 18,* 271–298.

Zambrano, M. M. (1985). *Mejor sola que mal acompanada: For the Latina in an abusive relationship.* Seattle: The Seal Press.

Chapter 12

Substance Abuse in Women: Relationship Between Chemical Dependency of Women and Past Reports of Physical and/or Sexual Abuse

Gail B. Ladwig and Marcia D. Andersen

INTRODUCTION

Women who have histories of sexual assault, childhood sexual abuse, and/or incest (both blatant and insidious) are a high-risk group for becoming chemically dependent (Ryan & Popour, 1983). Ryan and Popour indicate that the extent of rape and incest among chemically-dependent women appears highly underrated and in some rehabilitation programs it is as high as 70–90%. Investigators have reported from 28% (Wasnick, Schaffer, & Bencivengo, 1980) to 44% (Benward & Densen-Gerber, 1975) of drug-dependent women having been victims of incest. This contrasts with only 5% of the general population who are victims of incest, according to Benward and Densen-Gerber. Reed, Bischner, and Mondanaro (1982), and Ryan (1979) reported that drug-dependent women experienced a greater incidence of rape and incest than women in the general population.

Wasnick et al. (1980) also report that over one third of women who are chemically dependent report high rates of incest and other forms of sexual and family violence. As there are many factors associated with chemical dependency, this statistically high rate of sexual abuse may be another factor to consider. The possibility exists that chemical dependency and sexual abuse may both be related to other common denominators such as self-perception and/or status of powerlessness.

Although issues of sexuality concern an overwhelming majority of drug-dependent women, treatment programs appear to be unresponsive to these concerns (Reed et al., 1982). Sexuality issues related to intimacy, self-image, and body image are often intertwined in women, especially if there is history of sexual assault or incest (Reed, 1985). Appropriate assessment and intervention requires that the imputed high-risk individual be identified and taught methods other than substance abuse to deal with her past and present stressors (Ryan & Popour, 1983). If indeed those with a history of family violence and sexual abuse go on to become substance abusers, then they need to be identified and appropriate interventions need to be planned.

Purpose

The purpose of this study was to look at the histories of female incarcerated felons who are chemically dependent or who are chemically dependent prior to their conviction. In reviewing the histories, we looked for self-reporting of past family violence and/or sexual abuse. We are not suggesting cause and effect but are reporting on a possible association. A finding of a high association between family violence and/or sexual abuse might lead to the design of more effective intervention programs for this population.

LITERATURE REVIEW

The literature suggests many reasons why people abuse drugs (Segal, 1986). The researchers, while acknowledging many possible causes, focused primarily on studies that described histories of abusive relationships, which may lead to psychological problems associated by some theorists with substance abuse. Gold (1980) emphasized the low self-esteem, conflict, anxiety, and powerlessness experienced by the drug or alcohol abuser. Brown and Cermak (1980) and Mandanaro (1976) suggest that children growing up in abusive environments have psychological problems such as low self-concept, distrust, aggression, anxiety, and unfulfilled dependency needs. The researchers explored studies that deal with abusive relationships and chemical dependency, particularly in the female population.

Incest, Sexual and Family Violence

Investigators report high rates of incest and other forms of sexual and family violence among drug-dependent women (Ray & Popour, 1983). In a study done by Wasnick et al. (1980), out of 50 drug-dependent women, 46% reported being raped. Of these, 70% of rapes occurred prior to drug use. In addition to being victims of incest and rape, many drug-dependent women report being abused and neglected as children (Reed, 1985). Reed proposes that incest and sexual violence may be important etiological factors in chemical dependency.

Boundary Inadequacy

Colgan and Riebel (1981) report a high correlation between boundary inadequacy and alcohol and drug dependence. Coleman and Colgan (1986) examined 340 subjects of whom 122 fell into a category described as alcoholic. In this group of subjects the female alcoholics reported the greatest amount of boundary inadequacy in their families of origin. Boundary inadequacy is also defined as a symptom of intimacy dysfunction that is displayed by invasion of boundaries through the physical abuse of children (Steinmetz & Straus, 1974), and the sexual abuse of children (Finkelhor, 1979b).

Invasion of boundaries (Coleman & Colgan, 1986) involves sexual and physical abuse. Questions used in this study, by Coleman and Colgan (1986), to determine boundary inadequacy included inappropriate expressions of affection, touching of children's genitals by adults in sexual ways, and physical neglect. The questions were framed to elicit frequency. Coleman and Colgan's (1986) study dealt only with alcoholics, as opposed to all types of substance abusers, which is a limitation, but it did show differences between that population and the nonalcoholic population. Alcoholic subjects were more likely to experience boundary inadequacy than nonalcoholic subjects ($F = 11.04$; $p < .001$), and females were also more likely to experience boundary inadequacy than males ($F = 5.11$; $p < .05$) (Coleman & Colgan, 1986).

Specific Concerns of Women

In addition to reviewing the literature for psychological stressors and their association with substance abuse and women, we looked for treatment approaches to meet these needs. Moore (1980) reports that only 3 out of 374 recent studies of alcoholism focused on women. Much of the nursing research that has been done involves investigations of nurses' attitudes toward alcoholics rather than research about the alcoholics themselves (Gurel, 1976; Schmid & Schmid, 1973). Miller (1984) reported on a nationwide survey of prison occupants in 1979. The total number of inmates interviewed as 11,397 (9,142 men and 2,255 women). Whereas results from extensive data analysis had been reported in group form with the U.S. Department of Justice in 1983, little had been mentioned of the 2,255 female inmates. Miller (1984) cross-tabulated the data and found higher proportions of women ever using heroin (36.9%) and using heroin daily (13.7%), compared to men who ever used (29.5%) and were daily heroin users (0.85%). He also described 61 other variables. Until Miller did his study, apparently, only the data concerning the male population had been analyzed. This would lend support to the idea that the specific needs of women and substance abuse are often not addressed, just as they were not addressed in this population.

Women have many unique treatment needs related to areas such as gender, role status, economics, and dependency, but for the purpose of this study we have focused on issues dealing with sexuality. In a study by Wasnick et al. (1980), 36 women discussed their prior drug treatment experiences. Of these women, 86% stated that counselors never addressed issues of sexuality or sexual concerns. Of the 10 women whose agencies had women's groups, only 2 reported that sexuality was discussed. Although issues of sexuality concern an overwhelming majority of drug-dependent women, treatment programs appear to be unresponsive to these concerns (Reed et al., 1982). Sexuality in the broadest terms is related to issues of intimacy, self-image, body image, and in this context, sexual assault or incest.

Smith et al. (1982) studied 130 detox clients (82 men and 48 women) entering the Haight-Ashbury Medical Center in San Francisco and reported that women more often than men noted sexual concerns prior to and during drug use. In a study of 50 female drug clients, 58% of the women experienced sexual problems prior to drug use, and 84% while in treatment (Wasnick et al., 1980).

Assessment Needs

Mondanaro et al. (1982) indicate that a sexual assault history should be part of the intake assessment; and sexual concerns, a part of substance abuse treatment. An attempt at classifying addicts and then developing treatment applications was done by Cohen (1986). Cohen's study used 520 addicted subjects and resulted in nine classifications, which involved 28% females. The total population reported abuse as children at .6 on an abuse scale of 0–2. This survey pointed to the many variables present in the addicted populations and the need for individualized treatment for each individual. It suggests that drug-addiction treatment should be matched to the addicts' needs and motivations. The implication is that a high rate of relapse might be due to the fact that the specific needs of the individual are not being addressed. Perhaps the use of a model that addresses a client's specific needs and motivations would be helpful.

CONCEPTUAL FRAMEWORK

Gold (1980) has developed a theory that emphasizes the low self-esteem of the substance abuser (see Figure 12-1). Substance use is reinforced because it gives the individual a sense of power regarding the area of conflict, thus reducing anxiety. Unfortunately, the substance-using activity itself may create a new source of conflict and contribute to the individual's low self-esteem. Eventually the substance abuse perpetuates the need to continue taking the drug. Using this

Predisposing Factor (Conflict)

Substance Abuse

Low Self-Esteem and
Self-Depreciation   Anxiety
                        Feeling of Powerlessness

Figure 12-1 Model of substance abuse. This is a dynamic process. It occurs within a complex intra-inter ecology/environment, and our current state of empirical knowledge has many gaps about the valid prediction of what facilitates, as well as what inhibits, the initiation into drug use, its continuation, cessation, abstinence following use, or total nonuse in one's lifetime.

model, the predisposing factor could be the abusive behavior inflicted on the client. There may be anxiety associated with abuse and a feeling of powerlessness.

These both predispose to low self-esteem and the substance abuse relieves these feelings. According to Reed (1985), this predisposition probably results from a number of factors such as lower status, self-devaluation, low expectations, and competition for attention.

INTERVENTION MODEL

The researcher has included an intervention model that might be useful in addressing addicts' individual needs and concerns. The literature indicated that often programs were not individualized or based on specific client needs. Personalized nursing is an intervention model based on the Andersen theory of well-being and knowing participation in patterning one's life. Well-being is defined as a person's sense of his or her contentment, health, happiness, and satisfaction with his or her current life (Andersen, 1986). Knowing participation exists when a client perceives she is involved in directing change in her life (Andersen, 1986). Patterning is the form and structure of one's day-to-day existence (Andersen, 1986). Personalized nursing's emphasis is on treating client-identified needs rather than needs identified by the health care provider. The model uses the social network system while focusing on the client's perceived needs in developing self-esteem, well-being, and positive coping skills (Andersen, 1986). Nurses assist clients to identify areas of stress related to health, drug use, and other life spheres. Nurses assist clients in the presence of their social network members to identify options for addressing their concerns directly. Nurses encourage planning and action rather than reaction and they can address physical and mental health problems (Andersen, 1986).

The nurses using this model recognize that any change in a client's life necessitates a change in the client's social network members' lives as well. An in-home social network group approach to treatment is used. This group approach encourages sharing of concerns, developing problem-solving skills, decreasing isolation, exploring new ideas, and improving relationships with others. Planned positive change can be supported by all members of the group (Andersen, 1986). The woman and her social network members identify a main concern in the presence of the group as related to substance abuse or the woman's reentry into the community (Andersen, 1986).

Personalized nursing uses an acronym to explain its concepts. The acronym is LIGHT:

Personalized nurses:

Love their clients.
Intend to heal.
Give nursing care gently.
Help their clients improve their sense of well-being (Andersen, 1986).
Teach a healing process to their clients.
"Dream it the way you want it, then do it."

Personalized nursing clients:

Love themselves.
Identify an immediate concern.
Give themselves a goal.
Have confidence.
Take action to improve their well-being (Andersen, 1986).

The use of personalized nursing as an intervention model could be effective in reducing the anxiety and powerlessness of victims of sexual and family violence. This would be particularly effective if an association between sexual and family violence and substance abuse is established.

The nurse values/loves the client, empowering the client to love himself or herself. The client can then make changes in his or her life.

RESEARCH DESIGN AND METHODOLOGY

This study was designed as a nonexperimental correlational descriptive survey that examined the history of physical and/or sexual abuse in a group of chemically dependent female felons.

Research Questions

1 What percentage of women in this sample report sexual abuse?
2 What percentage of women in this sample report sexual or physical abuse prior to entrance into prison?

3 What are the major concerns in life for the women in this sample? Are sexual and/or physical abuse among their major concerns?

4 What major life events occurring during initiation to drug use are reported by the women in this sample? Did these events include physical or sexual abuse?

Definition of Terms

Sexual abuse: Subjects reported "yes" when asked if they had been sexually abused.

Physical abuse: Subjects reported "yes" when asked if they had been physically abused prior to entrance into prison.

Major concerns in life: Major concerns (e.g., prison release, housing, etc.) in life that were identified by women in the sample.

Life events during initiation to drug use: Life events (e.g., peer pressure, personal pressures) during initiation to drug use that were identified by women in the sample.

METHOD

Setting and Sample

Data were obtained from Andersen's 1986 pilot study on drug-dependent women, which was funded by the Michigan Department of Corrections (MDC) and Wayne State University (WSU). The purpose of Andersen's research was to test the use of the personalized nursing LIGHT treatment intervention model with drug-dependent women who were in prison. The subjects for Andersen's study, selected as a nonrandom convenience sample, were drug-dependent women, incarcerated in the Michigan Corrections System. They all gave a history of substance abuse to psychologists during a prison entrance assessment. The experimental group consisted of substance-abuse offenders residing in medium and minimum security facilities. The women volunteered to participate in the treatment program and signed an informed consent. Women who participated in the treatment program expected to be released into the Detroit area.

The questionnaires of both the treatment group and nontreatment group were analyzed. The total sample for this project and Andersen's project consisted of 118 subjects.

These subjects were pretested using the Addiction Seventy Index (ASI) (McClellan, Luborsky, Woody, & O'Brien, 1980). The concepts of abuse were subjective in that no clear definitions of these phenomena were given to the clients.

Instruments

Data that ascertained drug use were based on subjects' self-report. During the study the Addiction Severity Index (ASI) was modified and clients were asked to recall their alcohol/drug use 30 days prior to incarceration. While it is recognized that this may be affected by a client's recall and may not be accurate, it provided a baseline for the study. Women could not be expected to answer truthfully about current drug use in prison because of potential punishment, so data from the 30-day period prior to prison entrance were gathered.

Data regarding sexual and/or physical abuse were taken from the pretest and close-ended questions asking "Have you ever been physically abused?" and "Were you sexually or physically abused prior to entrance into prison?" The second question is of particular significance in looking at a correlation between substance abuse and a *prior* history of physical and/or sexual abuse. Other information that will be analyzed were the open-ended questions "What are the major concerns in your life?" and "What events were occurring in your life when you first used drugs?" These responses were open coded according to a coding system that assigned specific numbers to specific responses so that the data could be entered into the computer. All responses were analyzed for relevance to this project.

RESULTS

Sexual Abuse

The final sample consisted of 118 subjects. The first question analyzed for this study was "Have you ever been sexually abused?" A total of 91 responses were recorded. Twenty-seven of the 118 subjects in the sample had responses reported as missing.

Table 12-1 gives data for the total responses, missing and those actually recorded. Nearly 20% responded "yes," they had been sexually abused.

Sexual or Physical Abuse Prior to Prison

The second question analyzed was "Were you sexually or physically abused prior to entrance in prison?"

This question contained a total of 112 responses, with only 6 of the subjects having data missing. This question asks for *prior* history of both physical and/or sexual abuse *prior* to prison entrance. The percentage of "yes" responses is higher than the question that just asks for information regarding history of sexual abuse. These data are not conclusive as to whether or not the addition of physical abuse made the response rate higher. Asking if the abuse was prior to prison may have had some influence on the subjects' response. Table 12-2 lists

Table 12-1 "Have You Ever Been Sexually Abused?"

Response	N	%
Yes	18	19.7
No	73	80
Missing	27	—
Total	118	

the results. Twenty-seven percent reported "yes," they had been sexually or physically abused prior to entrance in prison.

Major Concerns in Life

The subjects were asked to identify their major concerns in life. Sexual abuse and/or physical abuse were not identified as major concerns, as can be seen in Table 12-3, which lists all the major concerns identified and their percentage of responses.

The area of major concern for these subjects was prison release (36.5%). Family and children were also identified as major concerns (30.5%). This information would be worthy of further study.

Life Events During Initiation to Drug Use

The subjects were asked to identify the major events that were occurring in their lives during initiation into drug use. None of the respondents clearly identified sexual or physical abuse as major events. The closest they came to these were family problems, 6.8%, and personal pressures, 9.3%.

The highest percentages of respondents identified curiosity (35.6%) and friends/peer pressure (28.8%).

Table 12-4 includes all areas identified by subjects and the percentages.

Table 12-2 "Were You Sexually or Physically Abused Prior to Entrance into Prison?"

Response	N	%
Yes	30	27
No	82	73
Missing	6	—
Total	118	

Table 12-3   Major Concerns in Life

Response	N	%
Prison release	43	36.5
Employment/unemployment	15	12.7
Education	3	2.5
Housing	3	2.5
Health	3	2.5
Family/children	36	30.5
Become drug-free	7	6.0
Church/religion	1	0.8
Other	5	4.2
Missing	2	1.8
Total	118	100.0

Background Characteristics

Table 12-5 lists background characteristics of the sample group: age, race, when substances first used, type of substance first used, person who first initiated subject into using, and if subject ever had been in a treatment program before. These results might be useful in planning further research.

DISCUSSION

All 118 of the women in the final sample gave a history of substance abuse to psychologists during a prison entrance assessment. Of the 118 women tested, 19.7% reported histories of sexual abuse and 27% reported sexual or physical abuse prior to prison.

Table 12-4   Life Events During Initiation to Drug Use

Response	N	%
None	2	1.7
Partying	12	10.2
Friends/peer pressure	34	28.8
Family members doing it	3	2.5
Angry	2	1.7
Curiosity	42	35.6
Family problems	8	6.8
Personal pressures	11	9.3
Make me feel better	2	1.7
Missing	2	1.7
Total	118	100.0

The percentage of reported sexual abuse, 19.7%, may be important in providing nursing service to clients who are drug dependent. It suggests, along with Mondanaro et al. (1982), that a sexual assault history should be part of the intake assessment and sexual concerns a part of treatment.

The response of friends/peer pressure being a life event occurring during initiation to drug use, 28.8%, would substantiate the need for intervention within the client's social network and indicates the need for a model that would use the social network.

Andersen's LIGHT model employs the social network and was used with the clients in this study. The staff consisted of nurses who were trained in use of the model and trained in group therapy.

Table 12-5   Background Characteristics

Characteristic	n	Characteristic	n
Age at time of study (n = 118)		First drug used (n = 118)	
19	4	Alcohol	40
24	12	Heroin	23
29	47	Codeine	1
39	11	Darvon	1
44	6	Blues	1
49	1	Dilaudid	2
Missing	6	Percodan	1
Race (n = 118)		Valium	1
Black	90	Cocaine	3
White	22	Amphetamines	4
Missing	6	Marijuana	37
Age first used (n = 118)		Hallucin	1
1	1	Other	1
6	1	Missing	1
10	1	Person initiating use (n = 118)	
11	2	Sister	5
12	4	Uncle	1
13	15	Sister-in-law	1
14	13	Girlfriend	3
17	14	Brother	3
18	14	Friend	73
19	7	Brother-in-law	1
20	3	Relative	2
21	6	Cousin	6
22	1	Self	4
23	2	Boyfriend	10
24	2	Missing	9
25	1	Previous drug treatment (n = 118)	
29	1	Yes	79
30	1	No	36
Missing	2	Missing	3

The treatment program consisted of two components. The first component was a series of group discussions that met twice weekly for 10 weeks and were led by a nurse experienced in the use of the treatment model. The second component involved four home visits by a nurse over a period of 4 weeks.

During the intake interview, each client was asked to identify her focal concerns and to develop short- and long-term goals related to these concerns. The client's perceptions of individual situations and concerns is considered to be the beginning point for the LIGHT treatment process. Together the nurse and client developed a goal and a personalized plan of action for the client to use in resolving concerns.

Criteria for assessing reasonable treatment outcomes for both success and failure were selected using the ASI. This assessed seven areas of functioning often found to be impaired in drug-dependent individuals: drug use, alcohol use, medical status, legal status, psychiatric status, employment/support status, and family/social relationships (McLellan et al., 1980).

This index was used before and after treatment.

Limitations of the Study

The researchers had to use data already collected. This did not allow the opportunity to structure questions to specifically address the issues of sexual abuse, incest, and/or physical abuse recently or as children.

Recommendations for Further Research

While this study does not suggest causal relationships, it does suggest possible directions for further research.

Recommendations for further research to be considered are compare female substance abusers with a control group of female nonsubstance abusers, compare substance abuse between incarcerated females and nonincarcerated females who abuse substances, and when studying both of those groups, use a sexual assessment tool that has been tested for reliability and validity. Wasnick et al. (1980) used a sexual history questionnaire in its study. The questionnaire included 27 questions that would elicit very specific responses regarding sexual abuse, concern, and desire for help. It also asked questions regarding drug use and sex.

The review of literature suggests that there is an association between sexual and/or physical abuse and substance abuse. This study also shows an association between the two. Nurses are in an excellent position to be alert for and to identify women with these concerns. After nurses have been adequately trained they can assist women in helping to develop alternative coping mechanisms for their identified stressors.

CLINICAL RECOMMENDATIONS

Practicing nurses are encouraged to incorporate and expand upon the brief questions used in this study in all their nursing assessments. Questions such as the following might be asked:

1 Have you ever been sexually or physically abused? (Prompts: Recently? As a child?)

2 Are you currently being sexually or physically abused?

3 Do you feel safe in your current relationships?

Nurses could also use an indepth assessment instrument such as the Indicators of Potential or Actual Violence in a Family Assessment Tool (Campbell, 1984). This tool assists the nurse to assess a number of parameters of family functioning for at-risk responses.

Nurses working with substance-abusing women who are at high risk for physical and sexual abuse should educate themselves in coping strategies found to be effective for addressing violent situations. Nurses should assume any woman they treat is a potential abused woman. While no special formal educational preparation is necessary to sensitize nurses to problems of substance abuse and violence, continuing education courses addressing areas of interest for the nurse are advised.

Nurses need to become proficient in ways of empowering women to recognize the meaning of experiences, acknowledging the experiences in the present moment, avoiding denial of feelings, and moving beyond them into a world of safety, love, and LIGHT.

REFERENCES

Andersen, M. D. (1986). Personalized nursing: An effective intervention model with drug dependent women in an emergency room. *International Journal of Addictions, 21,* 105–122.

Benward, J., & Densen-Gerber, J. (1975). Incest as a causative factor in antisocial behavior: An exploratory study. *Contemporary Drug Problems, 4,* 324–340.

Brown, S., & Cermak, T. (1980). Group therapy with the adult children of alcoholics [Newsletter]. California Society for the Treatment of Alcoholism and Other Drug Dependencies, No. 1, p. 7.

Campbell, J. (1984). Nursing care & family violence. In J. Campbell & J. Humphreys (Eds.), *Nursing care of victims of family violence* (pp. 216–245). Reston, VA: Reston Publishing Co.

Cohen, A. (1986). A psychosocial typology of drug addicts and implications for treatment. *International Journal of the Addictions, 21,* 148.

Coleman, E., & Colgan, P. (1986). Boundary inadequacy in drug dependent families. *Journal of Psychoactive Drugs, 18,* 22–26.

Colgan, P., & Riebel, J. (1981). *Sexuality education for foster parents,* Vol. 1. Minneapolis: Foster Care Program, School of Social Work, University of Minnesota.

Finkelhor, D. (1979a). *Sexual abuse.* New York: Free Press.

Finkelhor, D. (1979b). The traumatic impact of child sexual abuse: A conceptualization. *American Journal of Orthopsychiatry, 55,* 530–541.

Gold, S. R. (1980). The CAP control theory of drug abuse. In Letter, P. J., Sayers, M., & Pearson, H. W. (Eds), *Theories on drug abuse: Selected contemporary prospectives,* Monograph of the NIDA, *30.* Rockville, MD: National Institute on Drug Abuse.

Gurel, M. (1976). An alcoholism training program: Its effect on trainees and faculty. *Nursing Research, 25,* 127–132.

McLellan, A. T., Luborsky, L., Woody, G. E, & O'Brien, C. P. (1980). An improved evaluation instrument for substance abuse patients. *Journal of Nervous and Mental Disease, 168,* 26–33.

Miller, R. (1984). Nationwide profile of female inmate substance involvement. *Journal of Psychoactive Drugs, 16,* 319–326.

Mondanaro, J., Wedenoja, M., Densen-Gerber, J., Elahi, J., Mason, M., & Redmond, A. (1982). Sexuality and fear of intimacy as barriers to recovery for drug dependent women. In B. Reed, G. Bescober, & J. Mondanaro (Eds.), *Treatment services for drug dependent women,* vol. II. (DHHS Publication No. ADM 82-1219.) Washington, DC: U.S. Government Printing Office.

Mondanaro, J. (1976). Mothers and methadone—Echoes of failure. *Journal of Addictions, 2,* 23.

Moore, C. (1980). Women and health. *United States public health.* (United States Public Health Report supplement September–October 1, 1984).

Reed, B. (1985). Drug misuse and dependency in women: The meaning and implications of being considered a special population or minority group. *International Journal of the Addictions, 20,* 13–62.

Reed, B., Bischner, G., & Mondanaro, J. (1982). *Treatment services for drug dependent women* (pp. 303–304). Rockville, MD: U.S. Department of Health and Human Services.

Ryan, V. (1979). *Differences between males and females in drug treatment programs.* Ann Arbor, MI: Women's Drug Research Project, University of Michigan.

Ryan, V., & Popour, J. (1983). *Five year woman's plan.* Developed by the Capital Area Substance Abuse Commission, for the Office of Substance Abuse (OSAS), Michigan Department of Health, IV, 4c, IV, 12c.

Schmid, N. J., & Schmid, D. T. (1973). Nursing students' attitudes toward alcoholics. *Nursing Research, 22,* 246–248.

Segal, B. (1986). Confirmity analysis of reasons for experiencing psychoactive drugs during adolescence. *International Journal of the Addictions, 18,* 22–26.

Smith, D. E., Moser, C., Wesson, D., Apter, M., Buxton, M., Davison, J., Orgel, M., & Buffum, J. (1982). A clinical guide to the diagnosis and treatment of heroin related sexual dysfunction. *Journal of Psychoactive Drugs, 14,* 1–2.

Steinmetz, S. K., & Straus, M. (Eds.). (1974). *Violence in the family.* New York: Harper & Row.

Wasnick, C., Schaffer, B., & Bencivengo, M. (1980, September). *The sex histories of fifty female drug clients.* Paper presented at the National Alcohol and Drug Coalition, Washington, DC.

Chapter 13

The Wake of Trauma: Long-Term Outcomes and Treatment Issues

Theresa F. Mackey

INTRODUCTION

This chapter examines some of the long-term outcomes of violence against girls and women, and considers treatment issues relevant to nursing practice. A variety of clinical issues are addressed such as the emergence and working through of previously repressed memories of childhood trauma, repeat victimization or "reenactment," severity of the stressor, and societal processes that promote and sanction violence against women. Since this chapter builds on and is an extension of Chapter 4, "A Model for Analysis of Outcomes Related to Trauma," it is assumed that the reader is familiar with that content as a conceptual base to the material that follows.

Violence in Childhood

Justice and Justice (1979) assert that prolonged experiences of incest have more serious repercussions than rape. They cite issues to be resolved in therapy, including betrayal of trust by an adult perceived to be a protector, a sense of helplessness with an absence of any or adequate social support, guilt from having been involved in the relationship, and chronic stress symptoms. As Herman (1981) noted, the betrayal of trust in childhood because of incest complicates intervention efforts:

> The major obstacles to forming a good working alliance are the same problems that often lead the patient to seek help in the first place: her feelings of shame and hopelessness and her fear of betrayal in intimate relationships. (p. 189)

Since the experience of abuse includes having had one's realities destroyed by people whom the victim trusted (Reiker & Carmen, 1986), the survivor does not know whom she can trust to help her restructure reality and a new belief system. This mistrust of those who should be trustworthy, including the therapist, is a central issue in treatment.

This issue is compounded when, in adulthood, in an effort to heal, the survivor takes a risk in trusting others and that trust is once again betrayed. There is legitimate reason for the survivor's persisting mistrust, as one outcome of this childhood trauma is vulnerability to revictimization in what has been described as the *sitting duck syndrome* (Kluft, 1990). Repeat or multiple experiences of betrayed trust are common and may occur with any number of people including family members, friends, associates or colleagues, and those in positions of power such as clergy, attorneys, employers, and health professionals (Rutter, 1989). The betrayed trust retraumatizes the survivor and challenges her preexisting impaired coping resources.

The broken trust generally includes an *accurate* perception of the woman having been abused or taken advantage of; a repeated experience of having her reality disconfirmed, including true feelings dismissed or minimized; her perceived social support destroyed; and, in some cases, suicide. Revictimization exacerbates treatment issues including loss and grieving; disturbances of the "self"; impaired cognitive functioning and information processing; emotional and social isolation; alienation from others; perceptions of the world as malevolent and meaningless; aloneness and loneliness; low self-esteem and low self-worth; and overwhelming feelings of helplessness, rage, and fear. The victim often displays disrupted task performance including workaholic coping responses; chronic depression; and, symptoms of a posttraumatic stress disorder with intrusive memories of both the childhood and adult events, and an increase in avoidance coping strategies (e.g., Burgess & Hartman, 1986; Hartman & Burgess, 1988; Kluft, 1989b; Pope & Bouhoutsos, 1986; Rieker & Carmen, 1986; Rutter, 1989).

In Chapter 4 of this book, Deb's account of the destruction wrought upon her life by childhood sexual abuse is painfully clear to adult survivors who struggle to stay alive amidst a world that is experienced as untrustworthy, rejecting, and hostile (see Chapter 4; Summit, 1984).

Consider then the major obstacles faced by a therapist trying to bring to the surface suppressed and repressed memories of sexual trauma and work these through, a process considered integral to the resolution of a posttraumatic stress disorder. Generally, these memories emerge only when safety in the victim-therapist relationship is established, and then these memories surface one at a time, like layers peeling from an onion. Throughout, the therapist facilitates the victim's control of the process. In discussing the recovery and verification of memories of childhood sexual trauma, Herman and Schatzow (1987) described two case examples, the first illustrating recovery of a memory, and the second illustrating recovery of repressed memories as well as verification of the memory:

Doris is a 37-year-old housewife and mother of four children. She sought treatment because of panic attacks during sexual intercourse with her husband . . . . She had always feared and disliked sex, but in the previous 2 years her anxiety had become so intolerable that the couple had ceased sexual relations altogether. Doris was extremely ashamed of this failure of what she considered her marital obligation and feared her husband might leave her in spite of his assurances to the contrary. A couples therapist, suspecting sexual abuse, referred her to group [therapy].

In group, Doris initially reported almost complete amnesia for her childhood. She spoke little until the 6th session, when she began to moan, whimper, and wring her hands. In a childlike voice she cried, "The door is opening! The door is opening!" She was instructed to tell her memories to go away and not come back until she was ready to have them. This she did, first in a whisper, and then in a loud voice. Her anxiety then subsided to bearable levels.

In the three weeks following this session, Doris was flooded with memories which included being raped by her father and being forced to service a group of her father's friends while he watched. The sexual abuse began at about the age of 6 and continued until the age of 12, when she was impregnated by her father and taken to an underground abortionist. During the time that she was retrieving memories, Doris required several emergency psychotherapy sessions and antianxiety medications. At the end of this period, her panic subsided and she experienced considerable relief. At 6-months follow-up, she reported feeling better about herself and was able to tolerate more intimacy with her husband. (p. 9)

Claudia is a 30-year-old, single, emergency room nurse. Although she has been highly successful in her career, she has been socially isolated for as long as she can remember, a fact she always attributed to her severe obesity. Three years prior to entering group therapy, Claudia was hospitalized in a controlled environment for weight reduction, losing over 100 lbs. When her weight fell below 200 lbs., she began to have intrusive flashback memories of sexual abuse by her brother, who is 10 years older than she.

In group, she recounted for the first time vivid memories of being handcuffed, burned with cigarettes, forced to perform fellatio, and having objects introduced into her rectum and vagina. She had especially clear memories of the wallpaper in the room. Reconstructing from this and other details, she estimated that she was 4 years old when the abuse began. The abuse could not have continued past the age of 7, since at that time her brother left home to enlist in the military.

Prior to the group session in which she planned to tell her story, Claudia became extremely agitated. She was unable to sleep and could not tolerate being alone in her apartment at night. For several days she did not return home after work, but spent the night at the hospital. She expressed the fear that when she told her story she would become her 4-year-old self and would not be able to return to adult functioning. During the narration she did indeed appear age-regressed: She trembled, sobbed, and spoke in a high, child-like voice. At the end of the narration, however, she was able to accept comfort from other group members and resume her ordinary adult persona. Following this session, she reported being able for the first time in many years to sleep at home in her bed without a night-light. (p. 8)

Verification by others of a memory of childhood sexual abuse is not required to establish that sexual abuse has occurred; however, some victims wish to obtain such verification. The verification process can be both a powerful strategy in trauma resolution, and it can also severely retraumatize the victim. Thus, clinical judgment indicates that a survivor's efforts at verifying these memories should be carried out within the context of therapy. A variety of methods can be used to verify memories of a childhood trauma such as corroboration of the history by the perpetrator admitting it, the testimony of other family members, and/or physical evidence (Herman & Schatzow, 1987). In the case of Claudia, the following occurred:

After a heroic military career, Claudia's brother was killed in combat in Vietnam. Her parents continued to make pilgrimages to his grave, and had transformed their home into a shrine dedicated this memory. His room, with all his belongings, had been left untouched. During a visit to her parents home, Claudia conducted a search of her brother's room. In a closet she found an extensive pornography collection, handcuffs, and a diary in which he planned and recorded his sexual "experiments" with his sister in minute detail. (p. 10)

Clinical research continues to investigate whether the severity of the stressor is associated with severity of the trauma outcome. For example, is the outcome significantly different between the victim who is burned with cigarettes during sexual violence and the victim who is gang raped by her father's friends? Is "just being fondled" less severe than sexual penetration? Herman and Schatzow (1987) found repression to be more severe when associated with onset at an early age, a long duration of sexual abuse (e.g., it began in early childhood, usually in preschool years, and ended during adolescence), and, violent and sadistic sexual abuse, a finding also cited in diagnoses of multiple personality disorders (Kluft, 1984a; Kluft, Baun, & Sachs, 1984b; Putnam, 1984, 1989).

Since working through memories of childhood trauma is so distressing, and for some results in decompensation, a combination of enhancing, supportive, and reconstructive approaches such as art therapy, dance therapy, visualization, the use of metaphors, and hypnotherapeutic interventions are helpful in the treatment process. Grove (1990a), for example, using information processing theories, stresses how the trauma is registered as a metaphor such as pain in the stomach, like a rock, or like a knife. He uses the client's metaphors as clues to connect with the internal experience, an experience that may not be registered as details, and teaches the client to restructure the experience or metaphor so that the internal experience becomes changed and releases knots of anger, guilt, and shame. The method of "healing by (content-free) metaphors" is one approach that helps clients heal childhood trauma while limiting experiences that retraumatize them in the process (Grove, 1990b).

Krystal and Zweben (1988, 1989) describe visualization techniques, derived from Jungian principles, that are useful in facilitating a client's regulation of emotions during treatment and in the processing of emotions such as fear, anger, and guilt. Kluft (1983) describes the use of hypnotherapeutic interventions as helpful to persons with multiple personality, and notes that adverse reactions are rare when treatment precautions are followed. Hypnotic techniques can assist the client in regulating the amount of distress endured commensurate with her resources and capacity to achieve self-efficacy and mastery. These techniques offer the client a sense of active collaboration and reduced sense of helplessness. They provide temporary respite by bypassing time, affect, and/or memory; attenuate affect and/or memory retrieval; provide sanctuary; and, permit distancing maneuvers (Kluft, 1989b).

VIOLENCE IN ADOLESCENCE AND ADULTHOOD

Domestic Violence

The fact that childhood trauma is associated with vulnerability to revictimization and psychiatric morbidity is observed in the phenomena of domestic violence and marital rape (Carmen, 1984; Finkelhor & Yilo, 1985; Weingourt, 1990). Carmen (1984) noted that, for numerous cases of women, childhood physical and sexual abuse was followed by rape and physical abuse by spouses and others in adulthood, yet a relative lack of attention has been given to this factor in psychiatric histories. The finding of increased vulnerability for revictimization is also reported by Herman in a study of incest victims (1981), and by Hilberman in a study of battered women (1980). Hilberman found higher levels of self-destructive behavior, including self-mutilation, suicidal behavior, a pervasive sense of helplessness, and lower levels of self-esteem among an outpatient sample of battered women as compared to a nonclinical sample.

Other studies (Dobash & Dobash, 1979; Green, 1978; Stark, Flitcraft, & Frazier, 1979) also report severe self-destructive behaviors among women as a sequelae to childhood victimization. In addition, domestic violence is a frequent finding in the records of psychiatrically hospitalized patients. For example, Post et al. (1980) found 48% of a sample of 60 adult inpatients to have a history of battering, and Weingourt (1985, 1990) notes that battered women may present for psychiatric treatment with symptoms of anxiety and major depression yet their battering history as a contributing factor may not be assessed.

For some theorists, revictimization (the combined history of childhood trauma and domestic violence) is conceptualized as a *reenactment*, a term not to be confused with masochism or sadism. The concept of reenactment originates from cognitive and information processing theories, and object-relations theory, which depict revictimization as associated with an earlier trauma that is denied; representing an attempt to master a prior unresolved trauma; and, having physiologic correlates (e.g., Hartman & Burgess, 1988; Krystal, 1982, 1985, 1990). Revictimization is not only a symptom of a preexisting unresolved trauma, it is also conceptualized as a socialized process and outcome. For example, Reiker and Carmen (1986) described the victim-to-patient process in which childhood trauma, dysfunctional family relationships, and life contexts (e.g., social inequality, the socialization of women) interact. The combined effect of these factors is a fragmented identity, and persistent doubts about one's own reality. This is derived from having been socialized to accommodate or "buy into" the judgments of others, particularly about "self" and the abuse. Mellody, Miller, and Miller (1989) describe the same phenomena. Reiker and Carmen (1986) noted that the most profound and prominent disconfirmations of the victim's reality, her true feelings connected to the abuse, and the meaning of her abuse include:

> It didn't happen; it happened but it wasn't important and has no consequences; it happened, but s(he) provoked it; it happened but it's not abusive." (p. 363)

Thus, the socialization processes for women and those associated with growing up in a dysfunctional family, including growing up in domestic violence and substance abusing families, places women at high risk. It sets them up as socially-sanctioned legitimate targets of domestic violence. Moreover, as a result of having attitudes and beliefs that blame the victim, society and mental health professionals historically have abandoned these "masochistic" battered women (Carmen, Russo, & Miller, 1981), further denying their reality and declaring the women's allegations are false or the violence was invited with comments such as "it couldn't be true," she is "simply wrong," she "must like it or she'd leave," she "must have done something to deserve it," she "made her bed, now let her lie in it." These and a litany of other mythologies persist, despite refutation by research.

For example, in a recent Michigan court case Macomb County Circuit Judge Deneweth gave a battered woman 5 years of probation and scolded her for stabbing her husband to death as the husband tried to strangle her. The judge told the defendant, "If you had an ounce of common sense in your head at all, you should have known what you were getting into. You put yourself in that position" (*The Ann Arbor News, 1990*).

Some writers have suggested this historical abandonment by professionals may be an attempt to avoid their own personal abuse histories, and their own unresolved pain that impairs their ability to respond to victims (i.e., the countertransference phenomenon). Commenting on this historical abandonment of battered women by health professionals, Carmen, Russo, and Miller (1981) note:

> . . . services for female victims of male aggression have largely been provided largely through the coordinated efforts of women themselves at a time when mental health professionals were often either blaming the victims or not noticing them.

Societal processes that initiate domestic violence are often perpetuated by negligent health care systems. So, like the child victim who turns to the paternal object believed to be protective and is betrayed, the battered woman is betrayed by the health care system when it fails to even identify her victimization. For example, using an emergency service to survey 481 women, Stark, Flitcraft, and Frazier (1979) found that "medicine's role in battering suggests that the services function to reconstitute the 'private' world of patriarchal authority, with violence if necessary, against demands to socialize the labors of love." The authors found the number of battered women that used the service was 10 times higher than what medical personnel identified. The authors identified a "staging process" that occurred before the battering was identified, and ended in consequences that reinforced the helplessness and hopelessness of these women. Some were sent back to the batterers, but medicated for their "symptoms" so that they would carry out their role functions as parents, housekeepers, and sexual partners. A few women were sent back to be murdered or to murder their partners and be criminally incarcerated. Others were tranquilized so that behaviors not consistent with sex-role stereotypes would abate, or they were given referrals that were "no choice" options.

In describing the double standard for mental health, derived from sex-role stereotyping that fosters adjustment to one's pathological environment, Broverman, Broverman, and Clarkson (1970) concluded that:

> For a woman to be healthy, from an adjustment viewpoint, she must adjust to and accept the behavioral norms of her sex, even though these behaviors are generally less socially desirable and considered to be less healthy than the generalized competent mature adult. (p. 6)

This position has been supported based on an analysis of a decade of gender research (Deaux, 1984). Deaux noted the need for a conceptual shift in gender research, one that considers the influence of interaction between gender (man or woman) and environment on subsequent choices. She found validity in the conceptualization that when society casts stereotypical images, those gender stereotypical expectancies are carried out (Skrypnek & Snyder, 1982).

Therefore, it is not surprising that the treatment received by the battered woman reflects gender stereotypes, and the interaction of both the provider's and the patient's gender with the social context of the health care system. This was described by Stark, Flitcraft, and Frasier (1979) who found that at first physical injuries were medically treated. However, when the patient's injuries persistently repeated, the failure to cure led the health care provider to label the patient (note the label now—the person, not society and its institutions) as personally responsible for her victimization.

Secondary problems deriving from the battering such as depression, substance abuse, and suicide attempts were treated as primary problems to be ameliorated so that the family could be kept together. The authors note that the political and economic constraints under which medicine operates in its care of battered women is an extension of societal patriarchy.

Many battered women present with a complaint of depression. Not only is depression more common in women than men, but these gender differences also cannot sufficiently be explained by biological, endocrinologic, and genetic factors (Weissman & Klerman, 1987). Rather, the powerlessness and societal alienation experienced by battered women (combined with social inequality that effectively prevents them from leaving a relationship) are more accurate explanations of the depression these women suffer. It is also consistent with epidemiologic data that links social inequality with depression among women.

Not all battered women have a history of childhood trauma. The absence of such a history would be expected to result in greater resources available to the woman in processing a battering experience, and in terminating a battering relationship. The phenomena of domestic violence experienced by women who have not had a history of childhood trauma, and violence between women who are partners are areas in need of further research.

Marital or Partner Rape

Marital rape is one expression of domestic violence. Many people believe marital rape is a contradiction in terms but it is a very prevalent reality that is, in some states, open to charges as a criminal act (Griffin, 1990; Russell, 1982; Finkelhor & Yilo, 1985). Finkelhor and Yilo (1985) aptly referred to the marriage license as a "license to rape." Contrary to popular and sanitized notions of marital rape as romantic, as in Gone With the Wind, most marital rapes are a frightening and brutal expression of the partner's rage. Finkelhor and Yilo found most marital rapes to center around themes common to rape in general: degradation, humiliation, power, anger, and resentment. The rape is one more extension of the depreciation and abuse sustained by a woman who is already denigrated in sexual terms such as "tramp" or "whore," or ridiculed for character flaws by being called "stupid" or "dumb bitch." It includes compliance with sex in the interest of survival due to threats of violence (Finkelhor & Yilo, 1985; Frieze, 1983). Most people, health professionals included, do not want to hear the "dirty" or "terrorizing" details of the violence that leaves these women physically disabled and psychologically traumatized for a long time, sometimes for the rest of their life. Finkelhor and Yilo (1985) share their pain with us in a few case examples:

- One had a six-centimeter gash ripped in her vagina by a husband who was trying to "pull her vagina out."
- One was raped at knifepoint by her estranged partner.
- One was forced to have sex with her estranged husband in order to see her baby, whom he had kidnapped (p. 18).

Immediate responses to the brutality are similar to those experienced by other rape victims, particularly acquaintance rape victims, and include anger, betrayal, humiliation, and guilt. Responses of anger, hatred, and a desire for revenge were found to be most common.

He threw himself on me like a dog. . . . He knew what he was doing. It wasn't that he lost his passion. . . . I would have killed him if I could have. I hated and despised him. Nothing he did later could make up for that. (p. 119)

Nausea and vomiting, symptoms common to rape trauma syndrome (Burgess, 1983), may accompany common feelings of being defiled, degraded, and used, and may also be associated with behavioral compliance in the interest of survival.

I felt like a two-bit French whore. What I was engaged in was nothing but prostitution. I was buying another hour of peace and quiet—that was all it was. (Finkelhor & Yilo, 1985, p. 120)

Contrary to popular myths that battered women and wives are sexually aroused by masochistic fantasies and acts of sexual violence, sexual arousal and orgasm in the midst of pain during marital rape is no different than other rapes (Burgess, 1983). Involuntary sexual response is a source of confusion and guilt for all victims, and prompts feelings of betrayal by one's body.

He would force me down on the bed and pin my arms. Then he would do things to me. Sometimes I responded. I felt betrayed by my own body when I did respond. Then he would act so proud of himself. I hated me at those times. It was like nothing belonged to me, not even my own body. (Weingourt, 1990, pp. 146–147)

The central defining issue in rape, *nonconsent,* defines marital rape. A society that sanctions marital rape, and continues to look for ways to blame and impose guilt on the victim, is evidencing societal regression (Bowen, 1976).

Long-term effects from marital rape are severe and enduring. These include sexual dysfunctions (e.g., reduced desire for sex with one's spouse or partner, a dislike of sex, inability to engage in sex without anxiety, and flashbacks to the rape during intercourse); disrupted ability to trust men, confusion about men and intimacy; a generalized increase of negative feelings toward men; social withdrawal from men; negative attitudes and feelings about one's self; a strong sense of helplessness; not wanting to be alone due to fear of the assailant's return; and a wide range of psychiatric disorders (Bart, 1975; Finkelhor & Yilo, 1985; Russell, 1982; Weingourt, 1990). Because of the entrapment sustained, the victim's responses are similar to those of hostages (Hillman, 1981). These responses common among marital rape victims include nightmares; fear of the assailant even when he is no longer present; self-blame and guilt from being compliant, even though compliance was necessary for survival; and, believing there is no escape, dependence on the assailant for survival.

Children and marital rape. Finkelhor and Yilo (1985) found one fourth of the abused women had been raped in the presence of their children. Witnessing the terrorizing rape of one's mother is just one more way children are victims of violence. The witnessing of violence induces a posttraumatic stress disorder in some children. Aborting children who are conceived as a result of marital rape has, in recent history, been common. Being forced to carry an unwanted child to term is a daily and long-term reminder of the terrorizing entrapment of the rape itself, and of the violence in the relationship. Today in America we are challenging the constitutionality of abortion laws that control the destiny of women's bodies and lives, and the destiny of children conceived by and reared amidst violence against women and children.

RAPE

Rape and sexual exploitation are types of sexualized violence that involve a range of criminal acts (e.g., from fondling to penetration), a range of force or coercion (e.g., from physical violence to intimidation and unethical professional practice), and nonconsent issues (e.g., mental incapacity). The following presents findings related to both types.

The magnitude of rape as a social problem becomes increasingly clear when the prevalence of rape is compared with other social concerns. Kilpatrick, Veronen, and Best (1985) noted that in 1980 there were more rape victims in the United States than combat veterans.

In discussing treatment issues a critical question is: What factors influence the fact that for some victims, and not others, trauma-specific symptoms persist for years and effectively destroy the quality of their life? While this section primarily addresses research results in the field, much is lost when only aggregate data are examined. It is all too easy to distance ourselves from the pain and suffering of victims and examine only aggregate data. Before presenting the results of research in the field, two questions are explored in relation to victim self-reports: when is rape, rape? and, does the severity of the stressor influence the severity and duration of postevent symptoms?

When is Rape, Rape?

For some victims it is years before they acknowledge that they were raped. One might ask whether rape is a crime defined by the woman, by legal criteria, or both. In each of the following cases the woman defined herself as having been raped; however, some may not agree with her definition and thus not provide rape-specific treatment. Consider the following situations:

Case 1: Joyce is a 25-year-old woman who recently divorced her husband due to his psychological battering and cruelty toward her and their two children. After working a series of jobs cleaning homes and waitressing, Joyce obtained a job selling vacuum cleaners. She thought this job offered better employment and benefits. For several weeks Joyce's supervisor personally provided her with field training. He then called Joyce one evening and told her to come to the office to sign some papers or she would not receive her commission. Wanting to keep her job, she went to the office even though it was after hours and other employees were gone. Once at the office the supervisor locked the door behind her and shouted at her, "Give me some oral sex." Joyce was so afraid of him that she did not scream or fight him off, but complied. The supervisor claimed Joyce consented to his sexual advances. Was Joyce raped?

Case 2: At age 36 Dawn became pregnant with her second child. After a long, nonproductive labor her physician said a cesarean section (c-section) was necessary and Dawn felt she had "no choice." In the delivery room she told the *female* physician, to no avail, that the spinal block was ineffective, that she was not anesthetized, and not to proceed, yet the physician proceeded with the c-section. In describing this experience Dawn said, "I can't think of anything more sexually assaultive than to be so helpless, and have your sexual organs and body assaulted during labor and delivery!" Was Dawn raped?

Does Severity of the Stressor Affect Outcome?

There are times when, after hearing a victim describe the trauma sustained, it seems like the worst case scenario until the clinician listens to another victim recount another abhorrent rape. The severity of the stressor is considered by some to be a variable that influences unresolved trauma. But how, precisely, does the victim, or researcher as observer, define and measure *severity* and *stressor*? These terms are not uniformly operationalized in research studies. Further, what is severe to one person may not be severe to another. Severity may include, for example, weapons and violence, hostage entrapment, degradation, witnessing the rape of significant others, numbing or "freezing" with inability to defend one's self, and meaning of the event to the victim. Consider the following case examples:

Case 1: Mrs. M. and her daughter Julie took on a part-time job delivering newspapers to help the family income while the husband/father was laid off work. They completed a "morning run" in the dark of night and loaded up newspaper machines outside shopping malls. At one of their work sites a gang of three young men pulled up behind their truck and caught them off guard. Mrs. M. reports that she was thrown onto the flatbed of the truck and raped by one of the men; her daughter, Julie, was thrown on to the gravel street and raped by another man. Mrs. M. was restrained and pinned down by one of the rapists with a weapon and physical force while they raped her daughter. During this time she heard her 16-year-old daughter's voice regress to age 3 as she cried out repeatedly, "Mommy, help me! Mommy, help me!" Mrs. M. said, "I couldn't do a damn thing to help her or stop it." Mrs. M. can barely talk through her sobbing tears as she shares her pain. Does severity of the stressor affect outcome?

Case 2: Audrey is a 27-year-old woman who is currently enlisted in the marines. Before entering the service she served on her local police force where she taught rape prevention and self-defense in the community. While in the marines she enrolled in course work and decided to study for an examine off-base where it would be quieter. As she exited her car a gang of youths kidnapped her, blindfolded her, and took her into the wilderness where they raped her for several hours. She reports that "when they were done with me they gasolined my body and talked about setting me on fire. I thought I was dead for sure. My life swept before me. But, I played dead and they left me in the wilderness presuming I was dead. It took me hours to find my way out of the wilderness to safety." Does severity of the stressor affect outcome?

Case 3: Linda is a 35-year-old, divorced woman with one child. She and her ex-husband (Dan, a police officer) were in the process of trying to reconcile their former marriage and decided to spend the evening together at a motel. They were awakened in the middle of the night with a man standing at the bedside. He threatened to kill Linda unless Dan did as he was instructed. The man took Dan to the bathroom where he tied him up with a sheet. He then returned to the motel room where he repeatedly raped Linda, and after several hours departed. The couple are certain that the only access to the room had to be via a master key as they had locked the door. Postevent problems included Dan sustaining ridicule from his colleagues on the police force for not defending Linda by attacking the assailant. Does severity of the stressor affect outcome?

Outcomes of Rape Trauma: Mixed Results

Early descriptive research in the field depicted profiles of response to a rape in terms of a rape trauma syndrome (Burgess & Holmstrom, 1974), while more recent research has focused on the response pattern as consistent with a post-traumatic stress disorder (Burgess, 1983). Research in the field continues to investigate what factors are associated with poorer adjustment postevent over time; however, the findings reflect inconsistent outcomes when the following variables are examined:

Victim characteristics. McCahill, Meyer, and Fishman (1979) found age of the victim to be significant. Adult victims had more adjustment difficulties postevent than adolescent or child victims. They also found employment status related to adjustment difficulties, with less distress experienced by unemployed victims. Morelli (1981) found no significant relationship between race and recovery rates for Black and White women. However, Ruch and Chandler (1983) found ethnicity and marital status significant factors with marriage and non-Caucasian race being predictive of the most postevent trauma. McCahill, Meyer, and Fischman (1979) found married women living with their husbands to report the most postevent adjustment difficulties. Kilpatrick, Vernon, and Best (1985) found no significant association between any demographic factors and the distress level (low vs. high) reported by victims. Similarly, Mackey, Sereika, Weissfeld, and Hacker (1991) found no significant association between demographics and depression of among victims years postevent.

Preevent history. Preevent factors reported to be associated significantly with poorer adjustment following a rape include some form of prior or current psychiatric history, and having received psychotropic medication in the past or currently (Frank, Turner, Stewart, Jacobs, & West, 1982; Frank & Anderson, 1987); a history of prerape adjustment problems (McCahill et al., 1979); pre-rape problems with anxiety, depression, or physical health (Atkeson, Calhoun, Resick, & Ellis, 1982); substance abuse; suicidal ideation; and, prior sexual victimization (Becker, Skinner, Abel, & Treacy, 1982; Becker, Skinner, Abel, & Cichon, 1986; Burgess, 1983; Burgess & Holmstrom, 1974, 1979b). However, in predicting factors associated with psychological distress postevent Kilpatrick, Veronen, and Best (1985) found no significant association between personal preevent history (including psychological difficulties) and the distress level (low vs. high) of victims. Mackey, Sereika, Weissfeld, and Hacker (1991) found no significant association between any personal preevent factor among victims who were experiencing depression years postevent.

Intervening stressful life events. Ruch, Chandler, and Harter (1980) found a curvilinear relationship between stressful life events and rape impact, with victims reporting moderate life changes having less postevent difficulties than those with no changes or many changes. In predicting psychological distress postevent, Kilpatrick, Best, et al. (1985) found that victims in low distress tended to have had less life changes in the year prior to the rape (e.g., such as death of a close family member other than a spouse), and were also more likely to have a loving, intimate relationships with men. Mackey, Sereika, Weissfeld, and Hacker (1991) found no significant association between stressful life events one year prior to assessment of victims and their report of depression years postevent.

Rape situation variables. Contrary to the popular notion that severity of stressor influences the outcome, characteristics of the rape situation generally have not been found to be associated with poorer adjustment postevent (Winfield, George, Swartz, & Blazer, 1987). This finding is consistent across a number of studies (Atkeson et al., 1982; Mackey, Sereika, Weissfeld, and Hacker, 1991; Kilpatrick, Best, et al., 1985; McCahill et al., 1979; Ruch & Chandler, 1983). However, other researchers found fear of physical injury and of being killed during the rape associated with a posttraumatic stress disorder 15 years postevent (Kilpatrick, Saunders, et al., 1987). Some researchers have found that if the perpetrator is an acquaintance, the victim reports more affective disturbances postevent and is likely to evidence a posttraumatic stress disorder (Ross-Durow, 1989; Stewart et al., 1987).

Acute reactions to rape. Most rape research has focused on victim response patterns that occur within 1 month to 1 year postevent, as opposed to long-term outcomes. The reader is referred to an extensive review of these studies in other resources (e.g., Ellis, 1983; Holmes & Lawrence, 1983). By way of overview, during the immediate aftermath following a rape, victims experience high levels of anxiety, fear, and depression. These symptoms decrease in intensity over time and at a variable rate among these women.

While symptoms are reduced significantly for some women at three months, for others symptoms persist for a longer period of time. Acute trauma-induced symptoms that have a propensity to persist include anxiety and rape-specific fears; avoidance behaviors, including avoidance of therapy; intrusive memories of the event; nightmares; loss of self-esteem; depression, suicide ideation and attempts; disturbances in relatedness; impaired task performance and social adjustment; physiologic hyperarousal and somatic disturbances such as temporal mandibular joint pain, sciatic nerve and lower back pain, and headaches; sexual dysfunctions; aggressive and antisocial behavior; substance abuse; and, eating disorders.

Recently more attention has been given to substance abuse and eating disorders as outcomes associated with unresolved rape trauma and childhood trauma (e.g., Carter, Prentky, & Burgess, 1988; Hall, Tice, Beresford, & Wooley, 1989; Lindberg & Disted, 1985; Rohsenow, Corbett, & Devine, 1988; Root & Fallon, 1988). Substance abuse is not only a coping strategy postevent, it is a method of coping used by some victims to live through an experience of sexual abuse, rape, or prostitution and may predict sexual victimization among both children and adults (e.g., Burnam, Stein, Golding, & Seigel, 1988; Covington & Kohen, 1984; Curtis, 1986; Herman, 1986; Jehu, Gazan, & Klassen, 1984–1985; Silbert, Pines, & Lynch, 1982).

Long-term responses to rape. Four areas of follow-up assessment on the long-term adjustment of victims are generally reported: social support as a mediator of stress, including disturbances in relatedness; sexual dysfunctions; affective disturbances; and, a posttraumatic stress disorder.

Social support and disturbances in relatedness. Early studies noted that when social support was perceived by the victim as helpful it appeared to facilitate the recovery process, and these women coped better with the assault than women who were alone (Ruch & Hennesey, 1982; Ruch & Chandler, 1983). Popiel and Susskind (1985) found that a girlfriend who provided reassurance was the most helpful person in the support network. However, while the most stressed victims received the most support, the amount of overall support did not predict subsequent adjustment, nor did support act as a mediator to weaken the correlation between stress and adjustment. Ruch and Chandler (1983) found that victims who were living independently viewed their family as less supportive than women living with parents. Ellis (1983) noted it was common for social support networks to experience severe strain postevent, or to collapse completely. In the absence of support many victims left home, college, work, and friends, and they became isolated and distressed. Atkeson et al. (1982) assessed victims at intervals over one year postevent, and found that the level of depression was significantly higher among those with limited social support as compared to victims with greater social support and nonvictims. Similarly, Ipema (1979) found that victims unable to express their pain, grief, and fear were, by three months postevent, more depressed, fearful, isolated, and unable to resume preevent routines than victims who were able to share their trauma. Burgess and Holmstrom (1979a) found that victims who felt they had not recovered four to six years postevent reported no strong social ties, social drifting, isolation from family and friends, and no stable partner relationship. Several studies have found that greater adjustment problems are experienced by victims who are married and live with husbands, as compared to victims in other living situations, due to reaction of the husbands to the rape and how the victim perceives the reaction (McCahill et al., 1979; Ruch & Chandler, 1983). Sales, Baum, and Shore (1984) found that victims lacking positive family relationships experienced a persistence of more symptoms, and a greater severity in the symptom level, than victims with positive family relationships. Relationship disturbances with parents postevent are common as outcomes associated with rape trauma, as are problems in sexual and marital adjustment with partners, and severed relationships by separation, divorce, or emotional cut-off. (An extensive review of studies on family responses to rape was done by Foley [1985].) Thus, the victim is not only isolated during the assault, she is also often without support postevent in resolving this life crisis, unable to disclose and share the meaning of this trauma with persons identified as "significant," and may have her entire network effectively destroyed in the wake of the trauma.

Sexual dysfunction. Sexual dysfunction postevent is a trauma response noted to endure for years among victim samples, and the dysfunction occurs in all categories of this disorder (desire, arousal, and orgasmic functioning). The most immediate response to sexual trauma is avoidance of and abstinence from sexual intimacy, and for many victims these responses remain active. Sexual dysfunctions are particularly common if the victim also reports a history of childhood sexual abuse, and in cases where the perpetrator is known (Becker, Skinner, Abel, & Treacy, 1982; Becker, Skinner, Abel, & Cichon, 1986; Mackey, Hacker, Weissfeld, Ambrose, Fisher, & Zobel, 1991; Ross-Durow, 1989). At follow-up 4 to 6 years postevent, 30% of victims (n = 81) did not consider themselves to be recovered sexually (Burgess & Holmstrom, 1979b).

Unresolved sexual trauma included reports of changes in sexual frequency, flashbacks to the rape, vaginismus, sexual aversion particularly to acts forced during the rape, orgasmic dysfunction, and physical pain or discomfort upon resuming sexual relations. Sexual behaviors ranging from a reluctance to initiate sexual activity to increased sexual activity and indiscriminate sexual behavior were also noted. In general, the more symptoms of sexual trauma experienced by the victim, the more protracted and unresolved she reported her recovery from the rape.

Feldman-Summers, Gordon, and Meagher (1979) found victims reported lower rates of sexual satisfaction postevent, as compared to a matched control group, even though the groups did not differ with regard to the frequency of sexual activity or orgasm. Areas unaffected by the rape included affectional and autoerotic behaviors, i.e., behaviors not commonly forced upon victims during a rape. Becker et al. (1982) found 56% of a victim sample (n = 83) to report sexual dysfunction postevent, with 71% of the participants identifying the sexual assault as the precipitant to the dysfunction. Areas most commonly affected included fear of sex, desire dysfunction, and arousal dysfunction while dyspareunia and anorgasmia were less commonly reported, and no subject reported vaginismus. Victims with a history of incest more frequently reported primary and secondary anorgasmia. The authors noted that the passage of time did *not* appear to heal the effects of sexual trauma from either the rape or incestuous assaults.

In a subsequent study assessing the long-term effects of rape on sexual functioning, Becker, Skinner, Abel, and Cichon (1984b) found inhibition of sexual response, including fear of sex and desire and arousal dysfunctions, to be most common. The chronicity of assault-induced sexual dysfunctions postevent was one of their most impressive findings with 60% of the sample reporting these more than 3 years postevent. In a follow-up report utilizing data from the same sample, victims reported these dysfunctions as persisting as long as 40 years. A number of researchers have found long-term symptoms of depression, coinciding with a reduced capacity for interaction, to be associated with rape-induced sexual dysfunctions suggesting that depression is the pathway by which sexual trauma is expressed. However, while many clinicians implement treatment for depressive symptoms (e.g., cognitive restructuring) they often fail to assess for the presence of unresolved sexual trauma or institute treatment specific to the sexual violence (Becker et al. 1984a; Frank & Anderson, 1987; Mackey, Hacker, Weissfeld 1991; Nadelson, Notman, Zackson, & Gornick, 1982; Resick, Calhoun, Atkeson, & Ellis, 1981; Sales et al., 1984; Santiago, McCall-Perez, Gorcey, & Beigel, 1985; Sutherland & Scherl, 1970).

Finally, little attention has been given to the effects of sexual trauma on women who are not sexually active postevent. Mackey, Hacker, and Sogren (1991) found that victims who were not sexually active with a partner postevent were significantly more depressed, as measured by the Beck Depression Inventory, as compared to victims who were sexually active. Among these victims theme analysis revealed a higher frequency of concerns related to mistrust; avoidance of sex; the need for control; fears of emotional and physical closeness, AIDS and sexually transmitted diseases, pain, and pregnancy; and a lack of pleasure in anticipating sexual intimacy. The findings indicate the need for further research regarding the sexual trauma sustained by women who are raped, and interventions specific to assault-induced sexual dysfunctions postevent.

Affective disturbances. Chronic depression as a response to rape has been suggested by Kilpatrick, Veronen, and Best (1985). In their efforts to identify factors predicting psychological adjustment among rape victims, the authors found the symptom level of women at 3 months remained relatively stable over 4 years, and more of the variance between high versus low distress groups was predicted by the single mood score of depression. Hence, they challenge the notion of stage or phase theories of trauma resolution as they found no period without significant symptom patterns.

Several researchers found selected variables related to a protracted depression postevent. Stewart et al. (1987) found that if the perpetrator was an acquaintance then the victim was more likely to delay seeking immediate treatment (median = 7.5 months); and, the victim reported significant levels of depression, anxiety, fear, impaired self-esteem, and social adjustment. Santiago et al. (1985) found the only rape situation variable related to a higher degree of depression and anxiety years postevent was whether the victim had survived a prior sexual assault. Mackey, Sereika, Weissfeld, and Hacker (1991) found higher levels of depression among a sample of rape victims associated with nondisclosure about the rape due to fears of stigma. The authors concluded that, despite years of rape-myth educational programs, the societal socialization of women regarding rape mythology persists and impairs their sharing the traumatic event with significant others. Finally, Kilpatrick, Best, and Veronen (1985) found attempted and completed rape, and attempted molestation (defined as unwanted sexual advances other than oral, anal, or vaginal penetration) to be positively associated with suicide ideation and attempts, and nervous breakdown (self-defined). They also found that the majority of these problems emerged after the victimization experience. Postevent nearly one in five victims attempted suicide, and when compared to their preevent rate victims were four times more likely to attempt suicide postevent. This postevent rate for suicide attempts by victims was 8.7 times higher than that of nonvictims.

In a retrospective sample of randomly surveyed women, Kilpatrick, Veronen, Saunders, Best, Amick-McMullen, and Paduhovich (1987) found that women who had been raped years previously were more likely to be depressed than nonvictimized women. Of the sample, 46% of those who experienced one rape and 80% of those who experienced two rapes met the criteria for a major depressive disorder at some time during their lifetime.

These data clearly indicate the severity of rape as a traumatic event, and graphically depict the wake of the trauma. At this time it is unclear whether depressive symptoms are concurrent with a posttraumatic stress disorder (PTSD) or are secondary to PTSD and other anxiety disorders, and whether some victims develop depressive symptoms but not PTSD.

Posttraumatic stress disorder. Whereas early research focused on rape-related anxiety and fears, the decade of the 1980s began to focus specifically on rape-related PTSD through descriptive reports (e.g., Burgess, 1983; Foley & Grimes, 1987) and research. In a recent report Foa (1990) found 95% of women they assessed postrape met criteria for PTSD at one week postevent, and 50% of these women still met PTSD criteria at three months postevent. Kilpatrick, Saunders et al. 1987; and Kilpatrick, Veronen et al., 1987 found that among a random sample ($n = 391$) of women in the community, over 50% had been sexually assaulted and nearly 25% had experienced more than one rape. In the crime survey, mean time since a criminal event was 22 years, while mean time since experiencing a rape was 29.7 years. Lifetime and current crime-related symptoms of PTSD were highest for victims of completed rape; however, many victims of completed molestation (defined as unwanted sexual advances other than penetration, oral or anal sex) also developed or were experiencing PTSD symptoms. Among rape victims in the sample 60% met the criteria for having had PTSD at some time in their life, while 16% of single-incident victims and 20% of two-incident victims currently met the criteria for PTSD. PTSD among rape victims was highly associated with the victim fearing for her life and believing she would be physically injured. Consistent with earlier findings, PTSD was not associated with demographic data such as age, race, income, or education. Current research and treatment are focusing on the psychobiology of trauma (e.g., Hartman & Burgess, 1988; Giller, 1990; Krystal, 1990; Vanderkolk, 1985).

CONCLUSION

The expectation of many people is that victims resolve or adjust to the abuse and violence they have sustained, and indeed many do. As predominantly female health care providers, to facilitate trauma resolution nurses need to dialogue openly about case data. This is an initial step in processing their own "trauma" by hearing about the suffering of other women. Too often nurses work in emotional isolation from each other and keep an intellectual distance from the pain of what clients share about their victimization experiences. To release the sadness of self that working with this violence stirs in the soul is to release creativity and energy toward helping victims of violence.

Several measures need to be developed within health care agencies if women are to receive the level of care that is needed:

1 There is clearly a need for skilled clinicians to help victims recover repressed memories so that these can be cognitively and affectively processed, and integrated into the self.

2 Institutional changes to ensure case identification and explicit trauma specific treatment plans are essential, and should be tied to accreditation requirements.

3 Continuing education should be provided on response to and treatment of physical and sexual trauma. Continuing education on victimology also should be linked with certification and license renewal.

4 Prevention and treatment of violence in in-patient settings should be mandated as a requirement in every treatment facility and nursing school curriculum.

Health care and educational systems with these advances in place would be much better equipped to provide the intervention women require in order to become survivors.

REFERENCES

Ann Arbor News (1990). Woman get lecture from judge on abuse. June 25, 1990, p. 10.

Atkeson, B., Calhoun, K. S., Resick, P. A., & Ellis, E. (1982). Victims of rape: Repeated assessment of depressive symptoms. *Journal of Consulting and Clinical Psychology, 50,* 96–102.

Bart, P. (1975). Rape doesn't end with a kiss. *Viva, 2,* 39–42, 100–101.

Becker, J., Skinner, L., Abel, G., Axelrod, R., & Treacy, E. (1984a). Depressive symptoms associated with sexual assault. *Journal of Sex & Marital Therapy, 10,* 185–192.

Becker, J., Skinner, L., Abel, G., & Cichon, J. (1984b). Sexual problems of sexual assault survivors. *Women & Health, 9,* 5–19.

Becker, J., Skinner, L., Abel, G., & Cichon, J. (1986). Level of post-assault sexual functioning in rape and incest victims. *Archives of Sexual Behavior, 15,* 37–49.

Becker, J., Skinner, L., Abel, G., & Treacy, E. (1982). Incidence and types of sexual dysfunctions in rape and incest victims. *Journal of Sex & Marital Therapy, 8,* 65–74.

Bowen, M. (1976). *Family therapy in clinical practice.* New York: Jason Aronson.

Broverman, I., Broverman, D., & Clarkson, F. (1970). Sex-role stereotypes and clinical judgments of mental health. *Journal of Consulting & Clinical Psychology, 34,* 1–7.

Burgess, A. W. (1983). Rape trauma syndrome. *Behavioral Sciences & the Law, 1,* 97–112.

Burgess, A. W., & Hartman, C. (1986). *Sexual exploitation of patients by health professionals.* New York: Praeger.

Burgess, A. W., & Holmstrom, L. L. (1974). Rape trauma syndrome. *American Journal of Psychiatry, 133,* 413–418.

Burgess, A. W., & Holmstrom, L. L. (1979a). Adaptive strategies and recovery from rape. *American Journal of Psychiatry, 136,* 1278–1282.

Burgess, A. W., & Holmstrom, L. L. (1979b). Rape: Sexual disruption and recovery. *American Journal of Orthopsychiatry, 49,* 648–657.

Burnam, M. A., Stein, J. A., Golding, J. M., & Seigel, J. M. (1988). Sexual assault and mental disorders in a community population. *Journal of Consulting & Clinical Psychology, 56,* 843–850.

Carter, D., Prentky, R., & Burgess, A. W. (1988). Victim response strategies in sexual assault. In A. W. Burgess (Ed.), *Rape and sexual assault, II.* New York: Garland.

Carmen, E. (H.) (1984). Victims of violence and psychiatric illness. *American Journal of Psychiatry, 141,* 378–383.

Carmen, E. (H.), Russo, N., & Miller, J. (1981). Inequality and women's mental health: An overview. *American Journal of Psychiatry, 138,* 1319–1330.

Covington, S., & Kohen, J. (1984). Women, alcohol, and sexuality. *Advances in Alcohol & Substance Abuse, 4,* 41–56.

Curtis, J. (1986). Factors in sexual abuse of children. *Psychological Reports 58*(2), 591–597.

Deaux, K. (1984). From individual differences to social categories: Analysis of a decade's research on gender. *American Psychologist, 39,* 105–116.

Dobash, R. P., & Dobash, R. E. (1979). *Violence against wives: A case against the patriarchy.* New York: Free Press.

Ellis, E. (1983). A review of empirical rape research: Victim reactions and response to treatment. *Clinical Psychology Review, 3,* 375–490.

Feldman-Summers, S., Gordon, P. E., & Meagher, J. R. (1979). The impact of rape on sexual satisfaction. *Journal of Abnormal Psychology, 88,* 101–105.

Finkelhor, D., & Yilo, K. (1985). *License to rape: Sexual abuse of wives.* New York: Holt, Rinehart & Winston.

Foa, E. (1990, March). *The development of post-traumatic stress disorder and its treatment in rape victims.* Paper presented at XXII Banff International Conference, Alberta, Canada.

Foley, T. (1985). Family response to rape. In Burgess, A. W. (Ed.), *Rape and sexual assault: A research handbook* (pp. 159–188). New York: Plenum.

Foley, T., & Grimes, B. (1987). Nursing intervention with sexual assault and rape victims. In G. Stuart & S. Sundeen (Eds.), *Principles and practice of psychiatric nursing* (pp. 971–1010). St. Louis: C. V. Mosby.

Frank, E., & Anderson, P. A. (1987). Psychiatric disorders in rape victims: Past history and current symptomatology. *Comprehensive Psychiatry, 28,* 77–82.

Frank, E., Turner, S. M., Stewart, B. D., Jacobs, L., & West, D. (1981). Past psychiatric symptoms and the response to sexual assault. *Comprehensive Psychiatry, 22,* 479–487.

Frieze, I. H. (1983). Investigating the causes and consequences of marital rape. *Journal of Women in Culture and Society, 8,* 532–553.

Giller, E. (Ed.). 1990. Biological assessment and treatment of post-traumatic stress disorder. Washington, DC: American Psychiatric Press.

Green, A. (1978). Self-destructive behavior in battered children. *American Journal of Psychiatry, 135,* 579–582.

Griffin, M. (1990). In 44 states, it's legal to rape your wife. *British Journal of Law and Society, 9,* 21–23.

Grove, D. (1990a). *Metaphors to heal by.* Edwardsville, IL: David Grove Seminars.

Grove, D. (1990b). *Healing the wounded child within.* Edwardsville, IL: David Grove Seminars.

Hall, R. C., Tice, L., Beresford, T. P., & Wooley, B. (1989). Sexual abuse in patients with anorexia nervosa and bulimia. *Psychosomatics, 30,* 73–79.

Hartman, C. R., & Burgess, A. W. (1988). Information processing of trauma: Case application of a model. *Journal of Interpersonal Violence, 3,* 443–457.

Herman, J. (1981). *Father-daughter incest.* Cambridge, MA: Harvard Press.

Herman, J. L. (1986). Histories of violence in an outpatient population: An exploratory study. *American Journal of Orthopsychiatry, 56,* 137–141.

Herman, J. L., & Schatzow, E. (1987). Recovery and verification of memories of childhood sexual trauma. *Psychoanalytic Psychology, 4,* 1–14.

Hilberman, E. (1980). Overview: The "wife-beater's wife" reconsidered. *American Journal of Psychiatry, 137,* 1336–1347.

Hillman, R. (1981). Psychopathology of being held hostage. *American Journal of Psychiatry, 138,* 1193–1197.

Holmes, M. R., & Lawrence, J. S. (1983). Treatment of rape induced trauma: Proposed behavioral conceptualization and review of the literature. *Clinical Psychology Review, 3,* 417–433.

Ipema, D. (1979, September-October). Rape, the process of recovery. *Nursing Research, 25*(5), 272–275.

Jehu, D., Gazan, M., & Klassen, C. (1984–1985). Common therapeutic targets among women who were sexually abused in childhood. Special issue: Feminist perspectives on social work and human sexuality. *Journal of Social Work & Human Sexuality, 3,* 25–45.

Justice, B., & Justice, R. (1979). *The broken taboo: Sex in the family.* New York: W.W. Norton.

Kilpatrick, D. G., Best, C. L., Veronen, L. J., Amick, A. E., Villeponteaux, L. A., & Ruff, G. A. (1985). Mental health correlates of criminal victimization: A random community survey. *Journal of Consulting and Clinical Psychology, 56,* 866–973.

Kilpatrick, D. G., Saunders, B. J., Veronen, L. J., Best, C. L., & Von, J. M. (1987). Criminal victimization: Lifetime prevalence, reporting to police and psychological impact. *Crime & Delinquency, 33,* 479–489.

Kilpatrick, D. G., Veronen, I. J., & Best, C. L. (1985). Factors predicting psychological distress among rape victims. In C. R. Figley (Ed.), *Trauma and its wake: The study and treatment of post-traumatic stress disorder* (pp. 113–141). New York: Brunner/Mazel.

Kilpatrick, D. G., Veronen, L. J., Saunders, B. E., Best, C. L., Amick-McMullen, A.,

& Paduhovich, J. (1987). *The psychological impact of crime: A study of randomly surveyed crime victims.* (Final report, Grant No. 84-IJ-CX-0039). Washington, DC: National Institute of Justice.

Kluft, R. P. (1983). Hypnotic crisis intervention in multiple personality. *American Journal of Clinical Hypnosis, 26,* 73–83.

Kluft, R. P. (1984a). Aspects of the treatment of multiple personality disorder. *Psychiatric Annals, 14,* 51–55.

Kluft, R. P., Baun, B. G., & Sachs, R. (1984b). Multiple personality, intrafamilial abuse, and family psychiatry. *International Journal of Family Psychiatry, 5,* 283–301.

Kluft, R. P. (1989a). Treating the patient who had been sexually exploited by a previous therapist. *Psychiatric Clinics of North America, 12,* 483–500.

Kluft, R. P. (1989b). Playing for time: Temporizing techniques in the treatment of multiple personality disorder. *American Journal of Clinical Hypnosis, 32,* 90–98.

Kluft, R. P. (1990). Incest-related syndromes of adult psychopathy. Washington, DC: American Psychiatric Press.

Krystal, H. (1982). The activating aspects of emotions. *Psychoanalysis & Contemporary Thought, 5,* 605–642.

Krystal, H. (1985). Trauma and the stimulus barrier. *Psychoanalytic Inquiry, 5*(1), 131–161.

Krystal, H. (1990). An informational processing view of object-relations. *Psychoanalytic Inquiry, 10,* 221–251.

Krystal, S., & Zweben, J. E. (1988). The use of visualization as a means of integrating the spiritual dimension into treatment: I. A practical guide. *Journal of Substance Abuse Treatment, 5,* 229–238.

Krystal, S., & Zweben, J. E. (1989). The use of visualization as a means of integrating the spiritual dimension into treatment: II. Working with emotions. *Journal of Substance Abuse Treatment, 6,* 223–228.

Lindberg, F., & Disted, L. (1985). Survival responses to incest: Adolescents in crisis. Fifth International Congress on Child Abuse and Neglect (1984, Montreal, Canada). *Child Abuse & Neglect, 9,* 521–526.

Mackey, T., Hacker, S., & Sorgen, A. (1991). *Depressive and sexual dysfunction symptoms among sexually-active and not-sexually-active sexual assault victims* (unpublished paper).

Mackey, T., Hacker, S., Weissfeld, L., Ambrose, N., Fisher, M., & Zobel, D. (1991). Comparative effects of sexual assault on sexual functioning of child sexual abuse survivors and others. *Issues in Mental Health Nursing, 12,* 89–112.

Mackey, T., Sereika, S., Weissfeld, L., & Hacker, S. (1991). Depressive symptoms among sexual assault victims. *Archives of Psychiatric Nursing,* (in press).

McCahill, T. W., Meyer, L. C., & Fischman, A. M. (1979). *The aftermath of rape.* Lexington, MA: Heath.

Mellody, P., Miller, A., & Miller, J. (1989). *Facing codependency.* San Francisco: Harper & Row.

Morelli, P. H. (1981, March). *Comparison of the psychological recovery of Black and White victims of rape.* Paper presented at the meeting of the Association for Women in Psychology, Boston.

Nadelson, C., Notman, M., Zackson, H., & Gornick, J. (1982). A follow-up study of rape victims. *American Journal of Psychiatry, 10*, 1226–1270.

Pope, K. S., & Bouhoutsos, J. C. (1986). *Sexual intimacy between therapists and patients.* New York: Praeger.

Popiel, D. A., & Susskind, E. C. (1985). The impact of rape: Social support as a moderator of stress. *American Journal of Community Psychiatry, 13*, 645–676.

Post, R., Willet, A. B. & Franks, R. D. (1980). A preliminary report on the prevalence of domestic violence among psychiatric in-patients. *American Journal of Psychiatry, 137*, 974–975.

Putnam, F. (1984). The psychophysiological investigation of multiple personality disorder. *Psychiatric Clinics of North America, 7*, 31–41.

Putnam, F. (1989). *Diagnosis and treatment of multiple personality disorder.* Washington, DC: American Psychiatric Press.

Reiker, P. P., & Carmen, E. H. (1986). The victim-to-patient process: The disconfirmation and transformation of abuse. *American Journal of Orthopsychiatry, 56*, 360–370.

Resick, P., Calhoun, K., Atkeson, B., & Ellis, E. (1981). Social adjustment in victims of sexual assault. *Journal of Consulting and Clinical Psychology, 49*, 705–712.

Rohsenow, D., Corbett, R., & Devine, D. (1988). Molested as children: A hidden contribution to substance abuse. *Journal of Substance Abuse Treatment, 5*, 13–18.

Root, M., & Fallon, P. (1988). The incidence of victimization experiences in a bulimic sample. *Journal of Interpersonal Violence, 3*, 161–173.

Ross-Durow, P. (1989) *Depression and post-traumatic stress disorder in women subsequent to erotic contact with health care professionals.* (Unpublished master's thesis, The University of Michigan School of Nursing).

Ruch, L. O., & Chandler, S. M. (1983). Sexual assault trauma during the acute phase: An exploratory model and multivariate analysis. *Journal of Health & Social Behavior, 24*, 174–185.

Ruch, L. O., Chandler, S. M., & Harter, R. A. (1980). Life change and rape impact. *Journal of Health & Social Behavior, 21*, 248–260.

Ruch, L. O., & Hennesey, M. (1982). Sexual assault: Victim and attack dimensions. *International Journal of Victimology, 74*, 94–105.

Russell, D. (1982). *Rape in marriage.* New York: Macmillan.

Rutter, P. (1989). *Sex in the forbidden zone: When men in power—therapists, doctors, clergy, teachers and others—betray women's trust.* Los Angeles: Jeremy P. Tarcher, Inc.

Sales, E., Baum, M., & Shore, B. (1984). Victim readjustment following assault. *Journal of Social Issues, 40*, 117–134.

Santiago, J., McCall-Perez, F., Gorcey, M., & Beigel, A. (1985). Long-term psychological effects of rape in 35 rape victims. *American Journal of Psychiatry, 142*, 1338–1340.

Silbert, M. H., Pines, A. M., & Lynch, T. (1982). Substance abuse and prostitution. *Journal of Psychoactive Drugs, 14*, 193–197.

Skrypnek, B. J., & Snyder, M. (1982). On the self-perpetuating nature of stereotypes about women and men. *Journal of Experimental Social Psychology, 18*, 277–291.

Stark, E., Flitcraft, A., & Frazier, W. (1979). Medicine and patriarchal violence: The social construction of a "private" event. *International Journal of Health Services, 9,* 461–493.

Stewart, B., Hughes, C., Frank, E., Anderson, B., Kendall, K., & West, D. (1987). The aftermath of rape: Profiles of immediate and delayed treatment seekers. *The Journal of Nervous and Mental Disease, 175,* 90–94.

Summit, R. L. (1984). Caring for the child molestation victims. In *Protecting our children: The fight against molestation,* A National Symposium (pp. 139–147). Washington, DC: U.S. Department of Justice.

Sutherland, S., & Scherl, D. (1970). Patterns of response among victims of rape. *American Journal of Orthopsychiatry, 40,* 503–511.

Vanderkolk, B., Greenberg, M., Boyd, H., & Krystal, J. (1985). Inescapable shock, neurotransmitters, and addiction to trauma: Toward a psychobiology of posttraumatic stress. *Biological Psychiatry, 20*(3), 314–325.

Weingourt, R. (1985). Wife rape: Barriers to identification and treatment. *American Journal of Psychotherapy, 39,* 139–192.

Weingourt, R. (1990). Wife rape in a sample of psychiatric patients. *Image, 2,* 144–147.

Weissman, M. M., & Klerman, G. L. (1987). Gender and depression. In R. Formaneck and A. Gurian (Eds.). *Women and depression: A life-span perspective.* New York: Springer.

Winfield, I., George, L. K., Swartz, M., & Blazer, D. G. (1990). Sexual assault and psychiatric disorders among a community sample of women. *American Journal of Psychiatry, 147,* 335–341.

Chapter 14

Battering in Pregnancy

Judith McFarlane

The first violence occurred when I told him I was pregnant. He was drinking his morning coffee. He threw the coffee cup on the floor, grabbed my arms, pinned me against the wall and punched me in the stomach. He never said anything.

One in 12 pregnant women experiences battering during pregnancy. Battered women are four times more likely to deliver a low birthweight infant. This chapter reviews the scope and prevalence of battering during pregnancy, the health consequences on mother and child, and the nursing interventions to prevent battering and promote maternal and child health.

A NATIONAL DISGRACE: BATTERING DURING PREGNANCY

Battering of women is pervasive. Based on national survey results, 1.8 million women are beaten by their husbands each year (Hotaling, Finkelhor, Kirkpatrick, & Straus, 1988). Stated another way, one of every eight husbands

---

This chapter is dedicated to all nurses everywhere who intervene to protect and promote health and physical safety of pregnant women and their unborn children. Pregnant women ask for no more and deserve no less.

assaults his wife at least once a year. Battering is the foremost cause of injury to women. Studies of battered women report 40–60% of battered women are abused during pregnancy (Walker, 1984; Stacey & Schupe, 1983; Fagan, Stewart, & Hansen, 1983). Reports of abuse during pregnancy include blows to the pregnant abdomen, injuries to the breasts and genitals, and sexual assault. The abused women report miscarriages, stillbirths, and preterm deliveries following a battering incident (Martin, 1976; Hilberman & Munson, 1978; Dobash & Dobash, 1979). Until recently, studies of battered women during pregnancy were taken from retrospective accounts of battered women, usually women in shelters. The time lapse since the reported battering was frequently lengthy. None of the studies compared reports of intentional injury during pregnancy to the women's obstetrical record or the child's birth record. The pattern or severity of injuries sustained during pregnancy were not addressed.

To determine the prevalence of battering during pregnancy among a healthy population of prenatal clients, recent studies include an assessment by Hillard (1985) of 742 prenatal clients. One abuse-focused question was asked. Hillard reported 11% of the women were abused in their present or a past relationship and 4% reported battering during the current pregnancy. The battered women tended to be older, be of higher parity, and have a lower educational level. Emotional problems were recorded for 43% of the battered women as compared to 5% of the nonbattered women. Twenty percent of the abused women had attempted suicide.

A subsequent random sample of 290 pregnant women from public and private clinics in a large metropolitan area were assessed for battering (Helton, McFarlane, & Anderson, 1987a). The 290 Black, White, and Hispanic women ranged in age from 18 to 43 years. Most were married and 80% of the women were at least five-months pregnant. Nine abuse assessment questions were asked of each woman. Of the 290 women, 8% reported battering during the current pregnancy (1 out of every 12 women interviewed). One third of the women battered during pregnancy had sought medical attention for injuries sustained from the abuse and 29% reported the abuse had increased following knowledge of the present pregnancy. One fourth of the women battered during pregnancy had been assaulted during the first trimester. All abused women were living with the batterer. The primary predictor of battering during pregnancy was prior abuse with 87.5% of the women battered during the current pregnancy having experienced abuse previously.

To establish the prevalence of battering during teen pregnancy, Bullock and McFarlane (1988, 1990) assessed more than 200 pregnant adolescents in two large metropolitan areas. Twenty-six percent of the teens assessed answered yes to being in a relationship with a man who was physically abusive. Among the battered teens, 40–60% stated that the battering had either begun or escalated since pregnancy. Most (65%) of the battered teens had not talked with anyone about the abuse, and no one had reported the battering to law enforcement agencies.

Finally, a study by Amaro, Fried, Cabral, and Zuckerman (1990) assessed violent incidents among a cohort of 1,243 pregnant women. Participants were predominantly poor, urban, and minority group women. Seven percent of women reported physical or sexual violence during pregnancy. Victims of violence were at greater risk of having a history of depression and attempted suicide, having more current depressive symptoms, reporting less happiness about being pregnant, and receiving less emotional support from others for the current pregnancy. Additional analysis that compared victims to nonvictims found victims more likely to use alcohol and drugs and partners of victims were more likely to use marijuana and cocaine. When incidents of violence were analyzed, 60% of the victims were subjected to one incident of violence during pregnancy, 25% were victimized twice, and 15% experienced three or more incidents. The majority (55%) of the incidents occurred in the first trimester. Thirty-six percent of the victims saw a physician for at least one of the violent incidents, and 10% were hospitalized, at least overnight, as a result of one of the violent occurrences.

HEALTH CONSEQUENCES OF BATTERING DURING PREGNANCY

Birthweight is the single most important determinant of survival and healthy growth and development for children. The Surgeon General set objectives for the year 1990 that included a goal to reduce low birthweight births to no more than 5% of all births with no racial or ethnic subgroup more than 9%. Despite major advances in the science of obstetrics, the incidence of low birthweight infants has remained at 6–7% of all live births in the United States (NCHS, 1990). Therefore, at the present rate of progress, the overall health objective for low birthweight will not be met until the year 2056 (Hughes, Johnson, Rosenbaum, & Lin, 1989).

In the absence of an etiology, risk factors associated with low birthweight have been categorized by the National Institute of Medicine (1985) as including the following maternal characteristics: demographics, medical care, behavioral and environmental factors, and absent or inadequate prenatal care. Recently, stress has emerged as a significant variable and the National Institute of Medicine has noted the need for research on the relationship between stress and infant birthweight.

Battering is stressful. To determine if an association exists between battering before or during pregnancy and infant birthweight, 589 postpartum women at private and public hospitals were randomly interviewed and asked if they had been physically abused (Bullock & McFarlane, 1989). For the total sample of 589 women, 12.5% of the battered women delivered a low birthweight infant compared to only 6.6% of the nonbattered women. The difference was statistically significant. When the battered women at the private hospital were treated as a subsample, the percentage of battered women delivering a low birthweight infant was 17.5% as compared to only 4.2% among nonbattered women. The difference was statistically significant. (At the public hospital battered women delivered a higher percentage of low birthweight infants than the nonbattered women, but the difference was not statistically significant.) When variables associated with low birthweight (i.e., tobacco and alcohol use, age, and race) were mathematically controlled, a strong connection was still evident between battering and low birthweight.

Presently a cohort of 1,200 pregnant women stratified by ethnicity and representative of teens and adult women are being followed by this author and a coinvestigator. The objectives of the study are to establish the pattern and severity of battering during pregnancy and associated consequences on maternal health and infant birthweight. The women are interviewed repeatedly and assessed for physical and emotional abuse as well as risk factors of homicide. Both quantitative and qualitative measures are being used. Data will be available in 1992.

NURSING INTERVENTIONS TO PREVENT BATTERING

The Surgeon General's Workshop on Violence and Public Health (1986) recommended screening and treatment for physical abuse during routine prenatal care. The recommendations advise that battered women be classified as high-risk for health complications during pregnancy. In January 1989, the American College of Obstetricians and Gynecologists (1988, 1989) sent information about battered women to its 28,000 members for the purpose of facilitating identification and follow-up. Despite increased awareness of violence by health care providers, minimal assessment, surveillance, and risk group identification occurs in the clinical settings (Centers for Disease Control, 1988, 1989; Mercy & O'Carroll, 1988).

Nurses are in a unique position to assess for battering during pregnancy and initiate education, referral, and advocacy. It is only during pregnancy that healthy women come into regular scheduled contact with nurses. Pregnancy provides an optimum time to inform all women about the potential for battering and assess the safety status of each client.

Assessment for Battering

Violence evokes a mixture of feelings from every person. Once a decision is made to begin assessing pregnant women for abuse, all staff must receive thorough inservice education. Special educational materials for preventing battering during pregnancy were developed by the March of Dimes. The educational materials and evaluation data are described in several publications (McFarlane,

1989; McFarlane, Anderson, & Helton, 1987; Helton, McFarlane, & Anderson, 1987b) and are listed in Appendix 1. Before assessment for battering is begun, it is essential to have administrative support and a definite plan of care for women answering positive for abuse. The process of establishing a screening program for battering is addressed in a related article (Lazzaro & McFarlane, 1991).

Nursing assessment for battering must be conducted privately and with assurances of confidentiality. At the same time, the assessment process must be a part of the standard, essential prenatal care regime and approached in a nonjudgmental, direct manner. Suggested assessment questions developed by the Nursing Research Consortium on Violence and Abuse are presented in Appendix 2. The assessment is presented in English and Spanish.

Some health agencies have instituted abuse assessment by self-report as part of the client's health history (Bullock, McFarlane, Bateman, & Miller, 1989). Battering is a highly sensitive and personal topic. Abused women are embarrassed by the violence; they may fear judgment and condemnation when they report the abuse. Self-reporting does not permit the development of rapport or trust. Because a therapeutic relationship is essential for the disclosure of personal, sensitive information, a nurse interview is recommended when assessing for battering. When self-reporting of battering was compared to nurse interview, the author measured a fourfold increase in positive responses to battering when the assessment questions were asked by a nurse (McFarlane, Christoffel, Bateman, Miller, & Bullock, 1991).

Interventions for Battering

Assessing for battering carries the responsibility for intervention following a positive response. Crisis intervention steps can be followed. The focus of crisis intervention is present oriented and directed toward restoration to a precrisis level of functioning (Aguilera & Messick, 1986). Regardless of the nature of the crisis, the intervention steps remain the same, specifically: assessment, therapeutic intervention planning, intervention implementation, and resolution of crisis and planning for an anticipated future. Regardless of the situation, crisis intervention always remains the same. The only changes are the facts surrounding the specific crisis and the appropriate selection of community resources.

The constancy of crisis intervention practice can be used to defuse the emotionally charged area of abuse and can enable staff to intervene more effectively when abuse is encountered. To prepare staff to assess and intervene for battering, examples can be drawn from the crises staff nurses encounter daily with pregnant clients. For example, minor crisis situations of elevated blood glucose and hypertension are daily occurrences in the prenatal setting as are major crises, such as no audible fetal heart tones, or an ultrasound that suggests congenital anomalies. When staff have adequate knowledge about the condition, coupled with crisis intervention theory, they can feel secure in their role to intervene in the client's behalf. Information on battering can be presented as another potential situation in which the nurse employs crisis intervention theory.

At a minimum, all health agencies must have referral sources available as well as information on legal and criminal options. Nurses need to know the law in their state on family violence and the penal code for assault. (Battering is considered assault, which is a crime in all 50 states.) Consulting local law enforcement agencies and the district attorney's office for specific information and procedures is essential. Nurses must be knowledgeable about how to direct the abused woman to file a criminal charge. Most shelters, social service programs, and law enforcement agencies welcome the opportunity to provide continuing education programs for nurses. A list of community resources must be kept current and available for nurses and clients. A recently published book by Statman (1990) lists national and state-by-state resources for battered women.

Battering is very embarrassing. The woman answering, "yes," to battering may minimize the abuse with statements such as "He only hits me when he drinks" or "He is a good father to the children." Most battered women want the violence to end, not the relationship. The woman may perceive few options, and the pregnant woman perceives even fewer. Discussing the cycle of violence with the woman helps her acknowledge the recurring pattern of violence. Dialogue responses for working with battered women are offered in Helton's (1987) *Protocol of Care for the Battered Woman* as well as Campbell's (1984) *Nursing Care of Victims of Family Violence.*

The most important consideration in the initial assessment of the battered woman is to protect her. Violence usually escalates over time in both frequency and severity. In this country, the majority of female homicides are caused by a husband, lover, or ex-husband. Each year, more than 1,000 battered women in the United States are murdered by their male partner (Browne, 1989). Research documents that the battered woman is in the greatest danger of homicide when she leaves the batterer or informs him that she is ending the relationship (Hart, 1988). One method for assessing for the potential of homicide is through use of Campbell's (1986) Danger Assessment. Appendix 3 presents the Danger Assessment in English and Spanish.

Frequently the plan for leaving a violent relationship includes the option of a shelter for battered women. Shelters are available in every state. A national toll free number is available that provides information regarding abuse as well as phone numbers of local shelters (1-800-333-SAFE).

Intervening with battered women is stressful. Campbell (1989) notes that battered women have as much difficulty terminating a relationship as women who are not battered. Frequently, battered women choose to stay in the violent relationship. Women who remain with the batterer require as much, if not more, nursing support and counseling. Nurses should advise the woman that, during, after, or when a beating is anticipated she may decide to leave home. Some advance planning is necessary. Nurses can suggest a woman pack an extra set of clothes for herself and her children, along with toilet articles and essential medications. A set of keys to the house and car should be stored with a friend or neighbor. Extra cash, a checkbook, and savings account number should be hidden or kept with a friend. Battered women should be advised to have copies of identification papers for herself and the children, such as birth certificates, social security card, voter registration, and driver's license. Identification papers will be important to obtain financial assistance and enroll children in school. Most importantly, the battered woman needs to know exactly where she could go and how to get there even if the battering occurred in the middle of the night.

Regardless, if the battered woman feels her or the children's safety is in danger, she needs to get out of the situation even if there has been no advance planning. Injuries from battering may require emergency treatment, and if the woman seeks medical care following a beating, she will need to describe the current and past beatings and obtain a copy of her medical record. A medical report of injuries will be helpful if she decides to seek legal assistance.

Parker and McFarlane (1991) discuss additional nursing intervention strategies for survivors of abuse. A related article by McFarlane (1991) discusses battering during teen pregnancy. Finally, an article by the Nursing Research Consortium of Violence and Abuse (Parker et al., 1990) discusses a protocol of safety for nurses completing research on abuse of women.

HOPE FOR THE FUTURE

Battering is no longer a private matter. Physical assault is a crime in every state. The public has increased awareness of the extent of the problem and is demanding action from police, social services, and the health care provider. Year 2000 Health Objectives cite the reduction of violent and abusive behavior as one of the 21 priority objectives for the nation (DHHS, 1990). Battering was defined by Surgeon General Koop as a "Crime Against the Future." Indeed, it is only during pregnancy that healthy women have regular scheduled contact with nurses. If the cycle of violence is to be interrupted and the health and safety of pregnant women promoted, it is essential that nurses take the initiative and begin to assess, intervene, and redress this health malady. Certainly, pregnant women ask for no more and deserve no less.

REFERENCES

Aguilera, D., & Messick, M. (Eds.). (1986). *Crisis intervention, and methodology* (5th ed.). St. Louis, MO: C.V. Mosby.

Amaro, H., Fried, L., Cabral, H., & Zuckerman, B. (1990). Violence during pregnancy and substance use. *American Journal of Public Health, 80,* 575–579.

American College of Obstetricians and Gynecologists. (1988). *The abused woman.* Washington, DC: Author.

American College of Obstetricians and Gynecologists. (1989). *The battered woman.* Washington, DC: Author.

Browne, A. (1989). *When battered women kill.* New York: Macmillan.

Bullock, L., & McFarlane, J. (1988). A program to prevent battering of pregnant students. *Response, 11,* 18–19.

Bullock, L., & McFarlane, J. (1989). Battering/low birthweight connection. *American Journal of Nursing, 89,* 1153–1155.

Bullock, L., McFarlane, J., Bateman, L., & Miller, V. (1989). Characteristics of battered women in a primary care setting. *Nurse Practitioner, 14,* 47–55.

Bullock, L., Maloney, L., & McFarlane, J. (1990). Preventing violence during teen pregnancy. *School Nurse, 6*(1), 10–12.

Campbell, J. (1986). Nursing assessment for risk of homicide in battered women. *Advances in Nursing Science, 8,* 36–51.

Campbell, J. (1984). *Nursing care of victims of family violence.* Reston, VA: Reston.

Campbell, J. (1989). A test of two explanatory models of women's responses to battering. *Nursing Research, 38,* 18–24.

Centers for Disease Control. (1988, February). CDC Surveillance Summaries. *MMWR, 37* (No. 22–1), 1–4.

Centers for Disease Control. (1989). Education about adult domestic violence in U.S. and Canadian Medical Schools, 1987–1988. Editor's Note. *MMWR, 38,* 19–21.

Department of Health and Human Services. (1990). *Year 2000 health objectives.* Washington, DC: U.S. Government Printing Office.

Dobash, R. E., & Dobash, R. P. (1979). *Violence against wives.* New York: New York Free Press.

Fagan, J., Stewart, D., & Hansen, K. (1983). Violent men or violent husbands: Background factors and situational correlates. In D. Finkelhor, R. Gelles, G. Hotaling, & M. Straus (Eds.). *The dark side of families.* California: Sage.

Hart, B. (1988). Beyond the "Duty to Warn": A therapist's "Duty to Protect" battered women and children. In K. Yllo & M. Bograd (Eds.). *Feminist perspectives on wife abuse.* Newbury Park: Sage.

Helton, A. (1987). *Protocol of care for battered women.* White Plains, NY: March of Dimes Birth Defects Foundation.

Helton, A., McFarlane, J., & Anderson, E. (1987a). Prevention of battering during pregnancy: Focus on behavioral change. *Public Health Nursing, 4,* 166–174.

Helton, A., McFarlane, J., & Anderson, E. (1987b). Battered and pregnant: A prevalence study. *American Journal of Public Health, 77,* 1337–1339.

Hilberman, E., & Munson, K. (1978). Sixty battered women. *Victimology: An International Journal, 2,* 460–470.

Hillard, P. J. (1985). Physical abuse in pregnancy. *Obstetrics and Gynecology, 66,* 185–190.

Hotaling, G. T., Finkelhor, D., Kirkpatrick, J. T., & Straus, M. (Eds.). (1988). *Family abuse and its consequences.* Newbury Park, CA: Sage.

Hughes, D., Johnson, K., Rosenbaum, S., & Lin, J. (1989). The health of America's children. In *Maternal and child health data book*. Washington, DC: Children's Defense Fund.

Lazzaro, M., & McFarlane, J. (In press). Establishing a screening program for abused women. *Journal of Nursing Administration*.

Martin, D. (1976). *Battered wives*. CA: Glide.

McFarlane, J. (1989). Battering during pregnancy: Tip of an iceberg revealed. *Women and Health, 15*, 69–83.

McFarlane, J. (1991). Violence during teen pregnancy: Health consequences for mother and child. In B. Levy (Ed.), *Dating violence: Young women in danger*. Seattle, WA: Seal Press.

McFarlane, J., Anderson, E., & Helton, A. (1987). Response to battering during pregnancy: An educational program. *Response, 10*, 23–25.

McFarlane, J., Christoffel, K., Bateman, L., Miller, V., & Bullock, L. (in press). Assessing for abuse: Self-report versus nurse interview. *Public Health Nursing*.

Mercy, J., & O'Carroll, P. (1988). New directions in violence prediction: The public health arena. *Violence and Victims, 3*, 285–301.

National Center for Health Statistics. (1990). *Health, United States, 1989*. DHHS. Public Health Service. Washington, DC: U.S. Government Print Office.

National Institute of Medicine. (1985). *Preventing low birthweight*. Washington, DC: National Academy Press.

Parker, B., & McFarlane, J. (1991, in press). Nursing assessment of the battered pregnant woman. *MCN, The American Journal of Maternal/Child Nursing*.

Parker, B., Ulrich, Y., Bullock, L., Campbell, D., Campbell, J., King, C., Landenburger, K., McFarlane, J., Ryan, J., Sheridan, D., McKenna, L., Torres, S. (1990). A protocol of safety: Research on abuse of women. *Nursing Research, 39*, 248–250.

Stacey, W., & Schupe, A. (1983). *The family secret*. Boston, MA: Beacon Press.

Statman, J. (1990). *The battered woman's survival guide*. Dallas, TX: Taylor.

Surgeon General's Workshop on Violence and Public Health. (1986). U.S. Department of Health and Human Services. Washington, DC: Public Health Service.

Walker, L. (1984). *The battered woman syndrome*. New York: Springer.

APPENDIX 1

Educational Materials to Prevent Battering

The following materials were developed by nurses to prevent battering during pregnancy.

Protocol of Care for the Battered Woman A 20-page booklet for health providers that discusses the cycle of violence, sociocultural causes, assessment tools, and dialogue strategies to prevent violence. Available from: March of Dimes Birth Defects Foundation, Materials and Supply Division, 1275 Mamaroneck Avenue, White Plains, NY 10605; $5.00 per copy, prepayment required.

Crime Against the Future A 23-min video introduced by Surgeon General Everett Koop. The film discusses battering during pregnancy, assessment tools, research, and primary prevention strategies. Suitable for community and professional audiences. Available from the March of Dimes Birth Defects Foundation, Materials and Supply Division, 1275 Mamaroneck Avenue, White Plains, NY 10605; 16 mm-$150.00, 3/4' U-matic-$60.00, 1/2" VHS-$60.00, prepayment required.

Prevention of Battering During Teen Pregnancy A 10-min video on the stresses of adolescence and primary prevention strategies for battering during teen pregnancy. Suitable for teen, community, and professional audiences. Available from Texas Woman's University, College of Nursing, 1130 M.D. Anderson Blvd., Houston, TX 77030, Attention: Dr. Judith McFarlane, 1/2" VHS-$20.00 prepaid.

Relationships Without Violence A tested, self-contained curriculum for high school students on the development of skills for violence-free relationships. The curriculum of five learning modules is accompanied by video materials. Available from the Metropolitan Houston March of Dimes, 3000 Weslayan, Suite 100, Houston, TX 77027. Cost of the curriculum and 10-min video is $50.00, prepayment required.

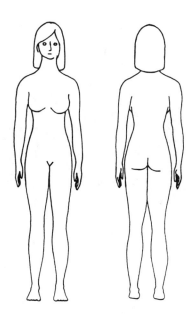

APPENDIX 2

Abuse Assessment Screen (Circle YES or NO for each question).

1 Have you *ever* been emotionally or physically abused by your partner or someone important to you? . . . . YES   NO

2 *Within the last year,* have you been hit, slapped, kicked, or otherwise physically hurt by someone? . . . . YES   NO
If YES, by whom? (Circle all that apply)
Husband   Ex-husband   Boyfriend   Stranger
Other   Total number of times _____

3 *Since you've been pregnant,* have you been hit, slapped, kicked, or otherwise physically hurt by someone? . . . . YES   NO
If YES, by whom? (Circle all that apply)
Husband   Ex-Husband   Boyfriend   Stranger
Other   Total number of times _____
Mark the area of injury on the body map.

4 *Within the last year,* has anyone forced you to have sexual activities? . . . . YES   NO
If YES, by whom? (Circle all that apply)
Husband   Ex-Husband   Boyfriend   Stranger
Other   Total number of times _____

5 Are you afraid of your partner or anyone you listed above? . . . . YES   NO

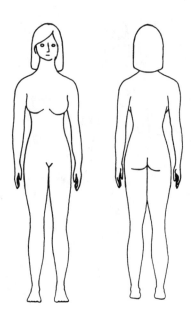

APPENDIX 2 (Español)

Evaluación de Abuso (Circula SI o NO por cada pregunta).

1 Ha sido emocionalmente o fisicamente abusada por su companero o por alguien especial? .... SI   NO

2 *Durante el ano pasado,* ha sido golpeada, bofeteada, pateada, o danada fisicamente por alguien? .... SI   NO
Si la respuesta es SI, por quien (Circule todos los que se apliquen).
Esposo   Ex-esposo   Amigo   Estrano
Otro   Numero de veces _____

3 *Desde el embarazo,* ha sido golpeada, bofeteada, pateada, o danada fisicamente por alguien? .... SI   NO
Si la respuesta es SI, por quien (Circule todos los que se apliquen).
Esposo   Ex-esposo   Amigo   Estrano
Otro   Numero de veces _____
En el dibujo de abajo marque la parte del cuerpo dañada.

4 *Durante el ano pasado,* ha sido forzada a tener actividades sexsuales? .... SI   NO
Si la respuesta es SI, por quien (Circule todos los que se apliquen).
Esposo   Ex-esposo   Amigo   Estrano
Otro   Numero de veces _____

5 Le tiene miedo a su companero o a alguna otra persona que ha circulado en alguna de las preguntas anteriores? .... SI   NO

APPENDIX 3

Danger Assessment

Several risk factors have been associated with homicides (murder) of both batterers and battered women in research that has been conducted after the killings have been taken place. We cannot predict what will happen in your case, but we would like you to be aware of the danger of homicide in situations of severe battering and for you to see how many of the risk factors apply to your situation. (The "he" in the questions refers to your husband, partner, ex-husband, ex-partner, or whomever is currently physically hurting you.)

Please check YES or NO for each question below.

YES NO

____ ____ 1 Has the physical violence increased in frequency over the past year?

____ ____ 2 Has the physical violence increased in severity over the past year and/or has a weapon or threat with weapon been used?

____ ____ 3 Does he ever try to choke you?

____ ____ 4 Is there a gun in the house?

____ ____ 5 Has he ever forced you into sex when you did not wish to do so?

____ ____ 6 Does he use drugs? By drugs I mean "uppers" or amphetamines, speed, angel dust, cocaine, "crack," street drugs, heroin, or mixtures.

____ ____ 7 Does he threaten to kill you and/or do you believe he is capable of killing you?

____ ____ 8 Is he drunk every day or almost every day? (In terms of quantity of alcohol).

____ ____ 9 Does he control most all of your daily activities? For instance, does he tell you who you can be friends with, how much money you can take with you shopping, or when you can take the car? (If he tries, but you do not let him, check here ___).

____ ____ 10 Have you every been beaten by him while you were pregnant?

____ ____ 11 Is he violently and constantly jealous of you? (For instance, does he say, "If I can't have you, no one can"?)

____ ____ 12 Have you ever threatened or tried to commit suicide?

____ ____ 13 Has he ever threatened or tried to commit suicide?

____ ____ 14 Is he violent outside of the home?

TOTAL YES ANSWERS ____

THANK YOU. PLEASE TALK TO YOUR NURSE, ADVOCATE, OR COUNSELOR ABOUT WHAT THE DANGER ASSESSMENT MEANS IN TERMS OF YOUR SITUATION.

APPENDIX 3 (Español)

Evaluacion de Danos

Varios factores de riesgo han sido asociados con homicidios (asesinatos) en ambos el abusador o la mujer abusada en estudios realizados despues de haber occurridas las muertes. No podemos predecir que sucedera en su caso, pero me gustaria advertirle del peligro de homicidio en situaciones de abuso severo y que usted se de cuenta de cuantos factores de riesgo se aplican en su situacion. (En las siguientes preguntas cuando hablamos de "el" nos estamos refiriendo a su marido, companero, ex-marido, ex-companero o quienquiera que la este actualmente danandola fisicamente.)

Por favor margue SI o NO a cada una de las preguntas que siguen abajo.

SI   NO

___ ___ 1 Ha aumentado la violencia fisica durante el ano pasado?

___ ___ 2 Ha aumentado en severidad la violencia fisica durante el ano pasado y/o ha sido amenazada con un arma o ha sido un arma usada en usted?

___ ___ 3 Ha tratado el de asfixiarla?

___ ___ 4 Hay alguna arma de fuego en su casa?

___ ___ 5 La ha forzado el a tener relaciones sexuales en contra de su voluntad?

___ ___ 6 Usa el drogas? Por drogas me refiero a "exitantes" o afetaminas, "speed," polvo de angel, cocaina, crack, drogas de la calle, heroina, o mezclas.

___ ___ 7 La amenaza el con matarla o cree usted que el es capaz de matarla?

___ ___ 8 Se emborracha el todos los dias o casi todos los dias? (En relacion con el alcohol.)

___ ___ 9 Controla el la mayoria de sus actividades diarias? Por ejemplo, le dice el quienes pueden ser sus amigos, o cuanto dinero puede llevar cuando va de compras, o cuando puede usar el coche? (Si el trata, pero usted no lo deja marque aqui ___.)

___ ___ 10 Ha sido golpeada cuando estaba embarazada? (Si no ha estada embarazada de el, marque aqui ___.)

___ ___ 11 Es el violento, o constantemente celoso de usted? Por ejemplo le dice el: "Si no eres mia no vas a serlo de nadie".

___ ___ 12 Ha usted amenazado o ha usted tratado con suicidarse?

___ ___ 13 Ha tratado o amenazado el con suicidarse?

___ ___ 14 Es el violento fuera de la casa?

TOTAL DE RESPUESTAS SI ___

GRACIAS. POR FAVOR HABLE CON SU ENFERMERA, BUSQUE SOPORTE O CONSEJO SOBRE LO QUE LA EVALUACION DE DANO SIGNIFICA EN SU CASO.

Chapter 15

Abuse of Women in the Health Care System

Janice M. Dyehouse

When a woman seeks health care, she enters a male-dominated medical system that has little appreciation of how she experiences and communicates her health concerns. Consequently a woman is often offered care that is based on stereotypical sex-biased responses. Physicians may trivialize her symptoms and prescribe unnecessary or inappropriate treatment. Such care is offered from a patriarchal stance rooted in the attitude that the "doctor knows best" with little recognition of the woman's experience or concerns. Thus, a woman is at a distinct disadvantage in terms of being listened to and responded to as an equal participant in exploring her health concerns and options.

Inherent in the relationship between the male physician and the female patient is a culturally-based power differential that stems from a traditional perspective that casts women as the "other." This leads the physician to define the woman's experience of illness and prescribe procedures and treatment based on a male medical model. Thus, women are at increased risk of abuse in a male-dominated system that does not value or understand woman's experience of health and illness.

This chapter is dedicated to my dear friend Irene, a social worker whose journey to recover from therapeutic abuse has provided me with an appreciation of the depth of trauma such abuse inflicts. I hope that by sharing the concerns described herein I will honor her courage for us all.

Historically women have been viewed by physicians as weak, passive, and incapable of understanding medical treatment and procedures. Frequently a woman's symptoms and concerns are not taken seriously or are attributed to her reproductive organs or psychological causes without exploring a biological basis. Women have been treated with medical and surgical procedures of unknown or limited effectiveness that could be potentially, or actively harmful (Corea, 1977).

The doctor-patient relationship often lacks mutual respect, trust, and cooperation. Lacking this, women's experiences and ways of communicating those experiences have been omitted from the development of medical knowledge and treatment. Women's health care is embedded in the male values of self-sufficiency, self-reliance, separation and individuation, and action-oriented solutions to problems. There is little regard for women's greater awareness and sensitivity to one's body or for an emphasis on nurturance of relationship and experience of emotion. Medical science has not focused on a woman's ways of experiencing and communicating illness, but instead has focused on her reproductive functions as her primary health care need. In fact women's reproductive organs have become a frontier for chemical and surgical expansionism, untested drugs, and reckless examinations (Ehrenreich & English, 1986).

The women's health movement developed in response to the male-dominated system and its growing lack of both concern and sensitivity to women's special health needs. Women's health at the core means taking women's lived experiences as the starting point of all health efforts (Opie, 1986; McBride, 1986). In 1980 a Committee of Women Physicians recommended to the American Medical Association that it address the issues of unnecessary surgeries, the overprescription of tranquilizer and antidepressive drugs, the need to improve medical alternatives in the treatment of menopause and the development of mutual respect and offer more adequate exploration of diagnosis and treatment (Weiss, 1984). In 1983, the Assistant Secretary of Health established the Public Health Service Task Force on Women's Health Issues. This task force was charged with assuring that the health needs of women are effectively addressed (Kirschstein, 1987).

While the women's health movement has impacted on health care offered to women, it is questionable as to whether these efforts have produced enduring results. In fact, medical professionals may be co-opting or exploiting the women's health movement for their own benefit (Dyehouse & Opie, 1990). Evidence suggests that physicians and hospitals are segmenting the health care market and targeting services to women. Women ages 18–64 comprise 31% of the population, but account for 61% of all surgeries. This represents a $280 billion dollar market (Coddington & Moore, 1987). In fact "specialized services for women are often the most profitable part of a hospital's activities" (Coddington & Moore, 1987). While there is an increased emphasis on providing services to women, there is little evidence to suggest that these new services are taking into account women's needs for education, information, mutual respect, or greater participation in health care decisions. Rather, the trend is to emphasize greater use of technology (Dyehouse & Opie, 1990). Thus, there is a growing concern that abuse toward women by organized medicine continues and, in fact, may be proliferating.

The purpose of this chapter is to examine current areas of woman abuse within the health care system and to explore strategies needed to remedy this trend. Six areas of concern in which women are at risk are: sexual abuse, pathologizing of women's characteristics, family system-based therapy, diagnostic labels, surgical abuse, and chemical abuse. Before exploring the specifics of these areas of concern, two issues that give rise to the differential treatment of women in the health care system will be discussed: the different ways in which men and women define and experience illness and the power differential between men and women.

FORCES THAT SUPPORT ABUSE OF WOMEN WITHIN THE HEALTH CARE SYSTEM

Sex Differences and the Experience of Illness

Demographic trends indicate that women generally outlive men by 7–8 years, but in their lifetime women experience more episodes of illness and have a higher rate of chronic illness and mental health problems (Hibbard & Pope, 1986). Questions can be raised as to why men and women experience illness/disease differently. Most authors attribute this sex difference to women's greater awareness of their body and to their increased concern for health. Women may not experience more illness but rather seek treatment more frequently and earlier.

Women are socialized to express their pain and vulnerability, freely acknowledge their emotional difficulties and feelings, ask for help, accept weakness in themselves, and report higher symptom intensity. Women are encouraged to identify with the role of the weak, vulnerable, or sick person and discouraged from expressions of strength (Rutter, 1989; Gentry, 1987).

Men, on the other hand, are socialized to be self-sufficient, self-reliant, stoic, and endure hardship and pain rather than ask for help. They are taught to deny illness and weakness and not to admit their vulnerability (Rutter, 1989). The American culture celebrates these traits.

Because men and women are socialized to define and respond to the experience of illness differently, some male physicians have tended to respond to women's more intense symptom descriptions, expressions of emotion, and awareness of their bodies by not taking their concerns seriously. From the male perspective women may appear neurotic and hysterical. Because women more readily seek and accept help, male physicians have often responded to women as weak, frail, incompetent, submissive, and needing outside direction. These two trends have combined to result in medical treatment of women that is frequently patriarchal and insensitive to the female experience. Thus physicians, because of their socialization, have been less inclined to listen to or explore women's experience. They have most often responded with action-oriented prescription of chemical or surgical intervention rather than with exploration, education, mutual respect, and participation in decision making.

Historically, from the male perspective, women have appeared neurotic and hysterical. Such a perspective greatly influences how symptoms are perceived (as not important), evaluated (as insignificant), and acted upon (with surgery or drugs). Treatment is aggressive and action-oriented rather than exploratory and educative.

The male perspective has influenced the amount and type of care women receive. This is demonstrated in symptom descriptions of the diagnosis of somatization or depression and, more recently, codependency. These conditions are consistently characterized by the ways women commonly describe themselves and have been socialized to behave. There are few characteristics that can be linked to denial of illness, self-reliance, or stoicism. These more masculine traits are socially valued; therefore, they are not pathologized by traditional medicine.

Because of their lack of understanding of women's experiences, awareness, and ability to express their pain, physicians have attributed these symptoms (contrary to their own experiences) to either women's psychological make-up or their reproductive organs. A variety of treatment approaches aimed at altering women's reproductive function have been developed. These attempts to alter women's symptom experience have fueled the current proliferation of hormone therapy, unnecessary hysterectomies, and cesarean sections. Women's reproductive organs have become the new frontier for surgical and chemical expansion (Ehrenreich & English, 1986).

Theoretical Framework/Power Imbalance

While the differences in the sex role stereotypes attributed to men and women are readily apparent, the power differential embedded in these descriptions and the consequences to women are often neglected. Because medicine is traditionally rooted in male values and ways of knowing, the male values of stoicism, enduring pain, denial of illness, self-reliance, and self-sufficiency affect the definition of illness. Thus women's experience of illness is often suspect and contrary to the medical definition. Male physicians remain in control of defining, interpreting, and prescribing medication for women whose experiences and values are invisible to them. Medical care is provided by men (or women who have been trained in a patriarchal medical system) who value toughness, aggressiveness, and who sometimes see disease as the enemy to be vanquished with drugs and surgery (Corea, 1977; Oakley, 1988).

By virtue of the gender-based power imbalance, physicians have substantial control over women's lives and their future health and well-being. Inherent in the physician/client relationship is women's trust of those in power to act in their own best interest in providing care and treatment. Important questions arise when the priorities set for medical research and development, technology, and the allocation of research funds are examined. The lack of women being included as research subjects, the question about unnecessary surgeries, the overprescription of drugs to women, and the sexual abuse of women by doctors and male therapists, all give rise to questions about whose best interest is being served. Traditional medicine's view of women's best interest is connected to a man's view of women's function in the world, generally focused on reproduction.

SOURCES OF ABUSE OF WOMEN IN THE HEALTH CARE SYSTEM

Abuse takes many forms. At times it is blatant; at other times it is subtle and hard to define. Nonetheless all forms of abuse are destructive to women's sense of self and can engender feelings of powerlessness. It is by listening to and taking seriously women's concerns that the depth of the problem is realized. The following discussion identifies forms of abuse currently operating in the health care system.

Sexual Abuse in the Therapeutic Relationship

The therapeutic relationship is central to the healing process in all health care, but it is particularly powerful in the mental health field. It is within this relationship that clients come to trust that past injuries and losses can be healed. No place is the violation of this trust more injurious than when a male therapist betrays a woman's trust by sexual exploitation.

The therapeutic relationship is one in which the therapist, as caregiver, in an emotionally charged and intimate exchange, has inherently greater power than the client. The therapist has the responsibility for maintaining clearly defined role boundaries with the client (Hill, 1990; Rutter, 1989). In the therapeutic relationship the woman trusts that the therapist will guide her development, that her trust will be used wholly to advance her interest, and that this trust will not be turned to sexual opportunity. Any sexual behavior by a man in power is inherently exploitative of a woman's trust. Because he is the keeper of that trust, it is the man's responsibility, no matter what the level of provocation or apparent consent by the woman, to assure that sexual behavior does not take place (Rutter, 1989). Under these conditions sexual behavior is always wrong no matter who initiates it (Rutter, 1989).

What makes the therapeutic relationship so powerful in mental health care is that it holds out the hope for the restoration of what has been lost or the healing of what has been injured (Rutter, 1989). The woman enters into this relationship trusting she will find access to new models of coping with life's problems. This relationship promises to help her transcend her limits and regain hope that wounded parts, unhealed, might be healed and the true self be awakened and recognized.

How a woman is treated by the male therapist in power determines how she experiences her femininity. It can be affirmed as a force to be valued and respected or a commodity to be exploited (Rutter, 1989). When the woman is sexually exploited she experiences, again, that her femininity and her true self are not valued and respected for who they are, but for what they can provide to men. Thus, betrayal of her trust through sexual exploitation reopens past wounds and leaves little hope for healing these injuries and losses. Both the woman and the therapeutic relationship have been violated.

Because women have had the courage to speak up, a clearer picture is emerging of how frequently women are being sexually abused by male therapists. While statistics are inaccurate due to underreporting and the code of silence, the *American Journal of Psychiatry* indicated that 13% of psychiatrists report involvement with their clients and 80% of those indicate they had sexual contact with an average of six patients (Rutter, 1989). Most of what is currently known about sex between male therapists and female clients comes from case studies (Bates & Brodsky, 1989; Gabbard, 1989; Plasil, 1985; Walker & Young, 1986). For his book, *Sex in the Forbidden Zone* (1989), Rutter reviewed 1,000 case reports of male therapists having sex with their patients. These cases were based on women he had either seen in his own professional practice, cases other professionals made available to him, or cases reported in papers given at professional conferences, reported in the professional literature, or of public record. It is alarming to consider that, while these figures probably underreport the problem, they are an index of how frequently the trust of the therapeutic relationship is violated.

Rutter (1989) offers a cogent explanation of how a male therapist might use the balance of power and trust for sexual opportunity rather than for the development and healing of the women in his care. He suggests that men's cultural training encourages them to challenge women's intimate boundaries. Men are socialized to believe that women should defer to their needs, and be available as a sexual partner, for emotional comfort, and as a helpmate. Males also believe women have special powers for healing, nurturing, and sex, which they are to bestow on men. Women's sexual powers are seen as a way of affirming the man's sexuality.

Because of these culturally ascribed beliefs about women's role as deferent to and supportive of male sexuality, the male therapist may misdirect the relationship. In emotionally charged and intimate therapeutic relationships, male therapists can find themselves responding to this belief system and ministering to their own needs for healing and affirmation from the women. Because greater power is invested in men, both culturally and within the therapeutic relationship, women are vulnerable to sexual exploitation as men play out these powerful stereotypes of sexual opportunity and lose sight of the women's interest. As Rutter (1989) emphasizes, even if the woman is seductive or initiates the sexual relationship, it is the male therapist's responsibility not to respond to this out of the male need for power, affirmation, or healing, but to respond in a way that shows the woman that she can be valued for herself and not just her sexuality. When the male therapist betrays this trust, the woman leaves more injured than when she began. The male therapist, in this case, has not supported the woman's own inner development, but often has left her without hope of finding a source of healing (Rutter, 1989; Hill, 1990). Women who are seductive in therapeutic relationships are blindly playing out part of the masculine myth that wants them to behave seductively. For the woman who was originally victimized as a child and who experienced a devaluation of her feminine sense of self, this relationship is nothing more than a repeat of the original victimization.

Rutter (1989) concludes that because of the imbalance of power in the therapeutic relationship, there is no such thing as consent. Women in a therapeutic relationship are not free to consent. Acquiescence to sex in these terms cannot meet the criteria for adult consent.

Why then does sexual exploitation continue in this relationship? Rutter (1989) offers two reasons. First, because of fear, shame, or guilt, women frequently do not report the occurrence; also when such events are reported, the woman is often "revictimized" by not being heard or believed. Second, he suggests that silence by other male professionals is based on the widespread envy in men when they hear of these sexual exploits.

While sexual exploitation in the therapeutic relationship continues in alarming proportions, forces are emerging to reverse this trend. Women in greater numbers are speaking up to report their experiences. This has allowed for an accumulation of knowledge and understanding. With this increase in data, women see they are not alone in their experience, which encourages others to add their voice of concern as well as facilitate the healing of this abuse. Both men and women have a new vision of relationship based on mutual respect and trust. Male therapists are gaining insight into women's behavior formerly perceived as seductive or reflective of women's sexual needs. Men are beginning to understand their inner needs and finding new avenues of healing.

Pathologizing of Feminine Characteristics

The current popularity of the codependency movement, which initially was intended to empower women, in fact pathologizes those characteristics and behavior that typify the socialized female role (Walters, 1990). The label of codependency describes women's overinvolvement as pathological. Recent works on the psychology of women have emphasized women's ability to nurture, enhance relationships, and accept dependency (Miller, 1986; Green, 1990; van Wormer, 1990). These feminine characteristics are in contrast to the dominant male values of self-reliance and self-sufficiency and, in fact, are devalued. In appraising the relative worth of the characteristics, Hill (1990) comments that the capacity for relationship should be considered at least as important as the capacity for individualization.

The concepts of codependency were initially intended to help women with an alcoholic spouse deal with the trauma and daily hurt experienced when living is such a relationship. However, they have come to stigmatize these women for their capacity for caring and support and to label the women themselves as sick. In fact, the women are now held as equally accountable for the alcoholic's behavior as is the alcoholic himself. Paradoxically, women have been credited with equal power in the creation of dysfunctional behavior at a time when they are seeking equal power in the outer world of work (van Wormer, 1989; Walters, 1990). While both men and women are dependent, male dependency on women is sanctioned and is not considered sick, whereas women's dependency on relationship is (Bradshaw, 1990).

The codependency approach uses a deficit model locating the problem with the individual. It is based on the disease framework in which there is a prescribed treatment and a submission to a higher authority with conformity to a fixed protocol. What is ignored are women's competencies and capacities, as well as the social origin of the problem (Walters, 1990). It does not take into account the social context of women's lives and the possibility that their alternatives are limited. The powerlessness inherent in many women's lives is ignored (Walters, 1990; Anderson & Holder, 1989; van Wormer, 1989).

By pathologizing women's capacity for relationship the importance of interdependence, affiliation, commitment, involvement, or taking care of others is devalued. In fact, in the male-dominated culture these characteristics are seen as weak and when exhibited in the family are viewed as dysfunctional. The capacity for the healing and growth potential of these characteristics has not been explored. Instead those who exhibit these characteristics have been pathologized and stigmatized (Walters, 1990).

Family System-Based Therapy

Some of the distortions in the codependency literature can also be identified in family system-based therapy. Although family therapy and the systems perspective are current treatment modalities that enhance the understanding of family dynamics and treatment, family system-based therapy blurs the power differential between men and women. Systems thinking blurs the difference between the actor (the alcoholic) and the audience (the family). In fact the audience is seen as coculpable or equally liable (Walters, 1990). As van Wormer (1989) notes this confuses the cause and effect relationship to a dangerous degree.

Women's powerlessness is often labeled dependent. This is particularly problematic when examining family patterns underlying addiction. These patterns are maintained by an imbalance concerning who is responsible for what or whom. Those who help are considered equally responsible for the problem as is the one with the problem (Walters, 1990). The woman receives little recognition and support as she struggles with the abusive and controlling behavior of the addicted husband but rather is seen as codependent, a label of pathology.

On the other hand, when the woman is the addicted member, the husband is seldom held accountable for the wife's problems. In disorders commonly displayed in women, there have been no terms coined to describe a potentially destructive role for the women's father/husband (Anderson & Holder, 1989). Women are frequently misdiagnosed as having a psychiatric disorder, depression, or hysteria and are sent to the psychiatric hospital (Bepko, 1989).

Family therapy, from a systems perspective, frequently does not take into account the gender-based power imbalance of the family. Often interventions are designed that maintain the power differential or the woman is provided insufficient empowerment to function equally in the relationship. Family therapists instinctively respond to the greater receptivity of women by asking them to do more of the caring and more of their share of nurturance, more of the adapting, even when the women are seriously disturbed (Anderson & Holder, 1989). The lower expectations for the husband/father perpetuate an already unequal balance in the family system and may even operate to keep already troubled women stressed and dysfunctional (Anderson & Holder, 1989).

Without addressing the power imbalance in the family and attempting to redress this imbalance within and outside the family, women remain vulnerable to continued abuse and violence. Recovery for women entails being freed from the dictates of the female role so she can take appropriate responsibility for herself. She needs to be empowered with experiences for self-definition, confidence, and direction within the therapeutic situation, as she has not been in other relationships.

Diagnostic Labels

Women seem to suffer more episodes of depression, anxiety, hysteria, and eating disorders than do men. In fact, women are disproportionally represented in most psychiatric diagnostic categories. They seek treatment for anxiety more often than men (Sturgis & Reda, 1984). This may result from women's willingness to express feelings of fear, since they are socialized to internalize and express emotion. The woman's social context is relevant in the development of depressive symptoms, as we find differences in incidence of the disorder between married and unmarried, working and unworking, and childless and women with young children. Thirty years ago a symptomatic woman was likely to be labeled "hysteric" or "neurasthenic"; now she is more likely to be called depressed.

Social factors influence a diagnostic label and the way it is applied. Years from now, it may be concluded that in the 1980s depression was as over-diagnosed as hysteria was a few years earlier (Anderson & Holder, 1989). Thus, the question is raised: Is depression inherently a woman's problem or does it arise from the context and powerlessness of a woman's life?

As was demonstrated by the classic Brovermans' (Broverman, Broverman, Clarkson, Rosenkrantz, & Vogel, 1970) study, men and women were viewed as having different characteristics, with male characteristics being more highly valued and more closely approximating what is thought to be the mentally healthy adult. Since feminine characteristics are at variance with what is considered mentally healthy, it is not surprising then that more feminine behavior and characteristics are used as descriptors for various diagnostic categories, e.g., depression, anxiety, masochism, and somatization. More recently, codependency and "self-defeating personality disorder" are diagnostic labels that reflect behaviors that are socialized with the female role.

Scant attention has been given to the consequences that women experience from this labeling. However, it is well known that women are more likely to be prescribed minor tranquilizers and sedatives as well as hospitalized for psychiatric care (Anderson & Holden, 1989). What is less well documented are the effects of these experiences on the women's sense of power, control, and self-efficacy. Little is written from the women's point of view concerning the etiology and treatment of these issues (Anderson & Holder, 1989).

While psychiatric care and the therapeutic relationship purport to provide healing of past wounds and losses, based on the experiences of women, it appears that many are worse off for their experience. Moreover, virtually no effort is made to change the cultural values and social conditions of women's lives that perpetuate these problems.

Surgical Abuse

Concerns regarding surgical abuse of women involve the inappropriate and overuse of hysterectomies, cesarean sections, and mastectomies.

Hysterectomy is the most common major operation performed in the United States (Morgan, 1984; Opie, 1986). It is estimated that approximately 50% of the women in the United States will have hysterectomies before age 65 (Morgan, 1984; Opie, 1986). According to the Centers for Disease Control (1980), as many as 500,000 of the 3.5 million hysterectomies performed on reproductive-aged women between 1970–1978 were done for questionable reasons (Greenspan, 1981).

Questions arise concerning the necessity of this surgery. Morgan (1984) noted that insured women undergo twice the number of hysterectomies as uninsured women and that salaried physicians perform one fourth fewer hysterectomies than physicians who charge on a fee-for-service basis. Also, in the United States there are twice the number of hysterectomies per capita than in Great Britain. The number of hysterectomies appears to be associated with the number of gynecological surgeons.

The increase in the rate of hysterectomies may be partially due to improved detection of diseases or the occurrence of new diseases for which a hysterectomy is the most appropriate treatment. However, a study by the CDC estimates that 5–15% of hysterectomies are unnecessary (Greenspan, 1981). The use of this surgery as a solution to the woman's problem further supports the notion that male physicians generally do not take the time or have the understanding of the function of the woman's reproductive system to explore other options with her.

Concurrent with the increase in the number of hysterectomies is the dramatic increase in the number of cesarean sections used for the delivery of newborns. Increasingly the childbirth experience has become a physician-centered process with the mother no longer an active childbearer. The ultimate removal of women as central to this process is the surgical removal of the infant through cesarean section.

The rate of c-sections rose 222% from 1968 to 1976 and accounts for 5–16% of all births; what was initially considered an emergency procedure has become commonplace, performed on approximately one in every six women giving birth (Marieskind, 1984). The increased risk of this procedure for mother and infant is reflected in the higher rate of complications, both psychological and physical, and the higher death rate and economic cost when compared to vaginal deliveries. Cesarean sections are performed when the surgery is believed to offer a better outcome than would be expected by a vaginal delivery, either in absolute or relative terms. As Marieskind (1984) notes "Analysts of the rapid rise of c-sections are beginning to question the necessity for the large increase, in the face of considerable risks, especially in the absence of causal evidence of improved outcomes. Also questioned are the beliefs, practices, and decision-making process that have contributed to this rise" (p. 116).

Those critics more skeptical of the rise in this procedure suggest that cesarean sections are done for the mother's or physician's convenience, as well as for economic incentive of the physician since, there has been a decline in the number of births per obstetrician, from 260.7 in 1963 to 144.9 in 1976. C-sections are a way of increasing the physician's income as well as allowing for a greater control of time. The added length of stay is also attractive to hospitals, particularly in light of the declining birthrate and empty obstetric beds (Marieskind, 1984).

While there are legitimate reasons for performing cesarean sections, it is questionable whether these reasons can account for the dramatic rise in this procedure. Such factors as economics, physician training and beliefs, malpractice fears, and technological innovations all affect decisions and practices and must be examined (Marieskind, 1984).

Mastectomy for the treatment of breast cancer is a third surgery that is borne solely by women. While there have been many modifications in the treatment of breast cancer over the past 10–15 years, these changes have not led to a decline in the death rate from breast cancer. Yet in the face of this, for 1990, the National Institutes of Health allocated only $17 million to study this problem that affects one in nine women.

Surgeons have modified practices to favor lumpectomy and now seldom resort to radical mastectomy, a very disfiguring procedure. It is disturbing to note, however, the findings of a recent study dealing with the mastectomy experience from a woman's point of view (Hailey, Lavine, & Hagen, 1988). In this study, while the women indicated that their physician took enough time and took their emotional needs seriously, more than half of the women reported they were offered no treatment options, no literature about the procedure, and no information about prosthesis. More than half the women reported that they were not adequately prepared for the experience and that the mastectomy was a major trauma. The majority of women experienced emotional distress and depression as a result of the surgery.

Chemical Abuse

Chemical abuse of women takes two forms: overprescription of tranquilizers and sedatives and indiscriminate prescribing of insufficiently tested drugs and hormones. It is beyond the scope of this chapter to review the extensive literature surrounding this topic. Rather, some key inequities and problematic treatment rationales will be highlighted.

Women are two to three times more likely to receive a prescription for major and minor tranquilizers, or sedatives than men (Anderson & Holder, 1989; Ogur, 1986; Fidell, 1984). Eighty-five percent of these prescriptions are written by nonpsychiatrists and one third are written when there is no evidence of mental or emotional problems (Anderson & Holder, 1989).

Evidence suggests that women are more willing to express emotional pain and discomfort, and this is viewed as a weakness from the male point of view. Women are offered prescriptions as a way of abating or ignoring the concern. Pills may be used to suppress negative emotions, anger, fear, or emotional pain. Since communication based in feminine socialization is less familiar to the male physician there is greater potential that it will be misunderstood as a pathological emotional state needing drug therapy (Ogur, 1986). When physicians resort to prescriptions of psychotropic drugs in response to women's expressions of concern they reinforce the stereotype that women are unable to actively participate in the solution and resolution of their problems. Rather a need for outside intervention is implied.

For years powerful hormones have been prescribed for the treatment of menopausal symptoms. To date there is insufficient research to document the long-range consequences of these drugs. Research examining alternate ways of managing these issues is limited. Women have been subjected to inadequately tested hormonal drugs.

Current medical attitudes pathologize a normal segment of a woman's development—menopause. The prevailing paradigm is the biological or deficit model in which menopause is seen as a disease resulting from the loss of estrogen and thus needing medical intervention and monitoring for replacement therapy (Voda & George, 1985).

There is a paucity of research on the normal events of menopause from a woman's perspective. Voda's (1981) research attempts to describe hot flashes and the meaning that women assign to this experience. Generally women did not see hot flashes as a disease, but as a turning point signaling the end of childbearing (Voda, 1981).

Others (Muhlenkamp, Waller, & Bourne, 1977; Uphold & Susman, 1981) have attempted to develop an integrated and holistic approach to understanding how biological and psychosocial factors interact and shape a woman's experience of menopause. To date menopause is an important aspect of human development that is virtually unexplored. Little is known of the normalcy of this transition. This area is lacking in clear definition and description of the parameters involved. Feminist researchers are rethinking and questioning the current conceptualization of this stage of female development.

RECOMMENDATIONS FOR NURSING

In summary, the traditional medical approach to the health care of women is rooted in the imbalance of power through which the physician controls the gender-based definition of illness and pathology, directs scientific research and ultimately, the prescription of treatment. It is this imbalance of power that perpetuates abuse of women in the health care system. Women are vulnerable to the misuse and abuse of this power. Consequently the remedy for this abuse is to equalize the power in the situation by giving women access to knowledge and information. This is based on mutual respect and participation in decision-making, as well as increasing physicians' understanding of women's experience of their bodies and illness and taking seriously the growing body of scientific knowledge concerning women's health.

The feminist perspective takes as its starting point women's lived experiences for all health efforts (McBride, 1986; Opie, 1986). The "givens" of society are not unquestioned "truths." Rather what is true emerges from women's inner experiences. Affirmation is given to the experiences of women who have thus far been invisible and silenced (Hill, 1990). Feminists describe and take seriously the feminine reality. This viewpoint needs to be brought into the mainstream of medical and scientific thinking. It needs to influence the type of research priorities developed as well as the type of treatment and care offered to women. Because of feminism and the women's health movement, women's experiences are beginning to be taken seriously, and challenges are being raised about what happens to women in the health care system.

More research is delineating the women's experience of normal growth and development. This research provides an understanding of the normalcy of women's experience and questions what has heretofore been labeled as pathological. It will provide a basis for redefinition and conceptualization of woman's experience of health and illness. Based on these new definitions, more appropriate treatment and education strategies can be developed to facilitate woman's coping with illness and promotion of health. Nursing has the opportunity to provide leadership in developing research agendas that will contribute to the recognition of woman's experiences of health and illness. Nursing can delineate those strategies that will enable women to participate in their own care in a productive and meaningful way.

Nurses can challenge the medical model bringing into the mainstream of health care those strategies that support a woman's need for education, participation in decision-making, and mutual respect. The male interpretation of woman's experiences of health and illness must be challenged and more appropriate treatment and coping strategies identified. Nurses can argue for a more integrated approach for health care for women taking into account a unique psychological sensitivity and awareness of the social context of women's lives.

Nurses need to be in the forefront in supporting and affirming woman's lived experiences in the face of sexual, chemical, and surgical abuse in the health care system. Nurses can add their collective voice in taking women's concerns seriously.

Nurses have the opportunity to educate the public and their clients concerning abuse as well as supporting women as they report and heal from abusive treatment. In particular, nurses can support individual and family treatment that empowers women in coping with life problems. Supporting strategies can enhance women's belief that they can take charge of their own health rather than passively responding to the external intervention without complete information and consideration of alternatives.

Nurses in their practice can actively develop alternatives to medical and surgical interventions. These options may be either viable alternatives to drugs and surgery or they may be the facilitation and support of the women as they manage their response to these interventions.

Nurses need to continue to object to the labeling and pathologizing of feminine characteristics. This can be accomplished through developing alternate conceptualization and descriptions of clients that empower them and respect their strengths rather than pathologizing them.

REFERENCES

Anderson, C., & Holder, D. (1989). Women and serious mental disorders. In M. McGoldrick, C. M. Anderson, & F. Walsh (Eds.). *Women in families* (pp. 381–405). New York: W. W. Norton & Company, Inc.

Bates, C., & Brodsky, A. M. (1989). *Sex in the therapy hour: A case of professional incest.* New York: Guilford Press.

Bepko, C. (1989). Disorders of power: Women and addiction in the family. In M. McGoldrick, C. M. Anderson, & F. Walsh, (Eds.). *Women in families* (pp. 406–426). New York: W. W. Norton & Company, Inc.

Bradshaw, C. (1990). A Japanese view of dependency: What can AMAE psychology contribute to feminist theory and therapy? *Women and Therapy, 9,* 67–86.

Broverman, I. K., Broverman, D. M., Clarkson, F. E., Rosenkrantz, P. A., & Vogel, S. R. (1970). Sex role stereotypes and clinical judgments of mental health. *Journal of Consulting and Clinical Psychology, 34,* 107.

Coddington, D. C., & Moore, K. D. (1987). *Market-driven strategies in health care.* San Francisco: Josey-Bass Publishers.

Corea, G. (1977). *The hidden malpractice: How American medicine treats women as patients and professionals.* New York: William Morrow and Company, Inc.

Dyehouse, J., & Opie, N. (1988). *Women's health care advertisements: Co-optation of the women's health movement.* Paper presented at the Women in the Year 2000 National Conference, Indianapolis, IN.

Ehrenreich, B., & English, D. (1986). The sexual politics of sickness. In P. Conrad & R. Kern (Eds.). *The sociology of health and illness* (2nd ed.). New York: St. Martin's Press.

Fidell, L. (1984). Women, drugs, and physicians. In K. Weiss (Ed.). *Women's health care: A guide to alternatives* (pp. 82–93). Reston, VA: Reston Publishing Company, Inc.

Gabbard, G. O. (Ed.). (1989). *Sexual exploitation in professional relationships.* Washington, DC: American Psychiatric Association Press.

Gentry, J. (1987, July/August). Women's health: A course of action; social factors affecting women's health. *Public Health Reports: Journal of the U.S. Public Health Service* (Supplement 2). Washington, DC: U.S. Department of Health and Human Services.

Green, G. D. (1990). Is separation really so great? *Women and Therapy, 9,* 87–104.

Greenspan, J. R. (1981). *Hysterectomy trends for reproductive-aged women in the U.S., 1970–1978.* Paper presented to the American Public Health Association, 109th Annual Meeting, Los Angeles, CA.

Hailey, J., Lavine, B., & Hogan, B. (1988). *The mastectomy experience: Patients' perspective. Women and Health, 14,* 75–88.

Hibbard, J., & Pope, C. (1986). Another look at sex differences in the use of medical care: Illness orientation and the types of morbidities for which services are used. *Women and Health, 11,* 21–36.

Hill, M. (1990). On creating a theory of feminist therapy. *Women and Therapy, 9,* 53–65.

Kirschtein, R. (1987). Women's health: A course of action. *Public Health Reports* (suppl. July–August, 7).

Marieskind, H. (1984). Caesarean surgery: Current treatment. In K. Weiss (Ed.). *Women's health care: A guide to alternatives* (pp. 112–123). Reston, VA: Reston.

McBride, A. B. (1986). Women's health: Where nursing and feminism converge. In J. Griffith-Kenney (Ed.). *Contemporary women's health: A nursing advocacy approach* (pp. 2–10). Menlo Park, CA: Addison-Wesley.

Miller, J. B. (1986). *Toward a new psychology of women.* Boston, MA: Beacon Press.

Morgan, S. (1989). Hysterectomy: Current treatment. In K. Weiss (Ed.). *Women's health care: A guide to alternatives* (pp. 102–111). Reston, VA: Reston.

Muhlenkamp, A. P., Waller, M. W., & Bourne, A. E. (1983). Attitudes toward women in menopause: A vignette approach. *Nursing Research, 32*, 20–23.

Oakely, A. (1988). Review of in the patient's best interest: Women and the politics of medical decisions, by S. Fisher, 1986. *Women and Health, 14*, 121–122.

Ogur, B. (1986). Long day's journey into night: Women and prescription drug use. *Women and Health, 11*, 99–115.

Opie, N. D. (1986). The contemporary woman and the health care system. In J. Griffith-Kenney (Ed.). *Contemporary women's health: A nursing advocacy approach* (pp. 11–27). Menlo Park, CA: Addison-Wesley.

Plasil, E. (1985). *The shocking autobiography of a woman sexually exploited by her analyst.* New York: St. Martin/Marek.

Rutter, P. (1989). *Sex in the forbidden zone: When men in power—therapists, doctors, clergy, teachers and others—betray women's trust.* Los Angeles: Jeremy P. Tarcher, Inc.

Sturgis, E. T., & Scott, R. (1984). Simple phobia. In S. M. Turner (Ed.), *Behavioral theories and treatment of anxiety* (pp. 91–141). New York: Plenum Press.

Uphold, C. R., & Susman, E. J. (1981). Self-report climacteric symptoms as a function of the relationship between marital adjustment and childbearing stage. *Nursing Research, 30*, 84–88.

van Wormer, K. (1990). Codependency: Implications for women and therapy. *Women and Therapy, 8*, 51–63.

Voda, A. M. (1981). Climacteric hot flashes. *Maturitas, 3*, 73–90.

Voda, A., & George, T. (1986). Menopause. *Annual Review of Nursing Research, 4*, 55–75.

Walker, E., & Young, T. D. (1986). *A killing cure.* New York: Henry Holt.

Walter, M. (1990). The codependent cinderella who loves too much . . . fights back. *The Family Therapy Networker* (July/August).

Weiss, K. (Eds.). (1984). Current crises and controversies in women's health care. In *Women's health care: A guide to alternatives.* Reston, VA: Reston.

Chapter 16

Health Care Agency Support for Nursing Intervention in Violence Against Women

Mary Jo Perley

In Chapter 5, Jacqueline Campbell's review of nursing research highlighted the perceived insensitivity of service agencies to the needs of women who are victims of violence. The term *insensitivity* is especially relevant, for it suggests both a lack of identification or "sensing" the problem by health care providers and a detached, impersonal approach that falls short of the supportive, compassionate care needed by these women. The traditional, prescriptive approach to care does little to empower women to seek appropriate support. Thus, it inadvertently contributes to the continuing cycle of victimization.

This chapter explores several important issues related to health care agency support for women who are victims of violence. While women receive care in a variety of settings, the discussion in this chapter will focus upon the primary and tertiary care settings where women have most frequent contact with caregivers: the primary care physician's office, the urgent care facility, and the emergency department. The first section of the chapter discusses system barriers to effective assessment and intervention. In the second section, a model for orientation and continued development of professional staff is outlined. The third section proposes system changes to formalize a program of identification, assessment, and intervention for women who are victims of violence. The final section explores issues facing nurses as members of a culture of domination in the health care setting.

ORGANIZATIONAL AND PROFESSIONAL BARRIERS

A variety of system issues interferes with the provision of sensitive care for women who are victims of violence. First, health care agencies are generally structured bureaucracies, which promote a sense of external control and help-lessness. Barriers of paperwork executed by busy, and sometimes insensitive, clerks may greet the woman who seeks care. Crowded emergency departments triage patients on the basis of physical trauma, often oblivious to the deep emotional stress that may accompany a minor wound. Medical personnel treat the independent symptoms, usually without recognizing the underlying patterns of abuse. Women may seek care in a variety of primary and urgent care settings, thus compounding the difficulties with assessment and intervention.

Second, health care practitioners are not educationally prepared to identify and appropriately manage this complex health care problem for women. Physician training focuses upon the "review of systems" approach to interviewing, with little attention to therapeutic communication. Patterns of symptoms suggesting violence may be overlooked as each complaint is addressed as an independent event in a woman's life. While nursing and social work students may receive broader exposure to issues of violence against women, actual patient experience may be limited. Thus, practitioners have little opportunity to practice skills learned in theory.

Once a practitioner enters the health care setting, there is an opportunity for additional education through orientation and professional development. Many institutions lack a comprehensive approach to victim assessment and intervention, however. Orientation may include a list of shelters and counselors, with little attention to the epidemiology of violence across a woman's life span and the skills needed for direct intervention. Thus, practitioners may never develop an appropriate level of comfort in addressing the very complex needs of this group of patients.

Personal attitudes and beliefs about domestic violence are a fourth impediment to sensitive care. King and Ryan (1989) discuss five myths that interfere with effective intervention:

- Violence among family members is a private matter.
- The abuse can't be that terrible or the woman would leave.
- Women who live in abusive relationships tend to become helpless.
- Alcohol causes battering.
- Battering occurs most frequently in certain racial and cultural backgrounds.

These assumptions lead health care institutions and providers to remain passive in assessment and intervention, thus overlooking many women who need help.

In addition to the widely held social beliefs about violence against women, health care practitioners may have unresolved personal issues stemming from their own family experiences or those of their friends or relatives (King & Ryan, 1989). These issues remain dormant until aroused by a challenging situation. At that time, the practitioner may unwittingly deny the intensity of the situation or intervene in a manner prescribed by past personal experiences, rather than the patient's needs.

Health care organizations provide little support for practitioners to work through their beliefs and feelings about violence against women. There are few opportunities to confront feelings in a multidisciplinary format with appropriate expert assistance. Emergency department personnel may tend to focus on the immediate physical concern, remaining detached from the sense of personal vulnerability created by the long-term trauma experienced by the woman and her family (Morkovin, 1982). There is a sense that nurses can transfer responsibility for the patient through appropriate referral. Thus, referral becomes a way of further avoidance, rather than intervention. The pressures of busy work schedules with limited personnel reinforce this detachment as a practical necessity.

Finally, the culture of health care does little to empower the practitioner to become an advocate for the patient. Rather, the nursing staff often see themselves as victims in an organization where decisions about their practice are made without their input; information is withheld and they are powerless to change the circumstances of the environment. Distrust of the organization may be subtly transferred to the patient, who is already wary of the motivations of others. Without a model of empowerment, nurses may attempt to rescue the woman through a prescribed course of action, rather than supporting her to make informed choices which are congruent with her own values, beliefs, and life experiences.

PROFESSIONAL ORIENTATION AND DEVELOPMENT

Professional orientation and development should focus on cognitive, behavioral, and affective dimensions of the care of the woman and family who are experiencing violence. Ideally, education and training should begin when all practitioners enter the organization and continue at regular intervals. A multidisciplinary approach, including nurses, physicians, social workers, chaplains, and other personnel who are most frequently in contact with patients, addresses educational needs most effectively. The program should include consciousness-raising about the dynamics and epidemiology of violence against women, strategies for assessment and case-finding, crisis management and therapeutic intervention, legal responsibilities, referral sources, and effective training that addresses the personal beliefs and experiences of the practitioners.

Consciousness-raising about the epidemiology of violence should include a discussion of the incidence and patterns of violence and their physical and psychological sequelae throughout the life cycle. Educational sessions often focus upon the *incidence* of the most obvious forms of physical violence, such as child and elder abuse, incest, rape, and domestic battering, while ignoring its *dynamics*. Brendtro and Bowker (1989) present a helpful discussion of these dynamics, pointing to the interrelatedness of various forms of violence with the need of the batterer to maintain control over the partner or other party.

A second level of consciousness-raising should address common misconceptions about family violence across the life span. Health care providers should be given an opportunity to compare their own concepts of the incidence and dynamics of violence with relevant data. King and Ryan's (1989) exploration of the myths and realities of abused women provides an excellent framework for discussion.

Case-finding should be a major component of professional staff orientation and development. Campbell and Sheridan (1989) offer a useful guide to emergency department intervention, including assessment of physical trauma, mutual violence, and nontraumatic indicators. Careful attention should be given to case-finding in other settings, as well. Practitioners should be taught to look for indicators of violence that go beyond the assessment of traumatic injury. Women may present for treatment of chronic pain, depression, sleep disorders, or other stress-related symptoms. They may experience spontaneous abortions precipitated by physical trauma or be seen after attempting suicide. They may be seen at the bedside of an infant who is premature or is failing to thrive or women may accompany a child who has suffered a traumatic injury. They may also be encountered at the side of an older parent with chronic long-term care needs. Health care providers should be taught to identify patterns of symptoms and illness as well as behavioral indicators such as depression, low self-esteem, passivity, dependence, resistance to change and overprotectiveness of the spouse or significant other.

Crisis management and therapeutic intervention should be an integral component of ongoing professional development. While most health care practitioners have some basic understanding of crisis intervention, they often lack the framework to understand the complex dynamics of the violent family. In addition to a basic review of crisis theory, staff should be encouraged to use the skills they have developed in caring for other patients as a foundation for care of the battered woman and her family. The dynamics of battering, and the psychosocial sequelae should be carefully reviewed. Health care providers should be helped to understand that passivity and mistrust by a woman are a part of the dynamics of battering and do not necessarily indicate a victim's acceptance of the abuse or a lack of personal strength to change.

Therapeutic intervention for the woman who has experienced family violence should not follow the traditional medical approach to care. The prescriptive nature of most medical intervention not only fails to develop the woman's strengths for the future, but is usually unsuccessful in matching intervention strategies with the woman's life circumstances. As a part of ongoing professional development, health care providers should be taught strategies to empower the patient, rather than making her more dependent upon the health care system for support. Practitioners should be taught how to interview, using open-ended questions that encourage a woman to explore her own circumstances. Strategies that assist the woman to develop her own independent plans should be reinforced.

Orientation of staff for therapeutic intervention should build upon the knowledge of the dynamics and epidemiology of battering and the foundation of crisis-management theory. The core components to any therapeutic intervention include an identification and triage of the problem, exploration of the woman's strengths and resources, support for the formulation of a plan, and appropriate referrals. Campbell and Sheridan (1989) and Tilden and Shepherd (1987) outline protocols for intervention in an emergency department which can be adapted to a variety of settings. King and Ryan (1989) provide relevant discussion of intervention in the primary care setting. McFarlane's discussion of intervention for battering during pregnancy (Chapter 14) provides another useful model for intervention. Common themes among these models include:

• The woman should be interviewed alone, away from the possible perpetrator. It is important for the practitioner to establish trust in a safe environment.

• Questions about family violence should be included in every woman's history and physical examination. Four critical questions include: "Do you feel your partner controls your behavior too much?"; "Does he threaten you?"; "Has your partner ever pushed, shoved, punched, or kicked you?"; "Have you every had unwanted sexual acts/contact with anyone?" These provide a quick profile of the potential for violent behavior, as described by Brendtro and Bowker (1989). Also, they give direct assessment of the incidence of battering and an identification of experiences, such as incest or rape, which may shape a woman's current coping patterns. In the primary care setting, these questions should be asked as a routine part of any interview. In an emergency, these questions form the foundation of triage for the patient.

• Assessment goes beyond identification of violence; it includes appropriate triage for a level of personal and family risk. Stuart and Campbell's (1989) instrument is useful in assessing a woman's risk for femicide. Women should be assisted to identify actions to provide safety for themselves and their children in the event of life-threatening aggression.

• Careful documentation is essential. Techniques such as body mapping and instant photographs provide graphic augmentation for carefully documented physical assessment. Patterns of symptoms in a patient's history often provide clues of a more serious problem. King and Ryan (1989) list injuries or behaviors of concern to clinicians.

• Women should be made aware of their options for assistance, including social service support, women's shelters, crisis hotlines, support groups and informal supports such as friends, relatives, and neighbors. The probability of intervention is enhanced when a referral is made while the woman is still in the health care environment. Follow-up appointments provide continuing linkages with the system. All referrals should be accompanied by written documentation.

Legal perspectives must also be included in a program of ongoing professional development. Staff should be aware that battery is a crime in every state. They must also be aware of the legal rights of battered women so that they may offer appropriate advice and guidance. The medical staff should also know their own legal obligations for reporting assault and other potentially life-threatening family situations. Campbell and Sheridan (1989) provide relevant discussion of the role of the nurse in assisting with a police interview. Since battered women may present in many settings, it is important that all health care professionals are aware of their obligation to accurately document their findings in the patient record, for use in future intervention.

Referral sources are an important component of professional development for health care professionals who care for women in violent families. It is important, however, that referral sources are more than a phone number in a directory. During education programs, the staff should become familiar with the personnel and policies of each agency. This should include the police department, women's shelters, crisis hotline, child protection services, social services, clergy and other agencies that may be used to assist women. When possible, a delegation of staff should visit agencies to gain firsthand experience with their services. These staff members may then serve as credible sources of information for their colleagues.

Affective training is an integral part of any effective program for support of battered women. If nurses represent a typical population profile, approximately 20% will have had personal experience with physical or emotional abuse in their lifetime. Assuming some self-selection into the helping professions by those who have lived in dysfunctional family environments, this estimate will certainly be much higher. King and Ryan (1989) note that these professionals may repress feelings about abuse and use personal myths to explain past experiences. Professionals who have not had personal experience with abuse may also have difficulty caring for women who have experienced violence in their lives. They may protect themselves from a sense of powerlessness over the problem and their sense of vulnerability by emotional distancing from the problem or psychological rejection of the patient (Morkovin, 1982).

Affective training can take many forms. The most common form of education is group discussion with a professional who is knowledgeable about the issues of violence against women. During group discussion, professionals are encouraged to explore their own feelings and experiences with violence. Social and personal myths are explored in a context of openness and support. Groups may become sensitized to the dynamics of battering through educational sessions and group discussion. Group members may choose to visit shelters to learn of the realities battered women face. As the group listens to the stories told by these women, they are encouraged to examine their own feelings and beliefs about caring for the women and their families.

An in-depth intervention may also be planned to assist practitioners who have had personal experience with abuse. Techniques such as writing in a journal may be helpful in assisting individuals to explore their feelings. One-to-one counseling will augment the journals by offering professional guidance for the integration of past experiences with current clinical encounters.

Finally, critical-incident debriefing is a vital part of ongoing professional development. The staff often feels a sense of failure when women return to the violent environment and are seen after being battered again. A regular debriefing program helps the staff cope with the frustration and sense of powerlessness. Multidisciplinary critical incident debriefings should follow any encounter with extreme or repeated violence. These sessions help to lessen the detachment and isolation from the patient by reinforcing the need to confront personal beliefs and feelings. Staff teamwork is enhanced as staff members wrestle with their own beliefs and feelings. This, in turn, leads to enhanced self-confidence and a sense of competence to care for women in the future.

SYSTEMS PERSPECTIVES

Health care organizations can address the needs of women who are victims of violence by committing resources for planning, education, and staffing. While there are a variety of environments where women seek assistance, this discussion is specifically directed to hospitals with emergency departments. Effective intervention at the point of contact for a woman in acute distress will shape her perception of the entire health care environment. In many institutions, however, effective intervention will only be achieved through significant system changes, as outlined in the following suggestions.

1 Establish a policy that all female patients will be asked questions about experiences with violence as a routine part of the patient history. The first step to intervention for women who are victims of family violence is identification. Research has substantiated that a significant number of women are never asked about abuse in their lives. They are embarrassed or afraid; therefore, they may never volunteer the information. Thus, it is important that all health care professionals be aware of the policy to ask these vital questions during an interview or emergency room department triage. Teaching institutions should take steps to

assure that these questions become as routine a part of the history and physical as inquiring about menstrual history.

2 Develop a unified system for recording and reporting clinical evidence of violence against women. Epidemiological studies suggest that many battered women may "fall through the cracks" of the health care bureaucracy. Large organizations with many primary and acute care treatment sites may have separate outpatient and inpatient charts. Patients may be treated in a private physician's office for sleeplessness and chronic pain and in the emergency room for a fractured arm. Patterns of symptoms suggestive of battery may go unnoticed without a unified record. When a single record-keeping system is impractical, a central reporting point is important. Within the past decade, child protection laws have mandated public reporting of suspected child abuse. These programs have been successful because they provided a central place for reporting violence, which is often treated at multiple sites in a community. A similar system could be developed in a single, large institution or community to serve as a repository of information about women who have been abused. This repository may be the social service department or a central point within the institution, such as the emergency department. It is important that the data be collected and appropriately analyzed to assess patterns of treatment and symptoms. It is also important that confidentiality be maintained.

3 Establish written protocols for the care of women who are victims of family violence. Most emergency departments have well-written protocols for the care of the rape victim. These protocols have been developed in response to increased awareness of the physical, psychosocial, and legal implications of rape. Every emergency department should also have multidisciplinary protocols, policies, and procedures for the treatment of battered women. These protocols should outline at least the following:

- injuries or behavior suggestive of battery
- additional clues from the medical history
- steps in interview and triage of patient, including assessment of risk for femicide
- procedures to assure the safety and trust of the woman
- steps for police intervention, when indicated
- steps to assist the woman to assess her own resources and develop a plan of action
- sample plan for patient management
- guide for appropriate documentation and reporting
- list of referral agencies

Special protocols should be developed for patients in the obstetrical setting. The work of McFarlane, described in Chapter 14, provides a framework that can be used to guide intervention in that setting. If women are treated at multiple sites within the same institution, the violence intervention protocol should be shared throughout the institution.

4 Maintain adequate numbers of personnel at all times who are trained to support women who are victims of violence. Women who have been battered or abused present with acute needs that must be addressed while they are in the health care environment, for optimal success. It is essential that trained support personnel be available to health care professionals at all times. In large emergency departments, this is often a social worker, who is assigned on call 24 hours a day. It is essential that these personnel are adequately prepared to intervene. In smaller institutions, networks of community resources may be used. It is especially important that emergency department personnel become comfortable with intervention when social service support is not available on the premises, since they may need to provide interim care until community resources can be mobilized.

5 Provide staff orientation and ongoing professional development programs about women and violence. The previous section outlined a comprehensive program for orientation and professional staff development. Health care organizations must provide the resources to make such a program a reality. Too often, budget constraints limit professional development activities. This, in turn, may isolate staff from effective intervention for the woman who is seeking care. Quality care for the woman who has been battered or abused should be as important as the care of the patient with a gunshot wound or a cardiac arrest. Resources must be allocated to prepare staff to intervene, and to provide continued assistance for affective training through group support and critical incident debriefing.

Orientation and professional development should be regularly extended to primary care practitioners and prehospital personnel. Trauma centers and education departments should include programs about the epidemiology and care of women who experience family violence in their regular outreach education series. An annual "awareness" seminar is another effective means of educating a wide variety of personnel. Sample protocols can be shared for practitioners in the ambulatory setting, to help establish a uniform standard of care.

6 Establish strong relationships with community agencies who support battered and abused women and their families. Health care institutions should establish close relationships with community service agencies, so that the women perceive a system of care, rather than disjointed efforts. These relationships are nurtured through familiarity with personnel and services and regular involvement of key personnel in education and training.

Administrators and providers from health care institutions and community agencies should meet regularly to exchange ideas and develop plans for better interagency function. The agenda for such meetings should include discussion of specific cases (hypothetical, if actual examples are not available). This can provide a forum for discussing the processes for referral, intervention, and follow-up. Mechanisms for feedback should be explored and put into place to enhance interagency communication. Opportunities for the provider staff to visit community agencies can foster a better understanding of available services.

A lack of awareness of services often leads to poor referrals, inadequate documentation, and lack of continuity of care for a woman who is extremely mistrustful and vulnerable. Strong alliances are forged when hospitals and primary care sites begin to see the community service agencies as important extensions of care.

PERSPECTIVES OF NURSES IN THE HEALTH CARE CULTURE

McBride and McBride (1982) have suggested that a woman's "lived experience" provides a key to understanding her health perceptions and behaviors. A majority of the research described in this text begins to capture the essence of the lived experiences of women as it describes the epidemiology and dynamics of violence against women. Yet, if the health care system dynamics that lead to insensitivity are to be truly understood, one must go beyond the analysis of organization systems and begin to look at its culture.

Nurses comprise a majority of health care providers in any organization. As a predominantly female group, the lived experiences of nurses in the organization significantly shape the type of care that is delivered to other women. Health care organizations are generally structured as bureaucratic business entities whose primary purpose is to support the provision of services to a defined population. The culture of any organization is shaped by the dominant ideological group. In the health care organization, two groups dominate because of their control over economic resources and patient access: the medical staff and the business managers. The ideological pattern of the first group is prescriptive control and the latter is bureaucratic control. These ideologies are often in conflict with the nurse's core values.

In two separate studies, this author has uncovered significant patterns of conflicting themes in the health care culture. In the first study of a rehabilitation hospital (Perley, 1986), the "team" metaphor, with a primary value on egalitarianism, was in conflict with the traditional medical model, with physician valued as the director or controller. In a second study of a woman's hospital (Perley, 1989), a woman's health theme, with primary value of self-advocacy, collaboration and lived experience, was in conflict with a reproductive biology theme, with a primary value of compliance, control, and science. The effect of the conflict between the explicit organizational values (teamwork and women's health, respectively) and the implicit ideology of the culture (traditional medical model) has far-reaching implications for professional nurses. In the former study, nurses appeared to subtly invest in the traditional medical model. Their linguistic patterns suggested objectification and fragmentation of the patient and their behavioral patterns suggested a learned helplessness over time in the organization. In the women's hospital, however, a different pattern emerged; nurses isolated themselves from patients, physicians, and other professionals and adhered to formal protocols and practice rituals. The value for compliance was displayed in rigid adherence to practice standards and routines for patient care.

What are the implications of this type of culture for nursing? While it is impossible to generalize beyond these two organizations, the patterns of behavior suggest that nurses who are "controlled" by the dominant ideology of an organization may begin to act as an oppressed group, adopting the behaviors of their oppressors. They may also divert their control needs from the organization to their colleagues and patients. It is clear that there has always been tension between the controlling, curative medical model and the empowering, caring, nursing model. This tension may manifest itself in behaviors that are harmful to patients who need nursing's empowerment.

If we are truly to change the approach to the health care of women who have experienced violence, we must begin by changing the lived experience of the nurses who are caring for them. The first step is to empower nurses to have control over their professional practice. Over the past decade, shared governance models have begun to reshape the concept of professional nursing practice. As nurses being to regain control over their practice, they will be less controlling of their patients and other health care personnel. They will, in turn, become less prescriptive in their approach and being to draw upon the strengths of their patients in a collaborative model.

A second step is to apply concepts of critical interpretive research to the nursing culture. Data about the organization culture should be presented to the staff, so that they may become critical analysts of their own system. As the patterns of dominance in their own culture are exposed, nurses can begin to better reframe experiences with an awareness of their own values. In turn, they will be able to identify ways that they dominate their patients. The collective awakening of nurses to issues of empowerment paves the way for truly lasting changes in practice patterns.

Finally, nurses can be helped to understand the common threads that are woven between their own experiences living in a controlling organization, which is subtly oppressive, and the woman who is living with a controlling partner who is overtly abusive. As the nurses tap into their wealth of strength and experience, they are better able to empower other women to discover options in their lives that will lead to better health. This enhanced sensitivity to the patient will ultimately lead to better use of health care services by women who have been dissatisfied with their care in the past.

REFERENCES

Brendtro, M., & Bowker, H. L. (1989). Battered woman: How nurses can help. *Issues in Mental Health Nursing, 10,* 169–180.

Campbell, J. C., & Sheridan, D. J. (1989). Emergency nursing interventions with battered women. *Journal of Emergency Nursing, 15,* 12–17.

King, M. C., & Ryan, J. (1989). Abused women: Dispelling myths and encouraging intervention. *Nurse Practitioner, 14,* 47–58.

McBride, A., & McBride, W. (1982). Theoretical underpinnings of women's health. *Women & Health, 6,* 37–55.

Morkovin, V. (1982). The professional confronted with human violence. *Topics in Emergency Medicine, 3,* 9–14.

Perley, M. J. (1986). *Organizational culture and social power: An analysis of a healthcare organization.* Unpublished doctoral dissertation, The Ohio State University.

Perley, M. J. (1989, November). *Exploring the culture of women's healthcare: An analysis of the organization culture of a woman's hospital.* Paper presented at the 75th Annual Speech Communication Association Meeting, San Francisco, California.

Stuart, E. P., & Campbell, J. C. (1989). Assessment of patterns of dangerousness with battered women. *Issues in Mental Health Nursing,* 245–260.

Tilden, V. P., & Shepherd, P. (1987). Increasing the rate of identification of battered women in an emergency department: Use of a nursing protocol. *Research in Nursing & Health, 10,* 209–215.

Chapter 17

Nursing Action to Prevent Violence Against Women

Carolyn M. Sampselle

From the material presented in the preceding chapters it is clear that violence is a significant health problem for women. The major themes of the content center around the increased risk of abuse that women of all ages share, the inadequate response of the legal and health care systems, and the negative context that is created by attitudes that devalue and objectify women. In fact, there is a danger that the statistics presented and the magnitude of the problem identified are so overwhelming that the primary response is hopelessness. However, nursing embraces a tradition of prevention. Thus, it is critical that attention be given to ways that this deeply entrenched problem of woman abuse might be addressed and, specifically, to nurses' contributions to its diminution and elimination.

Greater awareness of the markedly higher risk that is imposed upon women simply by accident of gender should alert nurses to the assess the risk status of all women clients. Familiarity with the content presented earlier should increase sensitivity to the signs of abuse that too often have gone unrecognized when

This chapter is dedicated to Julia who has chosen to survive with grace, humanity, and power and is an exemplary model to all who know her.

women present for health care. It is equally clear that intervention with women who have experienced physical and sexual abuse should embody a model of care that is empowering.

On the other hand, while increased case finding and sensitive intervention will work to interrupt the cycle of violence and decrease the sheer numbers of women who are maimed or murdered, it will do little to eliminate the source of the problem. Nurses are strategically positioned to intervene at the root of woman abuse and to effect significant progress in its prevention. Nurses in primary care settings such as school-based clinics and obstetric/gynecologic or pediatric practices encounter human beings at critical points of development. They are ideally situated to institute and implement prevention programs. Those who practice in emergency care and hospitals see the results of violence first-hand. They can be instrumental in raising public consciousness by articulating the pain and socioeconomic cost to the community. As respected health care providers, nurses have considerable authority by virtue of their expertise that can be mobilized to underline the seriousness of the problem.

Given the sexist myths and values that are deeply embedded in our society, it follows that prevention efforts must be focused on changing societal attitudes. Methods can be developed so that women can decrease their risk of violence, but realistically, it is futile to attempt to change the individual situation without altering the social context. Effective prevention requires an understanding that goes beyond simple knowledge of the facts in isolated cases. The target of intervention must be broadened to address the underlying attitudes that foster violence against women and allow this destructive behavior to continue.

This chapter discusses specific strategies that nurses can employ to alter the social dynamics that sustain violence against women. To accomplish this nurses must be familiar with tenets of feminist thought and incorporate these tenets into their practice. The initial focus of the chapter is upon feminist philosophy as the basic foundation of the health care of women. In later sections these philosophic tenets are applied to nursing practice with the goal of influencing societal attitude change.

THE INFLUENCE OF FEMINIST PHILOSOPHY ON NURSING CARE

A strong feminist point of view is evident in the preceding discussions of woman abuse. In fact, there is a growing belief that a feminist perspective is a prerequisite to effective health care of women (McBride & McBride, 1982; Sampselle, 1990).

Because nurses are themselves the products of a traditional, patriarchal culture, there is a significant risk that they will not question the prevailing attitudes that support woman abuse. Workers in rape crisis centers and shelters for battered women recount examples of nurses whose care reflects the patriar-chal, victim-blaming perspective. Such questions as: "What was she wearing?'', "Why was she out there so late?'', or "Why has she stayed with him if he beats her?'' typify this view.

The feminist philosophy that has been woven into the fabric of this text challenges both isolated gender-based social practices and, at a more basic level, questions the beliefs and values from which such practices arise. Concern about the impact of sexist values was expressed in *The Report to the President from the President's Commission on Mental Health* (1978):

> The rapidly changing role of women has left many traditionally trained mental health practitioners ill-prepared to deal with the new problems that women face as a result. . . . We are concerned by the failure of mental health practitioners to recognize, understand, and empathize with the feelings of powerlessness, alienation, and frustration expressed by many women. (p. 7)

Nurses must take this concern seriously. Practice that is not congruent with feminist principles deserves the censure implied by the President's Commission. Nurses are mandated by various professional standards (American Nurses Association, 1973; NAACOG, 1986) to protect the rights of their clients—rights that most nurses would acknowledge encompass the basic rights expressed in feminist philosophy. If nurses believe this, then nursing practice should reflect these values.

The feminist world view affirms the principles of gender equity, gender-free social roles, and personal sovereignty. An overview of the rationale for these principles follows.

Gender Equity

Feminist thought challenges the traditional view of male supremacy. This has enabled society to examine the damage done to women's sense of self when forced into the predetermined role of the "other" or the second sex (de Beauvoir, 1972). Making explicit the sexist biases in the writings of Marx and Engels has illuminated subtle bias in contemporary definitions of rape and pornography (MacKinnon, 1989). Taking an anthropological perspective, Eisler (1988) advocated, a partnership rather than a dominance model for human interaction. In such a model diversity is honored and sought after, rather than equated with either inferiority or superiority.

Feminists have also questioned patriarchal theology that holds woman to be a subsidiary of man (LaChat, 1988). The notion of a scriptural basis for male supremacy is challenged by the less often cited version of creation in which both man and woman were created simultaneously in the image of God (Genesis 1:27) and the assertion of the apostle Paul in the New Testament that in Christ there is neither male nor female (Galations 3:27–28). The movement within contemporary churches for incorporation of inclusive (nonsexist) language is a direct effort to enfranchise women as beings who reflect godly characteristics.

Gender-free Social Roles

The traditional belief that women are less capable than men has given rise to the view that women best serve society in a supporting role. Consequently, a woman's highest calling has been identified as the nurturer and supporter of a man so that he can accomplish activities that benefit society. An outcome of this view is the expectation that women will carry the primary responsibility for family well-being. This gender-biased expectation of woman as care provider is demonstrated in the disparate responsibility mothers think they have for their children's success (Caplan & Hall-McCorquodale, 1985); in the unequal division of household and childcare labor that persists despite women's outside employment (Berk, 1985); and in the differential demands placed on male and female offspring of elderly parents (Horowitz, 1985).

Feminist research provides evidence that counters the notion of gender-specific roles. In her review of biological and cultural influences on gender roles, Parsons (1980) concluded that the few biological differences between the sexes were not sufficient to limit women to the narrow supportive role that tradition prescribes. Rather, based on cross-cultural evidence, gender-role malleability and diversity is the norm. Socialization practices are indicted as placing far greater constraints upon women than those imposed by biological endowment (Block, 1982).

In industrialized society the more an activity is designated as woman's work the more devalued it becomes. This lower value is evidenced in monetary worth and in attribution of skill needed to accomplish the function. To the extent that the contributions of women are devalued, women will be extolled for their physical appearance rather than their accomplishments. Feminist philosophy takes issue with the notion that women contribute to society primarily via sexual and reproductive functions. As a corollary to this, as the routes for women's productivity have expanded, feminists have also challenged the traditional, limited ideals of feminine beauty. They have prodded the advertising and entertainment media to broaden the models presented for public consumption (Boston Women's Health Collective, 1984). Progress can be found in the growing numbers of women in the media who are not young, not thin, and not White.

Personal Sovereignty

Feminism recognizes that women should be accorded the same sovereignty over their bodies as men. This attitude challenges the assumption that men are entitled to visual and physical satisfaction at women's expense. It questions the harmlessness of just looking at pornography and views the objectification of women's bodies as inexcusable (MacKinnon, 1989).

When a woman is clear about ownership of her body it follows that she has the right to decide how it should be used. That is, she should be able to freely choose to engage in or to choose not to engage in any sexual behavior. Within this framework, date-rape is every bit as repugnant as an assault by a stranger. Such ownership also implies the right to protect one's self from sexually transmitted diseases or unwanted pregnancy.

The personal sovereignty that is entailed in ownership of one's body has direct implications for physical violence. Within this philosophy there are no acceptable reasons that justify battering or rape. Moreover, women who believe that self-ownership is rightfully theirs, communicate powerful messages about their unwillingness to tolerate violence. Men and women who embrace this view seek alternative routes for conflict resolution.

A more thorough understanding of feminist thought can also facilitate the nurse's insight into how patriarchal society's definition of what constitutes a real man contributes to the context of violence. The expectation is that "manly men" are perpetually ready for a sexual encounter, able to persuade a woman who says no, and able to take charge and show a woman who's boss. These values impart an attitude of entitlement that supports, from the male perspective, the appropriateness of audible appraisal of women's appearance, the belief that women are sexually excited by displays of power and control, and the sense of ownership. Operating from a feminist viewpoint, the nurse can gain insight into the subtle pressure that is exerted upon boys and young men to fit this mold. This also highlights the artificiality that is imposed on men and the cost that is exacted upon true intimacy between women and men.

An examination of personal values is the first step in applying the principles of feminism to nursing practice. The nurse is encouraged first to assess the extent of agreement with feminist philosophy. Then the question must be asked: Are the convictions that logically stem from such a world view actually practiced in one's personal and professional life? Moreover, familiarity with empirical findings about woman abuse and awareness of a feminist framework will heighten the nurse's sensitivity to gender-based inequities. This higher level of sensitivity is prerequisite to the questioning of well-established beliefs and can lead the nurse to dispute sexist statements and behavior.

NURSING'S INFLUENCE ON SOCIETAL ATTITUDES

Empowerment Through Practice

Nursing practice that empowers women in general is a basic element of women's health care. It is reflected in the nurse's view of the woman as key to health outcomes, in the language that the nurse uses, and in sensitive responses that raise the consciousness of both women and men with whom the nurse has contact.

Validating and valuing the woman's lived experience is foundational to empowerment (McBride & McBride, 1982). This is operationalized when the woman is truly welcomed as an active partner in her care. Language that reflects these values is already well established for many nurses: "You are the expert about your own body," and "What things have you already tried and how did your body respond?" Such attitudes are based on the consistent recognition of the critical contribution that women make to positive health outcomes. It also helps affirm their competence and contribution in the larger society.

Nursing practice that operationalizes the feminist point of view must use inclusive language. The written and verbal messages conveyed by the powerful symbol of language can influence the attitudes of women and society at large. Greater sensitivity to language usage cannot only increase clarity of thought and accuracy of communication, but it can influence the attitudes of both the sender and receiver to issues of justice (Diers, 1989). Thus, it is important for nurses to recognize exclusive or sexist language in client interactions and agency policies. Two excellent readings that can increase sensitivity to use of inclusive language are *Language, Gender and Professional Writing* (Frank & Treichler, 1989) and *Language, Gender, and Society* (Thorne, Kramarae, & Henley, 1983).

Nurses can further empower women by raising the consciousness of their clients. One strategy is to post offensive ads (with supplemental comments) in waiting rooms. This can make overt the sexist attitudes that are embedded in socialization. Images or copy that minimize or objectify women can help to stimulate greater awareness when the misrepresentation is highlighted. For example, the Virginia Slims campaign "You've come a long way, Baby" uses images of liberation and health, but covertly talks down to women and trivializes women's rights. Posting these ads with supplemental comments such as "Don't call me 'Baby' unless you answer to 'Sonny'!" or "I'll take my tennis without a smoker's hack, thanks!" is an effective means of consciousness-raising. In school-based clinics, contests could be held for students to nominate ads that are sexist or promote violence.

Empowerment also occurs when the nurse acknowledges the woman's ownership of her body during various physical examinations. For example, whether assisting with or conducting a pelvic examination, the nurse can introduce aspects of care that increase the woman's control of the situation. The location of the examination table so that the woman's head, not her genitalia, is first seen by someone entering the room sends an important message about the true focus of the agency. Greater power is maintained when the woman has the opportunity to first interact with her examiner while upright and seated. She can then be assisted into the examination position. Moreover, the traditional lithotomy position can be modified via elevation of the head to 45 degrees without interfering with the thoroughness of assessment. Having the head elevated allows for eye contact and communication as an ongoing part of the gynecologic examination and gives the woman the opportunity to be an active participant. Providing a hand or wall mirror for her use communicates that her body parts are not shameful, but worthy of her attention and understanding. These measures increase the woman's opportunity to gain greater knowledge and appreciation of her body. They also contribute to an atmosphere that promotes questions and discussion.

This atmosphere of respect can set the stage for further communication about related issues such as who should bear responsibility for acts of violence aimed at the woman. The insight that violence is the misuse of power by men rather than triggered by a woman's behavior is empowering in itself. The nurse can dispel the tendency to minimize woman abuse with comments such as: "There is never an excuse that justifies rape (or battering);" "What you are describing is a crime"; "There are laws against beating (or raping)."

Intervention in Specific Practice Settings

Nurses should consider the specific opportunities available to them to challenge the attitudes that support woman abuse. These opportunities will vary depending upon the clinical site and the agency clientele.

For example, clinicians who work with pediatric clients can encourage parents to question gender-specific childrearing practices. Child care education classes can incorporate content that enables parents to broaden their views of those behaviors considered acceptable for either gender. For example, providing dolls for boys allows them to model nurturing father behaviors, while building sets for girls widen female occupational goals. Both genders can be exposed to nonviolent processes for conflict resolution including strategies that facilitate taking the other's point of view. Preventive efforts with respect to child abuse can yield long-term dividends, as well. As children are helped to respect and care for their own bodies, expectations are established. Children learn that respect for one's body is a basic right throughout life for oneself and also a right that should be accorded to other individuals.

School nurses with an adolescent practice are in an excellent position to influence the factors teens use to define a positive self-image. The heavy emphasis that society places on physical appearance as a standard of achievement for girls can be questioned. Rather than accepting the unrealistic standards of perfection that are set forth by the advertising media, the vibrancy and attractiveness of good health can be affirmed. In this same vein, personal productivity and strength of character can be encouraged.

Adolescent boys and girls should be invited to examine prevalent macho myths. For example, the notion that use of a condom is a sacrifice the man should not be expected to make can be reconfigured into a symbol of maturity and caring. The message becomes: "Real men" don't give the women they love STDs or unwanted pregnancies.

In an obstetrical setting nurses can lay the groundwork for a more equitable distribution of household and child care labor (Darling-Fisher & Teidje, 1990). Couples can be helped to share experiences from each family of origin and to explore their expectations about child care participation during the antepartum and periodically during the early years of the developing family. For example, what is a reasonable number of hours for each parent to expend in child care when both are employed outside the home eight hours a day? Conversely, what are reasonable expectations for a single parent?

Nursing practice that reflects feminist philosophy must acknowledge the reality of the multiple roles women are expected to play (partner, parent, care-giver, and wage earner) and the strain that is often compounded by inequitable salary and differing workplace expectations. An unfortunate by-product of opening up outside employment to women has been an implicit message that they should be able to handle the added claims deriving from job and family. The nurse can be instrumental in helping set realistic expectations for gender equity in family care, whether decisions are being made about the care of children or the needs of older relatives. Rather than assume that the female relative will provide for the care of the frail elderly, the family should be encouraged to derive an equitable distribution of responsibilities.

Whatever the practice setting, nurses who conscientiously apply the princi-ples of feminist thought in their practice will encourage their clients of both sexes to reexamine traditional attitudes that devalue and objectify women. They will be able to delineate the links between these attitudes and the de facto acceptance of violence against women.

Nurses who are knowledgeable about attitudes that support woman abuse will identify further strategies for prevention. Additional guidance on the devel-opment of preventive intervention is available from:

National Organization for Victim Assistance (NOVA)
717 D Street, N.W., Suite 200
Washington, D.C. 20004   Tel: 202/393-6682
and
National Coalition Against Domestic Violence
1500 Massachusetts Avenue, N.W., #35
Washington, D.C. 20005   Tel: 202/393-8860

In summary, violence against women is rooted in societal attitudes about women's value and power. Through a practice that is grounded in a feminist philosophy, nurses can work to prevent woman abuse by challenging patriarchal attitudes. Their practice can empower women by increasing their awareness of the role that a view of women as lesser beings plays in this abuse. Enlightened care will support women to raise their expectations for themselves, their lovers, their daughters, and their sons. Through the planned application of the tenets of feminist thought, nurses can work to counteract the societal values that sustain violence against women.

REFERENCES

American Nurses Association Standards for Maternal-Child Health Nursing Practice (1973). Kansas City, MO: American Nurses Association.

Berk, S. (1985). *The gender factory: The apportionment of work in American households.* New York: Plenum.

Block J. H. (1982). Psychological development of female children and adolescents. In P. Berman & E. Ramey (Eds.) Women: A developmental perspective (pp. 107–124). USHHS, NIH Publication No. 82-2298.

Boston Women's Health Collective. (1984). *The new our bodies, ourselves* (pp. 5–10). New York: Simon & Schuster.

Caplan, P., & Hall-McCorquodale, I. (1985). The scapegoating of mothers: A call for change. *American Journal of Orthopsychiatry, 55,* 610–613.

Darling-Fisher, C., & Tiedje, L. (1990). The impact of maternal employment characteristics on fathers' participation in child care. *Family Relations, 39,* 20–26.

de Beauvoir, S. (1974). Introduction to *The second sex* (pp. xv-xxxiv). New York: Vintage.

Diers, D. (1989). On modern language. *Image: Journal of Nursing Scholarship, 21,* 122.

Eisler, R. (1988). Partnership not dominance: A model for the human race. *The World,* 7–9, 60–64.

Frank, F., & Treichler, P. (1989). *Language, gender, and professional writing.* New York: The Modern Language Association of America.

Horowitz, A. (1985). Sons and daughters as caregivers to older parents: Differences in role performances and consequences. *The Gerontologist, 25,* 612–617.

LaChat, M. (1988). Religion's support for the domination of women: Breaking the cycle. *Nurse Practitioner, 13,* 31–34.

MacKinnon, C. (1989). *Toward a feminist theory of the state* (pp. 171–183, 195–214). Cambridge: Harvard.

McBride, A., & McBride, W. (1982). Theoretical underpinnings for women's health. *Women & Health, 6,* 37–55.

Obstetric Gynecologic Neonatal Nursing Standards of Practice. (1986). Washington, DC: N.A.A.C.O.G.

Parsons, J. E. (1980). Psychosexual neutrality: Is anatomy destiny? In J. Parsons (Ed), *The psychology of sex differences and sex roles* (pp. 3–29). New York: McGraw Hill.

The President's Commission on Mental Health (1978). *Report to the President from the President's Commission on Mental Health,* Vol. 1, Washington, DC: U.S. Government Printing Office.

Sampselle, C. (1990). The influence of feminist philosophy on nursing practice. *Image: The Journal of Nursing Scholarship, 22*(4), 243–247.

Thorne, B., Kramarae, C., & Henley, N. (1983). *Language, gender, and society.* Rowley, MA: Newbury House.

Index